Les Pariablues

When the lost
are found
When the ground
yields a harvest
When the dead
come to life
There is reason to rejoice

D.N. Dettwiler

Copyright 2023 © D.N.Dettwiler

All rights reserved.

No part of this book may be reproduced, stored in a retrieval system, or transmitted by any means, electronic, mechanical, photocopying, recording, or otherwise, without written permission from the author.

ISBN: 979-8-9874996-3-4
ISBN (eBook): 979-8-9874996-4-1

Chapter 1

"*F*ather! Father! I found it, I *found* it!!" Princess Tebala, now ten years of age, races toward the throne room, interrupting all royal daily proceedings with a silver coin held high above her head for all to see. Behind her trail those who are already prepared to celebrate with her.

King Les Pariablues is just as excited as his daughter. He stands to his feet, catches his daughter in his arms and spins her around like he has done since she was little. He laughs and looks around at the servants standing in attendance. "What are you waiting for? What was lost has been found! We must celebrate. Prepare my table."

YEARS EARLIER

Fifteen years. Half of her life. The young woman sighs as she rises from her bed before the sun. She met him when she was just fifteen and they were married less than three years later. He was there holding her and there to take up their three children the moment she brought them into the world. Nicaia, Siohtion and

Onxwade. Now, he is gone. Sickness and death, the most terrible of thieves.

She realizes that it is noise in the kitchen that has woken her up, and why should she expect that it was any will of her own? She has tried to get herself to believe that the will to live is strong in her bones for the sake of her sons, but she feels empty and weary.

"Good morning, Mother," Nicaia says without pausing to look up when she comes through the doorway.

Even in her grief, she smiles. "Good morning." She stoops and kisses him. "You work so hard." Especially for a boy of only twelve. He's always been like this, as though he was born a man rather than a boy, accustomed to work from the cradle and uncomfortable with play. And now that he is the man of the house, he only carries himself with more dignity, or perhaps what he believes is dignity. She can barely think of a time when she has had to discipline him. He has always followed the rules and worked, worked to make sure that everything is in order. Very different from his younger two brothers who are ordinary boys: inquisitive, mischievous, cocky and adoring of their big brother who may as well be twice his age and a second father to them.

"I won't let the crop fail. You can count on it," he assures her, calling her out of her thoughts that he knows nothing of.

"I know, son, and I'll be working right beside you." The vineyard. That is what they are counting on to yield a harvest in return for their toil. Vaht inhales deeply. The vineyard that her husband so dearly loved. The vineyard that reminds her of her reason to live.

She still has her boys, and in them, she sees more and more of her husband come through every day. It is a beautiful thing.

And the smell of the vines, the feel of the soil under her bare feet, the feeling of the weeds on her hands as she evicts them from the earth to make way for the good plants...It's all a reminder of happier days, how she and her husband met. How he found her struggling to pull out a weed tree that had taken a particularly stubborn hold and helped her pull it out. How they became best friends and then fell in love and spent the best years of their lives together, even while they lived their lives as labourers eking out their existence on wages sparingly given by their master.

It is only the harvest before last that her husband signed the agreement with their master, Owner, as everyone calls him. This is just one of his many vineyards. The agreement? One-fifth of the harvest paid every year for ten years, as well as a down payment paid at the outset of the agreement and payment of three months' wages every year following until the sum is paid in full. Then the vineyard would be his. Last year was the first year he and his family made a payment, and it was a good one. In his absence, Vaht and her sons will fulfill the agreement. They must. This year's harvest will be just as good as last's. It has to be.

The house of King Les Pariablues was always full of joy. Though he was king, he was neither overly sober nor overly merry. He conducted himself with joyous dignity, celebrating often, ensuring that he conducted himself on his throne in a manner that ensured his people could rejoice with him. He was both just and merciful, even to the ungrateful. His character remained just as constant in his private chambers as when he was seated on his throne, as when he was sitting at the head of the feast or mixing and mingling among his guests, as when he would walk out on the streets, often unnoticed for his plain clothes.

And such was one of those days...

"Are you ready to go, Jeko?"

"Yes, Your Majesty," the middle-aged servant replies, giving his master and king a deferential nod. As his head moves, the purple sapphire studs that mark him as one of the king's servants catch the morning sunlight.

"Good. My blessing is on you this sowing season."

Jeko gives yet another nod. "Thank you, Sire. Ya!" And Votol, the mount on which the head servant of King Pariablues' house always rides gallops off into the sunrise, a black streak. The Sower leans forward, a satchel over each shoulder, and his legs work around several bulging leather saddlebags. Securely nestled in the bags are seeds for the entire empire.

The king turns away from looking after his chief servant. "Azaryada!"

"Here, Father," the crown prince says, coming to the king's side. They kiss one another on their cheeks.

Les smiles as he does when he looks upon no other. "Ah, my son. You're ready to go?"

"Yes, Father. It's a beautiful day for a walk."

"Indeed, come." And so the two of them set out without an entourage with the sunrise at their backs. King Pariablues cannot keep the smile off of his face. Such a fine young man his son is, just like his father. He is his only son, only child, the crown prince of a king without a queen. He has been without a queen for many years.

They make their way down the road, passing and being passed by many other travelers. Soon, they come upon one of the many small villages scattered over the landscape of the kingdom, most of them strung along the river and its branches that stretch over the kingdom. Jeko, as he goes to the east, will be stopping in every village he comes to for the yearly sowing.

At the village's center– a hill– there is a well. As any travelers might, it is there that the father and son top off their water skins before they finish passing through. All the while they watch; they listen; they smile and nod at their citizens who at this moment only see them as their fellows. The two take in the sight of the villagers' fields worked up and ready to receive seed from their king's chief servant, as well as orchards, vineyards and pastures.

"The soil is good here," Les says to his son once the village is behind them.

"Yes, Jeko will have good success here."

Nicaia slowly stands and watches as the sun slips below the horizon. He takes a drink from his skin of diluted wine (more like grape juice), just enough that quenches his thirst more efficiently than water. It is evening. He squints. Coming from the east are two travelers. Two men, one noticeably younger than the other.

"Greetings, young man!" the older says to him while still several paces away.

The boy gets a slight chill at being called out. He thought he would have time to observe who had come onto his family's property before being noticed. But as always, he puts on a show of confidence and steps out from among the rows of vines.

"Greetings," he says, chin level, back straight. "Is there something you wanted, sirs?" He does not break eye contact.

"What is your name?" the older one asks.

"Nicaia. This is my family's vineyard."

"It's a fine vineyard. My name is Pari, and this is my son, Azar."

Nicaia nods.

"We are on a journey and have decided to stop here for the night. Do you know of an inn or some house where we might lodge?" Azar asks.

Nicaia flexes his jaw. "We have room," he says, making the customary offer.

"Nicaia, who are these gentlemen?"

The boy turns and gives the woman a little nod to acknowledge her presence. For the narrowest slice of time, he does not recognize her in the dimming light with her hair so recently trimmed to shoulder length, the shorn part braided and buried with his father. Even still, he barely breaks eye contact with the strangers. "Mother, this is Pari and Azar."

"I am Vaht, and you are our guests?" she asks.

"If you sustain your son's invitation," Pari says. More customary formality. One who ranks higher in the household has the authority to overrule any offer made by another member of the household. However, to not make an invitation to a traveler is strange enough. To withdraw one is a mild offense.

Vaht gives the two men a little bow. "We would be honoured if you would grace our table with your presence." She finds herself smiling as the presence of both men warms her heart. They are good men, the rare kind that she knows to be such and doesn't have to second guess. Her husband was of the slightly less rare variety: a man of sturdy character that showed itself less readily. After all, he did not want to be seen as naïve and quickly taken advantage of. He had to act that way in particular around Owner. He was very careful when he signed the agreement to ensure that none of the terms could be twisted against him or anyone he loved. Ever since they met, he always protected her.

"Come, please, gentlemen. And Nicaia, the day is done. Leave the work until sunrise," she says with a hand on his shoulder, meeting eyes with her firstborn. She turns to the travelers. "My son is a very hard worker. He'll show you down to the river where you may meet my younger two sons before bringing you back to the house. By the time you arrive there, I will have the place prepared for you." It will give her time as well to ensure that the workers she is responsible to pay are given their daily due.

"And is your husband home, Vaht?" Pari asks.

"I am a widow," she says with forced steadiness. She finds comfort in Nicaia's presence and even more so as she grips his shoulder more tightly. "Nicaia is now the man of the house." She wonders why they didn't figure as much already from her shorn hair. Maybe they were just being polite.

"And a fine one from the looks of it," Azar says.

"Very, very fine," she says, pride and sorrow twirling together in a hot coil in her chest. She exhales slowly. "Please, accompany my son while I make preparations." She motions with her hand, embarrassed that though she can mostly smooth the quivering from her voice and lip she cannot keep her hand from shaking. She quickly turns away and hurries to meet her workers. Her strides are not hurried, but they are long and allow for the air to sweep against and cool her flushed cheeks. The weather is not warm, as it is sowing season, but she has been working all day.

Sweep, yes, that is what she needs to do. She was more than happy to invite the guests in. In fact, even if they were spies from an enemy land she would have seized them and implored them to stay under her roof just one night, give her just a few hours of purpose, two meals to prepare for guests that might help her remember the purpose she has in caring for the three boys she loves so well. She needs this. She cannot allow the loss of her husband to rob her of the three sons he gave her. She must love them with all she has so that she will stop hurting and will not blame him for leaving them.

Not blaming her husband is particularly difficult when Vaht looks at Nicaia. Being the oldest son without a father, he has been robbed of his childhood that he was already shunning. It does not seem fair. That is one of the reasons why she sent him to the river. She hopes that he will take a moment to join his brothers and enjoy himself. Deep down, she knows that he is not likely to take that moment, being so sober. But if she is not there to witness him turning away from the opportunity, she can imagine him once again in younger, happier and more carefree days as if he does indeed take the opportunity.

"Siohtion! Onxwade! We have guests. Come quickly!" Even as he calls, King Pariablues and Prince Azaryada note that the proud set of jaw and firm shoulders do not change in the young man. His two brothers don't seem to hear as they keep on splashing at each other. There are quite a few other children at the river.

Azaryada reaches out and puts a hand on Nicaia's shoulder, making him flinch. "There is no rush." The prince bends and undoes his sandals. "Why don't we join them?"

"You may, but my mother needs me." *And showing you back to the house is the least that they can do after playing all day.* He starts to walk away, but Azaryada keeps a firm grip on his shoulder for a moment longer.

"Your mother also cares about you. She won't be angry if you take a moment to enjoy the evening."

Nicaia stiffens but knows better than to think rudeness is acceptable behaviour toward a guest. So, he does not speak. In truth, he knows that the young man is correct. It is why she allows Siohtion and Onxwade days to play. She would allow him days as well, as if they don't need to work hard to ensure that the harvest is plenteous to prove to Owner that they are not allowing the agreement to fall to the ground. Owner is the only name that Nicaia has ever known the man by, and he does not care to know him by any other. As long as he is satisfied with the payments, everything will be alright.

"Please, excuse me," he says with one more glance at his brothers, ages eight and five. If there were no guests, he thinks he might drag them out of the river by their ears. As is, discipline must be postponed.

"I will accompany you, Nicaia," Pari says.

"Very well."

The man matches the boy's hurried pace up the bank. "Nicaia, look for a moment." He points to the west. "Just look. Isn't it beautiful?"

Nicaia exhales and nods. The man is smiling. Even if it does not put him at ease, it makes him pause a little, and that feels good.

Chapter 2

*V*aht opens the pipe and lets the water run. All of the houses in the village are supplied from the well on the hill. She pulls out the band that she tied her hair back with this morning and bows her head so that the water runs onto the back of her head. She closes her eyes and focuses on how it feels. She listens to her heart beating in her ears until it grows too quiet for her to hear anymore. Now, she opens her eyes and scoops up a handful of water from the trough that runs along the full length of one wall of the bottom floor of the modest house. Except for the stone staircase and this entry, both floors are covered with a woven carpet. Especially after a long day, the coolness of the stone on the bottoms of her feet is always soothing.

Vaht slowly looks up, running her fingers back through her soaked hair. She lets the drips fall at her feet for a moment before tying the band back in place. Next, she opens a little door in the trough just long enough to let the little waterfall fill the basin built into the floor of the entryway. She has a seat on the low stool and quickly washes her hands and feet with a little soap. She dries them and then drains the basin. The whole village shares a drainage system, just as it shares a well and piping system. She fills the basin again so that it is ready for her guests and then opens up the small door in the wall that divides the portion of the trough that runs along the entryway wall from the trough that runs along the rest of the east wall. She only allows herself a few seconds to anoint herself with oil from the little vial. Every house has a slightly different scent.

Vaht turns to sweeping, knowing that no matter how quickly she works she will not be able to have everything prepared by the time her two guests arrive. It will be alright, though. It will have to be. They know that it is just barely the end of the work day. However, she finds it difficult to concentrate, distracted by her hair. She feels silly for obsessing over something so simple as a shorter length. But it is not simple.

Every child until he or she is married never has a haircut. As a part of the wedding ceremony, each has their hair braided, cut to the shoulder and given to their parents. From then on, the man keeps his hair that length while the woman grows and then maintains hers around waist length. Upon widowhood, the bereaved wife braids her hair and cuts it off at the shoulder, burying her braid with her husband. In the opposite scenario, the husband cuts off his length of hair as close to his scalp as possible and shaves the rest, keeping it closely cropped ever afterwards unless he is married once more, just as the wife maintains shoulder length. In the case of a divorce, as a part of the formal agreement, the wedding papers are burned with the braids.

Vaht leans the broom against the wall. She needs to get the meal going. She is grateful for all of the preparations already done, as many thanks due to Nicaia as to herself. The vegetables are dried and need only to be boiled in broth to make soup.

The meat is wrapped in the bread dough and doused in a creamy sauce. Once the fire is lit, it does not take her long to get the dishes going. She even has a moment to sit on one of the cushioned chairs at the table to drink a good cup of wine. The table is just like the others in this village and the other villages: a sturdy board with one long edge built right into the clay and stones. Into the clay walls of the second floor painted wooden boards rather than stones are set vertically.

"Par yada!" *Here peace*, a common pronouncement for a guest to make upon their arrival at the dwelling, yet Vaht feels as though Pari not only means it but also can make it come to pass.

She jumps to her feet and comes to the door. "Yada ues," she says in customary reply, literally, *Peace you*, understood as the wish of peace from the host upon all guests entertained.

Nicaia has already stooped to wash the man's hands and feet as he sits on the same stool where Vaht sat moments ago. Pari puts his hand on the boy's head just before he stands and smiles at him. "Thank you."

Nicaia gives Pari a little nod and anoints him in the customary fashion. "Please, enter."

"Thank you again. It smells wonderful already," Pari says to Vaht, inhaling deeply.

Nicaia is quick with his own washing ritual and then refills the basin for Azar whenever he should come. This will be good experience for Siohtion and Onxwade to actually have guests to entertain, make them responsible, if that is at all possible.

"You honour me. Please, be seated," Vaht invites, motioning to the cushioned bench.

"Only if you and your son will join me," he says, eyes on hers. "You've been working hard all day. Please, rest."

Vaht exhales slowly. "Nicaia, come and have a seat."

Pari smiles at both of them as the woman sits on his right and the boy on his left. "Now, allow me." He slips a small box from his bag. He undoes the clasp to reveal a thin board that he unfolds onto the table. Next, he pulls out a small drawstring bag of pea sized wooden balls painted all different colours. Both Vaht and Nicaia watch in fascination as the man starts transforming the board, pulling up certain sections on hinges here and fitting more pieces from the box onto it there, and so on in a way that baffles both mother and son.

"Where did you get this?" Vaht asks.

"My son and I have always loved carpentry." He scrutinzes the set up and gives a nod of approval. "Now, see how this thing is on a stand? Here are the handles. They tilt it. So, we put one of these balls," he takes one from the bag, "and guide it through the maze." He demonstrates. As he does, Vaht notices his closely cropped hair, the sign of a widower. He slides the wooden masterpiece over to Nicaia. The boy bites his bottom lip. "Go on," Pari encourages, and it's enough.

Vaht rises to check on the pot of soup and the pan in the oven. "Azar is your son, Pari?"

"Yes, my only son."

"Have you been a widower for many years?"

"Yes. Was it recent for you?"

She nods as she diverts her eyes. She startles slightly with his hand on her shoulder for a brief moment. He says nothing, but he doesn't need to. "Thank you," she finds herself saying, and she hopes he understands that she's grateful for his silent comfort. She exhales and quickly checks on the dough in the oven before she turns to glance at her son. He is intently working with the game on the table. She gives Pari a smile. He is still a stranger, but he is already a friend.

"Par yada!!" comes the jovial call from Azar. Vaht feels the same way as when his father uttered the phrase. She gets the idea that neither father nor son waste any of their words and that every one of them has inordinate power.

"Yada ues!" Siohtion returns with a laugh like he hasn't let out since he lost his father. He was having a good day playing with his little brother– Onxwade– and the other village children, but these last few minutes with a race to finish them off with Azar carrying Onxwade on his back...well, it's been the best day ever. He wishes that Nicaia would still play with them, but all he does anymore is work and scowl.

Pari laughs. "Good to see you, boys." He smiles as he always does at the sight of his son. And to see him playing with these children– it warms his generous heart.

"Is supper ready yet? I told Azar that you always make good things," Onxwade says, eyes shining.

Was this not the day when Pari and Azar came and brightened her darkened life, she might be somewhat annoyed at her younger sons' muddy appearances, even though she wants them to play and knows that they cannot help but get dirty if they are going to play at the river. But today she laughs and nearly embraces them in all of their filth. She gives Azar brief a smile and shakes her head. He looks nearly as bad as the two of them.

"Don't worry," he says with a nod of his head, "I have a change of clothes."

"Good. Siohtion, make sure our guest is properly taken care of, and you and your brother too. You still have a little time before supper, but not that long."

Despite more laughter, the two boys and Azar emerge from the entryway looking respectable in time for the meal. Azar wears a wool jacket that matches his father's.

"What's that?" Onxwade asks the moment he sees what Nicaia is busy with at the table. He is concentrating as though the obstacle course is the only thing in the world. Siohtion is right behind Onxwade, just as curious.

"C'mon over here, and I'll show you," Pari says, setting up a similar challenge to what Nicaia is already busy with. Meanwhile, Azar takes a seat beside Nicaia without a word. Vaht cannot read his expression as he watches her son.

Soon the meal is served, and the marble obstacle courses are reluctantly set aside, though not too reluctantly with the inviting smells and grumbling stomachs. They open the meal with all present raising their common clay cups and bringing them together. Siohtion and Onxwade have to stretch more than the rest, especially the five-year-old boy.

"How about a story?" Pari says after everyone has a full plate.

Onxwade looks up at the man immediately, excitement almost making him get up out of his seat. Pari returns his smile. "For sowing season." He leans back in his chair with a little contented sigh. "A man went out to sow his seed. He scattered it far and wide. Some landed on the road. Some landed on rocks. Some fell where thorns grew. But some fell on good soil."

Nicaia bites his lip and keeps his eyes on his plate as he chews on his meat.

"Now, tell me, Onxwade, what do you think happened with the seed that fell on good ground?"

"It grew and grew and grew!" the little boy giggles, almost letting his fork fly right out of his hand in his excitement. He makes all but one around the table laugh along with him.

"Yes, it did grow. But do you think they harvested the same amount from all of the good ground?"

Onxwade nods enthusiastically. Vaht can't take her eyes off her boy. It's like these two travelers have brought them all back to life. "It grew!" he insists.

"It did grow," Pari says, looking at them all, "but not the same amount was harvested from every field at harvest time. Some ground gave a hundred times the amount that was planted, but other ground yielded sixty and other ground thirty times."

"What about the rest of the ground?" Siohtion asks.

"What do you think, Siohtion?" Pari asks.

Siohtion shrugs. "Maybe it didn't grow that much."

"No, it didn't grow that much at all. None of it produced a crop, even though at the start, well, some of it looked like it might. Let's start with the seed that landed on the road. Do you think it grew?"

"The ground's too hard."

Pari nods. "Exactly. The seed just sat there until the birds came and ate it. Then, for the seed that was planted among the stones it sprouted right away because it was barely under the soil. The seeds in the thorns started to grow too, but neither of these crops lasted. What was growing in the stones wilted under the heat of the sun without enough soil, and what started growing in the thorns was choked because the weeds were taking all of the things that it needed to grow. But there was a harvest. It just took a little while to see." He tips his cup back for a moment.

"Tell us another story," Onxwade says, mouth full of bread and meat, sauce oozing out through his lips.

Nicaia turns away in disgust.

"Ew," Siohtion says, not too quietly.

Vaht finds herself speechless for a second before she deftly helps Onxwade with her own fork to get the food into his mouth. "Wait until you're done chewing," she says, shielding his mouth from everyone's view with her free hand.

"Sorry," Onxwade mutters, and Vaht can't help but smile above his head because he still has food in his mouth when he says it. Somehow, she doesn't feel so embarrassed in front of these guests as she would in front of others. She plants a kiss in her little boy's hair.

"Ah, another story?" Pari says without flinching. He looks up for a moment. "Yes, I've got one. This one is about the stars in the sky and the sand on the shore..."

Pari keeps on telling them story after story throughout the meal. When they have all emptied their plates, some for the second (or third) time, Pari reveals something else from his bag. Onxwade leans in as the king in plain disguise unwraps a bundle of flat cakes wrapped in cloth.

"I bought these in the last village," Pari says as the smell of the honey covered pastries wafts upward.

"There were three dozen, but it seems that there are only two and a half now," Azar says. He hands one to Onxwade first and then hands one to Siohtion, then Nicaia and then Vaht.

Vaht sinks her teeth into the pastry. "Delicious," she says. "Thank you." Not just any guest gives something in return to their host.

Once they have enjoyed the cakes, Pari beckons them to join him outside so that he can continue his story about the sand and stars. Without a word, Nicaia stays behind, and no one seems to notice, except that Prince Azaryada stays behind too.

"Aren't you coming?"

"I have work to do, Azar."

"Let me help you."

"You're a guest."

"I wanted to talk to you anyway," Azar says, starting to gather dishes. "May as well work while we do that."

Nicaia turns to get the water ready for washing by opening another section of the trough on the north wall that has a place for a fire underneath. He lights one, and, once he stands, he finds Azar looking directly at him. He feels pinned in place.

Azar asks quietly, "Nicaia, did you have a question about the story my father told?"

"Which story?" He squirms, still feeling pinned.

"The sower."

Nicaia nods. "Why was the man so careless with his seed?"

"To reveal what every soil is made of."

Chapter 3

*J*eko's master carries a sleeping Onxwade into the house on his shoulder at the same moment as his chief servant lies under the stars with his wool blanket spread over top of him. With hands behind his head and a smile draped over his lips like a ribbon, the middle-aged man gazes upwards and counts the stars sprawled over the velvet canopy above. The glowing embers at his shoulder ward off the sharpest point of the night's chill, but Jeko the Sower has always savored a cool edge to the air he breathes.

His keen hearing serves him well as always, allowing him to hear the sound of crickets and other obscure night rustlings over the snoring of his horse at his elbow. Jeko cannot help but laugh inwardly at the familiar racket. Votol has never known a day when his black coat has not been washed and shined by his master. In return, Votol has been a faithful and swift steed for many of Jeko's years. They have spent many nights like this, and Jeko would not want it any other way. He loves his king and being in his house, but he favors the open country of his lord's realm to a soft mattress. That is also why he did not partake of any hospitality this night. Perhaps another day in another village. When the edge of the wind is not as sharply crisp and inviting.

Jeko allows his eyes to close while he keeps smiling. Today was a good day. And to end it in a clearing in the woods in between villages, well, it is glorious indeed. Sowing has a way of getting his spirits up. Not all of the villages will experience a good crop from the seeds sown, but it astounds him to see the results of King Pariablues' seeds. He laughs to himself at how many times he has seen something sprout after many seasons of fruitlessness. And the joy of the returns! Someday soon, he will take on an apprentice who will take over the work of sowing once he breathes the air of earth no more.

Meanwhile, King Pariablues and Prince Azaryada are doing some sowing of their own. He cannot wait to see how that turns out. Perhaps, the return will be years in coming, but Jeko knows that it will be more than worth the wait. And it is with these thoughts that sweet sleep wraps its temporary shroud around him until the first light of the sun seeps into the velvet canopy, turning it to silk.

"Good morning, Nicaia."

The twelve-year-old young man finds that his vision is quite blurry this early in the morning. He clears his throat, but his voice comes out raspy. "Azar." He clears his throat again. "You're up early." The smell of frying fish and warming bread fills his nose. He thought he smelled something when he stirred from sleep and stumbled down the stone steps.

"You are too."

"I have to be to start working," he says stiffly.

"What if I join you?"

"What?"

"Tending the vineyard."

"You? You're a guest."

"And?" Azar challenges.

Nicaia shakes his head. "You shouldn't be making breakfast. That's not your job."

"I'm not here to be served but to serve."

Nicaia shakes his head. Strange, but it fits with everything he's seen since last evening with Azar and his father, Pari. He sighs. It seems he won't dissuade their guest from helping out today any more than he could last night.

"Morning!"

"Keep it down, Onxwade," Nicaia snaps at his brother. "People are still trying to sleep."

"Good morning," Azar says.

Onxwade sticks his tongue out at Nicaia.

"Looks like this one is ready to eat," Azar plucks a small fish off of the pan and offers it to Onxwade on a clay plate.

The five-year-old's face bursts open with a smile.

"Careful, it's hot," Azar warns. "Just wait a minute."

Yeah, right, Nicaia thinks. *Like he knows the meaning of the word.* Yet, amazingly, Onxwade seems to heed Azar's words. If nothing else before this had given Nicaia cause to pause and consider the identity of their guests, this might have been it.

"Is there one for me too?" Siohtion asks as he enters, stretching.

Without a word, Azar finds another fish for Siohtion and then hands yet another plate with a fish to Nicaia. Nicaia stares at the plate in his hand. It smells delicious, so why is he so hesitant to eat it? He shakes his head. "I'll get some wine," he mutters, only to glance over at the table as he starts to set the clay plate down and blush. There sits the pitcher and next to it a pitcher of milk. Azar has done everything and now–

"Sit down and dine," he says with a smile that Nicaia avoids direct eye contact with.

Pari and Vaht join them at the table, and Nicaia feels pinned as the man blesses the meal with eyes pointed skyward. His cheeks will not cool. Pari does not belong in that chair. Nicaia eats little and flees the house quickly. He needs to get to work. There is so much to be done. Stroke after stroke, he angrily digs his hoe in. But the weeds are winning. The vines are being choked out.

As he works, it is not long before laughter is carried to his ears. He glances up. Onxwade and Siohtion are in the vineyard, though Nicaia has his doubts about the amount and quality of the work they are accomplishing, especially Onxwade, being as young as he is. At least it's not the harvest, which would only allow them to gorge themselves and rob from the year's store and payment.

Nicaia feels increasingly stifled as he works, and it is not just the sun warming the never cut hair of his head. Even at this distance, whenever he hears either Pari's or Azar's voice, he feels pinned, and he squirms with a renewed despising for them both.

He flinches as well at the memory of the words he and Azar exchanged last night. *Why was the man so careless with his seed?... To reveal what every soil is made of...To reveal what every soil is made of...To reveal what every soil is made of...*

Nicaia feels as though he will go mad, so he drops to his knees to attack the weeds with his bare hands. Yet, he can't escape the sound of his brothers' laughter. And his mother's. Why couldn't they just move on with their journey like guests are supposed to?

Replaced.

That's what he has been. He and his father. Pari is trying to take his father's place and Azar is trying to take his as the older brother.

Nicaia shakes his head, and gets to his feet. What can he do?

He decides to run to the river. They'll be gone soon enough, and until then he will take his time off that is long overdue.

"Nicaia, Nicaia!"

The boy stiffly turns at the sound of his name.

"What is it, Azar?" Is he honestly still here? Only family or friends ever stay longer than overnight as guests; that is just how things are done. Yes, some guests stay on as workers with their hosts, but their family does not need any more workers to pay, especially if they are named Pari or Azar.

"Would you like some lunch?" Azar offers.

"You made it?"

"Your mother did, actually," he says, continuing to come down the river bank toward him.

Nicaia sighs. "I'm not hungry." Sitting by to watch flowing water for a morning and moping never works up much of an appetite.

"I'll eat later," he mutters and stares at his feet. Even if he can't walk away, at least he doesn't have to look at him and feel even more guilty. He stiffens as Azar comes closer. Nicaia feels like his breathing is stunted as Azar touches his shoulder for a moment and then moves off. At last, with Azar gone, Nicaia exhales and glances down at the ground next to him. He gives an exasperated sigh when he sees the bundle. He stares at the cloth for a long time and then slowly opens it. Some of his favourite kind of cheese, the very best of what his mother makes, and a small clay jar of wine. He swallows and takes up the jar. He tastes it, and his eyes go large as his taste buds sing. There is no way that this came from their vines and yet...he inspects the little jar. Yes, yes it is one of theirs. He shakes his head and tries the cheese. It also seems better than usual.

What does it mean?

Nothing, he decides.

"Nicaia," Vaht gently puts a hand on her oldest son's shoulder, but she doesn't try any harder to wake him. Instead, she keeps her hand there and gazes down at him for a moment longer as he rests. She adjusts his cover and then kisses his forehead. He was out last night long after the sun went down and wouldn't even look at her when he came home in the dead of night. The work that he didn't do in the first hours of the day he more than made up for in the latter and beyond. She brushes a long strand of hair away from his face. He'll find breakfast when he wakes, if he even bothers to check in his hurried rush out the door. And he will be rushing when he discovers the sun has been up for hours before him. She won't let him work like he did yesterday, that is for sure, even if she must resort to tying him hand and foot.

Then again, Vaht knows better than to believe that she will succeed against her son's determination. Perhaps he will be in a better mood now that their guests are gone. They were gone before she stirred, leaving breakfast steaming on the table, not to mention the marble obstacle courses and a written note with two words on parchment, *Par yada.*

"Yada ues," she had whispered as though the wind could carry her delayed reply to the ears of her guests. And it was with those two words that Vaht told herself the visit was over, as custom. The same words used for both greeting and farewell.

It was all Vaht could do to get her younger two sons to keep their voices down so that their brother could sleep. And keep Onxwade from rushing in and jumping on his big brother's bed to wake him. At least the bedrooms are on the second floor, a little distance away from the kitchen. Then again, after the time the two of them spent with Azar, they are both more likely to mind her, and the disappointment to find that Azar and Pari have both left kept them more subdued than usual, at least this morning. Vaht knows it is only rational to prepare herself for the fact that such improved behaviour cannot last.

As the dew coats her bare feet and ankles on route to another day's work in the vineyard, she cannot help but miss her two guests. Very much. She wishes that she knew where they came from and where they went. Surely, they won't come back. That is just not the way of travelers…is it? It is not as though these are normal travelers. But, no, she must not get her hopes up. She must smother them before– before she inevitably learns from experiences that they are in vain. And she must help her sons do the same with theirs.

All the while, there is a tiny origami flower of folded parchment stashed away in her delicately carved wooden locket. Vaht fingers the slender wooden chain. She has worn it around her neck ever since the day her then future husband gave it to her. The first of his material gifts to her. And now it holds a secret treasure.

Vaht often marvels at how her boys still have energy at the end of the day. Today is no exception. Little Onxwade seems particularly excited at this late hour. She told herself that the five-year-old's memory of their guests might mercifully fade without her help, but it does not seem to be so. If only she could manage not to be miserable like Siohtion and Onxwade have managed in their guests' absence. Nicaia is another story. Though less withdrawn and irritable than when Pari and Azar were with them, he is still not himself. Then again, Vaht is not sure whether she can say for sure that she knows what that would look like in her son. He feels so distant, and she wishes she could draw him back in a way that he will not perceive as criticism when she is grateful for how hard he works. As long as he is around, their family will be well provided for.

But that is far too heavy of a burden for a boy of twelve to bear. It was difficult enough for her husband. She hopes that Siohtion will soon want to follow in his footsteps enough to pull more weight. If only she could be assured that Nicaia will share the load. It seems he has passed beyond the point of no return into solemn maturity. Far too solemn and unwilling to trust anyone else in order to relieve himself of at least some responsibility.

"Mommy, can I have a baby sister?" Onxwade asks suddenly, eager eyes shining as he sits up in bed while Vaht tries to tuck him in.

"What do you want a girl for?" Siohtion asks from the doorway.

"Mommy's a girl," Onxwade says.

"That's different," Siohtion says.

"C'mon, don't be silly," Nicaia says. "We can't have a boy or a girl. Dad's gone, and–"

"Enough! Everyone, just go to bed," Vaht says and flees from the room with an ache in her chest. She hates how she snapped at her sons, especially the youngest. She hears him ask Siohtion what Nicaia meant, but she doesn't wait to hear what he tells his brother.

She hates how Onxwade's innocent question stirs up so much within her. She wants nothing more than to dream with him about another little one who would give him seniority in the family. But instead, his words leave a bitter taste in her mouth and hot tears on her cheeks as she buries her face in her pillow and asks the husband who cannot hear her, "Why did you have to leave?!"

Chapter 4

"Mommy, Mommy!! Look, look, look!" Onxwade excitedly leaps onto his mother's bed.

Vaht almost sits bolt upright before she is awake. "What? What is it?"

"Look!" Onxwade holds out the coin. "It happened again!"

"I got one too," Siohtion says, running in behind his little brother.

Vaht tries to get a good look and struggles to get the lamp lit. She takes in the sight in the palms of her two sons. One silver rimmed copper coin lies in each.

"Nicaia got one too," Siohtion says.

Vaht starts to swing her feet over the side of her bed.

"Look inside your pillow, see if you got one!" But Onxwade is too impatient to let Vaht follow his instructions. He reaches inside her pillowcase. Sure enough, he finds a coin.

Vaht takes it from his hand. Onxwade giggles and runs out of the room. "Nicaia!!"

Siohtion follows Onxwade.

"What time is it?" she mutters to herself. She exhales. There is no question in her mind where the coins are from. Two weeks after Pari and Azar first visited, Vaht was eating breakfast with her sons, only to be interrupted with the most joyous, "Par yada!!" ever heard in the village. Her heart soared, and she leapt to her feet. She flew out the door with Siohtion and Onxwade to embrace their guests as though they had known each other for years.

"Yada ues!" the three of them had said all together. Vaht didn't even feel embarrassed about her emotional welcome until she caught a glimpse of Nicaia's disdainful glance moments later in the vineyard. He had slipped out the back door the minute the other three burst out the front and went to work in the vineyard only to avoid them as Pari and Azar worked together with the rest of them all that day.

All throughout that visit and the ones that have followed, Nicaia has been coldly polite, tolerating the father and son. And now it has been six months that Vaht and her younger two sons have lived in constant anticipation of hearing the greeting spoken in unison by Pari and Azar. After every visit, they have never failed to leave a gift, but this time they have gone above and beyond. This is the third time that they have given them each a coin of this kind inside their pillowcases. There is no other way to look at it now that Onxwade is dragging Nicaia back into the room with him. One silver rimmed copper coin each. Four weeks' pays when added together. One whole month. On three separate visits. The amount required by Owner this year to be added to the harvest.

She is stunned and humbled. *Why? Why are they so generous?* She feels guilt choking at her gratitude. How dare she just accept all this, expect them to come and give when she is the host and they are the guests? Who does she think she is? And what kind of sons have she and her husband raised that they would do the same? She feels her cheeks heat.

"Mom, that's enough to pay Owner!" Siohtion says, eyes shining.

"Let's save it then," Vaht says. No, she must not feel guilty. She must not let...pride, yes, that is what it is– She must not let pride rob her of the good gifts freely given. She never asked for anything from them, after all. "It will be all ready at harvest."

"Owner will be impest," Onxwade says with head up and a smile on his face, cutely smug in his use of a big word.

"Impressed," Nicaia corrects with an exasperated sigh.

"Here, give them to me, and I'll keep them safe with the others." She now holds the four coins in her palm. "Onxwade, Siohtion, it's time for breakfast. Why don't you get that going?"

Nicaia starts to leave, but she reaches out and grips his wrist with her free hand.

"What is it, son?" she asks, still sitting on the side of her bed.

"Guests don't pay."

"Why are you mad?" Onxwade asks, turning around.

"I told you two–"

"Yeah," Siohtion agrees, cutting his mother off. "They're giving us–"

"Exactly," Nicaia says. "Guests aren't supposed to do that."

Siohtion looks back with a swagger, proud of his comeback. "Azar said they're not here to be served–"

"Shut up!"

Vaht stands to her feet and clamps a hand down on her oldest son's shoulder before he can retaliate with more than just his tongue. She looks at him and sees anger in his eyes that is quickly turning to hatred.

"Sorry," Nicaia mutters to Siohtion. It is an apology given mechanically by a boy determined to follow the rules.

Siohtion sticks out his tongue at Nicaia.

"Enough, Siohtion."

"He started it."

"Yeah," Onxwade agrees.

"I told you and Onxwade to start breakfast. I'll talk to you later."

"But–"

"I'm not mad at you, Siohtion," Vaht says. "Please, your brother is working through a lot right now and needs you to be patient with him just as he needs to be patient with you. Now, please, go."

"Okay," Siohtion groans.

Vaht tightens her grip on Nicaia's wrist, but he tries to twist away.

"Let me go."

"Nicaia, listen."

"No, there's work to do."

She holds firm.

"Mom, the payment isn't taken care of, alright? We can't use that money for that. Don't you see what they're doing? If we use their money, they're the ones buying the vineyard. They're stealing it from us."

At first, the words hit Vaht with a chill because there's a part of her that agrees with her son. But now her better sense kicks in. "You're wrong, Nicaia. They're being generous. They care about us."

"And what are you going to say when they start making demands? They're putting us in their debt, and that's the truth." And, with that, he storms out of the house.

Vaht shakes her head. She leans up against the wall, feeling light-headed. But she welcomes the feeling because of what it means, something disconnected from her argument with her son. Slowly, she has let herself believe that it is true. And this morning, even as she is torn between grief and frustration over her oldest son's rejection of two of the best men she knows, she smiles at the thought that her husband has left herself and their sons one last gift. She can't wait to tell her three sons that she has already brought into the world the good news.

"Really, Mommy, really? Is it a girl?" Onxwade jumps up and down.

"Yes, really, see, right there." Vaht holds her little boy's hand over the small bump at her middle. "But we won't know whether it's a girl until the baby's born."

"It's a girl," Onxwade says. "It's going to be a girl."

"You can't decide that. And I want a boy," Siohtion says.

"But Mommy needs a girl," Onxwade protests.

Vaht stops listening to the happy argument between Siohtion and Onxwade in favour of shifting her gaze toward Nicaia. And, yes, there is a small smile on his lips. Maybe this will help him remember his excitement over Siohtion and Onxwade when they were on the way and then born. Maybe it will help him remember that he loves them as he gets the chance to care for another little one. Perhaps once the harvest is in, the stress of paying Owner for the first time without his father is over with and winter– the season of rest– sets in, he will be able to enjoy life again.

And perhaps by rest season, she will know what to do with Pari's offer, the offer to take them all as his family, just as Azar is his family. The more she sees of both Pari and Azar's characters, the more sure she is that she wishes to be Pari's wife. Pari and his son have blessed not only her but also the other workers in the vineyard and the entire village while having a special affection for herself and her sons. If only Nicaia could be just as convinced about becoming Pari's son and Azar's younger brother as she and his brothers are about becoming their family.

Nicaia stands with shoulders straight, chin up, and with himself set with purpose in between his mother, who stands in the doorway of their house with Siohtion and Onxwade, and the creditor who approaches with several servants.

"Where is the man of the house?" Owner demands of Vaht.

Nicaia takes a step toward the man, shoulder first. "I am the man of the house. Let us sit and conduct our business." Yes, he will conduct himself just as his father did last year. He keeps his chin up and motions to the table. He walks toward it and lays his parchment out, his family's copy of the agreement. But Owner is too insolent to follow tradition and take the chair across the table from Nicaia with his copy set before him. "Let us conduct our business," Nicaia repeats more forcibly and sits in his chair.

"What is this?" Owner laughs. "Where is the man of the house?"

"Sitting at the table waiting for you to do your legally binding part," Vaht says. "Now, do as he says."

"This is not the man I made out the agreement with. In fact, this is no man at all."

Every muscle in Vaht's body tenses as the man who has worked so many for countless hours and unfair wages attempts to make his point by running his fingers through the long strands that hang in rough braids over her son's shoulders. How dare he! And that smirk, that insinuation in his eyes that her son is just a boy. To think that he does not respect Nicaia when Nicaia has worked harder than Owner, who has lived several times as long as him.

"You know very well that he is the man of the house," Vaht says.

"We have the payment ready." Nicaia holds the small leather sack in his fist. "And a fifth of the harvest is set aside for you." All throughout the year Owner's most trusted servants have overseen the workings of the vineyard to ensure that he would get his payment.

Owner laughs. "I did not sign this agreement with you, boy. I did not sign it with you," he says, eyes narrowed at Vaht.

"You signed it with my husband on behalf of our whole family, and we have kept up our end of the bargain."

"In his absence? Am I to understand that you actually believe that payment from any other hand than his is acceptable to remedy this debt?"

"Dead men don't pay anything," Nicaia says.

"Which means that this agreement–" he snatches up Nicaia's copy. He rudely shoves Vaht and her younger two sons aside to get through the door of the house where he throws both copies in the fire. "Null and void."

"Get out! You have no right," Nicaia says. "You've had months to renegotiate." But of course, Owner has allowed them to work through the year as though he is honouring the agreement only to take everything.

Owner grips both of the boy's stiff shoulders. "I have every right. Your father knew that when he signed. He knew that if he could not pay the agreement would be over while the debt would remain."

Nicaia tries to get away, but Owner holds him fast, shoulders pressed to the wall and feet an inch or two off the ground.

"And what does this mean?" Vaht asks. She should've known this would happen. The table, set up like they were on level ground, was just wishful thinking. Owner was only playing with them from the beginning. He is powerful enough to do whatever he wishes in these parts. Siohtion and Onxwade stay close to her. She cannot let him harm any of her sons, but what can she do? Perhaps if it was just Owner, she could take a frying pan to his head, but five of his bulkiest servants have accompanied him. She does not stand a chance. And Siohtion and Onxwade cannot run and hope to escape either.

Owner releases Nicaia and looks him in the eye. "Well, according to my calculations," he pulls out a parchment and hands it over to Nicaia for his inspection, "paying three months' wages per year along with a fifth of the harvest, and having paid that one year already, you owe a total of seven years' wages when all is translated into monetary terms, which is the only acceptable payment for the family to make in the event of the demise of the man who signed this agreement. And it does fall to the family to pay what was agreed upon. Yes, I am merciful, if you have seven years' wages on hand then I will consider the debt made good. And so, do you have seven years' wages on hand, man of the house?"

Nicaia gives him a steely gaze in return.

He nods. "Well, that is a problem. Because I have my own finances to think about. I must have this settled. So, allow me to help you out, man of the house."

Nicaia continues to look back with the same hardened eyes, parchment crumpled in his hand.

"The truth is that you do have the means on hand to pay the debt."

"Do enlighten me," Nicaia says steadily, all hint of sarcasm carefully ironed out.

"And this is being generous because I like you: A woman ready to be a bride is worth three years' wages. A widow still of child-bearing age two and a half. Add to that the child on the way," Owner motions to Vaht with a glint in his eye, "another half year's wages. And you and those two, you're each worth a year's wages. So, that brings us to six years' wages worth. Add in the property you've already purchased and what can be found in this house and all that, well, I think that's about perfect. How about you, man of the house?"

Vaht looks at Nicaia and sees that his blood is boiling just as hers is. "You're evil," she hears herself say. There are no other fitting words for a man who would turn his own workers into merchandise to be sold for a profit to pay off a fabricated debt.

Onxwade and Siohtion look back and forth between their mother and brother, struggling to understand.

"It's simple math, Vaht. You'll fetch a good price."

Vaht's hands tremble. "No–!" Her scream is cut short with rough hands pinning her wrists to her back and pulling a leather sack over her head, the sign of a slave for sale. Its mouth is solid metal, a shackle. It veils the face, signaling a loss of identity, just another body to be put to work. Despair creeps into her heart, she can't feel Onxwade and Siohtion at her sides anymore. She knew this would happen, but she told herself it wouldn't until she believed it. She hears her boys struggling too, crying out for her. She should've known better. She should've–

"Par yada!!"

Vaht sinks to her knees with a cry. She has never been so grateful to hear those two voices pronounce those two words of greeting in her life. Tears roll down her cheeks because she knows that they mean it, but how can it be that they can bring it to pass now?

Chapter 5

The boy does not know how old he is. No one does. The only reference he has is the appearance of the rough men around him. Now that he has grown taller and is able to grow hair on his face, he figures that he can call himself a man, but he is not one of them. He has determined that he will never be. He cannot be.

As for his place of origin, he had no sense of direction back then. He has seen many burned-down ruins of villages, and every time he sees one he wonders whether that is the one he hails from.

As for his name, it has been so long since he's heard it that even he has forgotten it. As for his capture, the memories are vague and terrifying. He cannot smell smoke without choking or hear the creaking of a wagon wheel and not be hurtled back to the sounds of screams. And whenever a rare moment comes when all is still and quiet and dark, his heart beats quickly in anticipation of something awful to break it and end in him being torn from those he loves, sold for a mere day's wage.

He has told himself that, once a man, he will do something to stand in the way of these cruel men who have been his only companions– other than his miserable fellow slaves– for the better part of his life. But the more a man he finds himself to be in appearance, the more like a cowardly child he feels. *Better*, he thinks. No, these have not been his better years.

The best years of his life are the ones he only remembers scattered pieces of. As for how many years it was, time does not mean much to him. The seasons go by, and he endures the heat and the cold among the other hardships. Though they are scattered, he does still have pieces. He remembers his father and mother the clearest out of the blur. His memory has been so blurred by time that he is not even sure how many brothers and sisters he has. And the faces of his parents...But the physical details of their faces aren't all that important to him. What he remembers and fiercely refuses to let go of are the memories of their love. Unlike his masters ever since he was first taken prisoner, they only ever disciplined him justly, and no matter what, they always embraced him. He knew they would, even when he felt ashamed about something he'd done. And it is because of them that he refuses to be like these warring bands. No, he will not become like those who tore his family apart, though he is forced to run here and there at their every beck and call.

The blast of trumpets sends blood rushing into his ears. Even over the noise, he hears his breaths accelerating, even after all this time he is not accustomed to the battlefield. Today, it is an open field the five bands fight in. The boy cannot decide whether he likes the forest or the field better. In the forest, there are places to take shelter. In the field, he can at least see the enemy coming. Either place, fire can rage, and fire is what he hates more than anything he has encountered. He shivers at the thought. He can handle the standard beatings slaves must endure, but the masters who are cruel enough to use other punishments…they are the reason why he despises the element that rages and consumes.

The boy cannot count the number of times he has changed hands since he was first sold. Most of the time, he is pawned off for a day's wage along with several others for easy money, but other times his masters have haggled and gotten as much as an entire year's wage. Other times, he has been captured in one of the conflicts of the bands and has, by default, been subjected to a new master, the only price being the blood of the warring band members.

Miserable as his existence is, he has a strong will to live, and he knows that it is being a slave that has saved his life time and time again. *Avey peazuz galley*, they say. Literally, *A slave's loyalty is the wind.* Meaning, since a slave is buffeted by all, whoever happens to have command of him, he will obey, but only so long as he remains under that master's authority. In other words, it is understood that slaves serve out of fear. Not love. While warriors and servants are treated harshly and often made a public spectacle in their executions, captured slaves are simply absorbed into the number of slaves that the band already possesses without a second thought. For that reason, he is grateful he has not been made into a warrior. On top of that, being made a warrior would mean being forced to raid helpless villages.

As weapons are put to use once more, the boy feels the same numb frustration. The bands fight over made up borders. But at least fighting each other keeps them from any raiding on the villages.

The noise increases. The boy closes his eyes and waits with the other slaves. They have no choice. He does not know how it became custom, but slaves are always chained together by wrists and ankles in a ring (or rings depending how many there are of them) during a battle. Once the battle is over, the leader of the victorious band will take the key to the chains from his defeated foe and take the slaves as a part of his prize. The boy sighs inwardly, weary of the useless repetition.

The group of them are sitting down and facing each other. They are all silent. He remembers his first battles as a boy when an older slave let him huddle up against her. She was like a big sister to him. They were captured during one of those first battles and then quickly sold to two different masters. Since then, the boy has found it difficult to form attachments with any of his fellow slaves.

He wonders whether this will always be his lot, whether he will ever break out of this life and find a way to stand against this, this...he doesn't have the word for it. But though he cannot put a name to the face, his sense of justice is just as strong as it would be if he had the proper vocabulary.

It is chaos around them, but the boy has seen more chaotic battles than this. He always hopes– and prays to whatever greater king might be listening, one who actually cares unlike all of the ones he's heard of– that one of these times a battle will end with no single band member left standing. He has imagined it many times and kept it in mind as a glimmer of hope.

He pictures it now with eyes still closed: All of the band members lying in their own blood as they deserve and then the rings of slaves standing to their feet and finding the keys. Finally free, they help each other and share what water, food, clothes and wealth there is to be found from their former masters and finally build a civilization for themselves where no one is locked up or beaten or burned or sold without cause ever again.

Sometimes, they sit chained in these rings for hours. Sometimes days. Sometimes the water skin in the middle runs out or there is not one at all and there is death.

The boy loses track of time, numb to the terrible noises around him. His eyes don't even snap open in alarm when rough hands seize him. He's used to it. He's used to pain, which he can and will handle when it comes next. He's dragged along, knowing that his glimmer of hope has yet been deferred to another day. He suddenly realizes that the key was not used on his chains. The links were broken loose. The other slaves are being dragged off as well. The battle is still raging, but he is not surprised that they have been taken before it is over. It is not the first time. Perhaps the band leader who took them will try to claim himself the victor of this battle through their capture, but the boy doesn't care. He just wants the bands to destroy each other.

The boy's hands are pinned behind him. "This way!" comes the demand with more dragging to reinforce it.

Where are we going? Away from the battle from the looks of things. This gives the boy the idea that some band members are deserting, taking slaves as bounty while the rest of their band keeps fighting. The boy doesn't know the reason, but he does know that he has changed hands again, and that is enough. It's simply the story of his life, always moving. And so what if it is with someone else as his owner? He would be moving whether he stayed in the same hands or not.

"Move it!" one of the warriors barks at one of the other slaves who has fallen. Just a girl.

"All of you, keep on moving!"

And so they keep on, passing fields that should be ripe for harvest. However, the bands have been through these fields already, and that means that the crops have either been burned, trampled or stolen for the bands' consumption and sale. In some cases, that sale is back to those who tended the crops all year.

The boy keeps stumbling forward with the others. What choice do they have? The only question now is what will be done to them. On and on they run, the warriors never slacking, always shoving them onwards. There are about a dozen warriors with one slave each. But the odds aren't with them. How can they be when more than half of the slaves are women and girls while the boy guesses that he is about the oldest out of the males. No, slaves never have a fighting chance. And so they stumble on. And on. Sometimes on the road, sometimes through the fields, sometimes through wooded areas.

"Water," one of the slaves gasps, falling forward.

"If you want us to go on," rasps another.

Both slaves are struck on the cheek and reprimanded harshly, but their cries earn them all a little liquid refreshment. Not nearly enough to cure a parched throat. Meanwhile, the warriors each take liberal drinks before shoving them onwards. It's not a particularly warm day, the season being harvest time, but the hurried movement is enough to produce sweat. *They can't push us all night. They'll want to sleep*, the boy tells himself.

And he is right. After the sun slips below horizon, the warriors pile the slaves on the ground, securing them in a tangle of rope. The night turns cold, making it necessary for them to huddle together while the warriors enjoy a small fire and blankets.

Thirsty, hungry and exhausted as always, the slaves try to sleep. Morning comes all too soon. And so their journey continues. Except, they are not forced to go on much farther on their feet. In exchange for a horse and wagon, three of the slaves are given to a farmer as labourers in the harvest while the other nine ride on the bed of the wagon with the warriors. The boy keeps his head in the crook of his arm as he lies down on the planks with eyes closed, ill at ease with the creaking of the wagon. At least they are given some food and drink with the wagon that the warriors don't keep all to themselves. They spend another night in a camp and then finally come to a city the next evening.

The boy knows this place. It is one of the major slave trade markets, a place where agreements on price can take hours to settle, especially if the buyer wishes to see the merits– such as strength– of the slave demonstrated. It is a place where slaves are humiliated and used to bring their sellers great wealth. It is here that slaves can be sold for ten times or more the price they would be elsewhere.

"I'll take that one."

The boy slowly takes in the sight of the man who has just pointed him out.

"Best of the lot."

There is a gleam in the eye of the boy's seller. "Alright, Samaritan, bid away."

He stiffens and keeps his eyes averted; uninvited eye contact has never done him any good. Definitely a wealthy man. A high ranking servant. One who knows more freedom than he could ever dream of himself. But the boy does not envy his position. Those in positions like his are often just as cruel as the band members, sometimes more so. The band members put slaves through pain for sport, the servants do it out of spite and a sense of entitlement to their positions, as though they are the masters of the house.

Just like that, the racket of haggling begins, but few challenge the first bidder, especially once it is apparent that he is exceptionally experienced and particularly unaccustomed to not having his way. All at once, with only the warning of the jingle of the gold, the man clamps his hand on the boy's shoulder and jerks his chin up so that he is looking the servant in the face.

"Yes, sir," he responds mechanically.

"Yes, master," he hisses. "My name is Koje, chief servant of King Les Pariablues. You belong to me and you will do my bidding without a word."

The boy nods and bows as expected. *Koje, huh?* He has heard of King Les Pariablues before, and none of it has been good. Koingsung: the king of the Samaritans he's called by those looking for a euphemism for their distaste. But he has never served in a king's house before. Even through his skepticism from a lifetime of finding all men in power relatively the same, his interest is piqued about this king. It is something new, if nothing else. *Kuri vivi*, as they say. Or, *Curiosity is life*. And he has found that to be true.

The boy knows that it takes more than being of the right social status to keep alive. It takes a will to live– which he has– and that will needs nourishment. Curiosity has been one of the things that has sustained his.

"Get up!" Koje shoves him into the saddle before chaining his ankles to the stirrups and his wrists to the saddle's horn. The boy has always admired the beasts, always enjoyed caring for them as best he could. After all, used as they are for evil by the bands, they are glorious creatures who have no choice about what they are used for...much like him. As such, that care at times has included letting them loose in a way he cannot be blamed that they may be used more nobly.

The chief servant mounts his own chestnut horse. There is a chain running from the horn of his saddle to where the boy's wrists are shackled. And so the horses ride together. The boy keeps his head down as they ride out of the city with two others attending Koje. As they ride, the sun sets before them, and the boy marvels at the colours. That is one of the other things that has kept him alive. The sky and waiting for every new piece of art that appears there.

If there is a good greater king out there, then it must be he who does things like that and gave me eyes to see it. He has thought that so many times before, but now he has a new thought. *Is it possible that that greater king sees me at all?* He lets that thought turn over a few times in his mind as the city fades from view behind them and their four horses start galloping. *I'd be amazed if he did see me, even that would be something else. It's not like I'm much of anything. But maybe if that greater king can paint the sky, then maybe he can do something to set us free too. Maybe that will happen someday after all.*

But the boy doesn't particularly believe that it will happen. It is just something to add to his glimmer of hope. A sweet maybe in the midst of bitter uncertainty.

Chapter 6

*"P*ar yada!!"

The call rings out for the second time, King Les Pariablues and Prince Azaryada proclaiming the words in unison. And indeed, they have come here to bring peace. Peace, but also a sword.

"Get to your feet, woman." One of Owner's bulky servants jerks Vaht up by her wrists. Startled by the sudden pain, she cries out.

"Yada eu–" A hand smacks over Onxwade's mouth. "Ow!"

"Silence, slave," growls the gruff voice.

How dare you! Vaht's anger rises as only a mother's can for her baby, especially when she cannot see or move to answer his cry of distress.

"Release them!" Pari commands.

Vaht shivers. She's always thought that both Pari and his son speak with authority, but this level of firmness whispers of something even more significant than has ever occurred to her throughout the time she has known them. The unknown of it terrifies her, yet it is an exhilarating terror because all that she has ever seen of Pari and Azar until this point has been good. Surely, she is about to see more of their goodness.

"And what are they to you, King Les Pariablues?" Owner demands spitefully.

"They are mine."

There it is again: that vibration of authority. Vaht hears herself gasp. **Pariablues** and **Azar**yada. *How didn't I see it before? Only the king and his son can merely speak and it is. And it is. But how can it be?* She feels like she can't breathe, and how can she with a leather bag over her head?

"This woman's husband bought this vineyard as an inheritance for his sons, and so it will be, along with the rest of your property, for them and their siblings and children forever."

Evening light hits Vaht's eyes and clean air floods her lungs. She looks into the face of King Pariablues, her king, her defender. He turns and hands Nicaia an official parchment. The boy, now free as well, cannot take his eyes off of the words written by quill and ink. They are no longer slaves.

Vaht now sees the king and his son in their full royal attire. They're magnificent. And she cannot deny the veracity of the royal entourage or the signet rings on their fingers. They are indeed the king and crown prince. She is indeed but a lowly citizen of their realm.

"You can't do this! You cannot take what is mine," Owner protests.

"I gave it to you to begin with. I was the one who had the seeds sown. And now I am giving it to others to steward."

"But it is mine!" Owner cries.

"You have accumulated a great debt," King Pariablues says, drawing out another parchment. "This is your account."

"I don't have the means to pay."

Vaht watches in wonder as the man who has tormented her for years slips down to his knees. Surrounded by the king's soldiers, Owner's bulky servants cower as well.

"On the contrary, the sale of yourself and your property and the work you will do following will do some to alleviate what you owe."

"No!"

"Take them," the king commands. "Keep them in prison until I come and judge them from my throne."

And now, it is just the king, the prince, Vaht and her three sons in the house while royal attendants wait outside. She feels as though her lungs collapse with her knees. She bows her head as she becomes aware of whose presence she is in and what he has done for her. "I am not worthy."

He takes her hands, bows on a knee in front of her so that they are looking eye to eye.

"Yada ues," he says tenderly.

And there is that authority once more. Gratitude refuses to stop drawing from the wells of her eyes.

"Yada ues," he repeats.

Peace, peace upon you…How can it be? Yet she knows that it is so.

"Yada ues," she hears Prince Azaryada echo, putting a hand on the heads of each of Vaht's three sons: Onxwade, Siohtion and Nicaia, in that order, meeting their eyes as he does.

"I am yours," Vaht says.

"And I am yours." He rises, brings her to her feet, and sits her down.

She watches, stunned, as he washes her feet, while Azaryada washes the feet of her sons before anointing them each with oil. It seems to Vaht that the washing not only removes the grime of the day but the layers of grief and sorrow of the months and years. The moment the fragrance catches Vaht's nostrils, she can't believe that she didn't realize sooner that the distinct scent known as royal has been in her house so many times. How didn't she realize it until now?

Vaht understands the gesture and wonders to what degree each of her sons comprehend that their guest is now their host. In fact, in a way, Nicaia has been right all along, King Les Pariablues has been the host the entire time, but Vaht knows that her son, who now sits in silence staring at the inheritance deed, has yet to understand that it is not out of greed or selfish ambition that the king has taken them and all they have as his own. But perhaps, Nicaia can start to see the truth of the king's generosity now. Then again, though Vaht wants to believe the best about her son, she has her doubts that her oldest will be so easily convinced.

Vaht's heart pounds as her eyes meet King Pariablues' again. He is smiling, smiling at her. He hands her a stack of folded material. "Go and prepare yourself, my bride."

With trembling hands, she takes the clothes made to fit a queen to her room. At every step she mounts she feels as though she will slip and fall on her face. She moves quickly to set the clothes on her bed before she can drop them. Her hands are shaking as she draws water for her basin and quickly washes herself. She moves as quickly as she can, excitement coursing through her veins. How can it be? Or, in her language, a question spoken in a single word, *Comastasia? Comastasia? Comastasia?*

Yadmin, the answer echoes through her mind. Love. But, you see, reader, we do not have a word in our language that evokes in our mind a concept that aptly captures the meaning of the word that has Vaht smiling. Yadmin speaks of courage, of loyalty, of eternity, of unbreakable commitment, of tenderness, of goodness in every way. It is a word rarely used because of how cherished it is. And it is for this reason that Vaht almost feels ashamed to be thinking it over and over as she is. The last thing she wants is to wear it out. It seems so fragile, but, no, yadmin is a word that speaks of the greatest strength, so how can she– feeble and fumbling as she is– break it?

She cannot.

And so, knowing that she will be accepted with open arms by her bridegroom, she finishes washing herself and brushing her hair. She lets it hang loose at shoulder length and pulls on the new clothes. They smell wonderful, like they were washed in the royal anointing oil. She holds the fabric to her nose and breathes deeply. The moment she has the clothes on, she smiles and twirls.

She laughs aloud. She never thought she would feel this kind of joy. She wishes that she knew another word like yadmin to describe this joy. Surely, there is one, but she is too common to know it.

"Common!" she laughs in glad scorn. "But the king loves me. So there." She lets the smile blossom. She descends the stairs like a deer, bare feet hitting the stone with a spring. She no longer fears falling on her face. "I'm ready, Pari." Her breath catches. She just called the king...Tears spring to her eyes. *Comastasia? Yadmin. Yadmin, Vaht. Yadmin solue.*

Only because of love.

She glances at her three boys. They are clothed like the princes they now are, like Azaryada. The king takes her hand again and leads her to the doorway. It looks as though the entire village has gathered at their doorstep. Of course, she heard the wedding music through the walls as she was getting dressed. Carefully, King Les Pariablues reaches out, takes a strand of her hair and makes a small braid the length of his shortest finger. He binds it at the top and bottom with two short strands of beaten gold, cuts the hair, then places the braid inside a small crystal vial strung on a golden chain around his neck. The setting sun catches the vial at just the right angle to cast rainbows around them. All the while, more and more people pick up the melody of the music made with bells and tambourines and stringed instruments and hands clapping and feet stomping and whatever is on hand.

"Daddy!" Onxwade exclaims and jumps into the king's open arms.

Pari laughs and perches the boy on his hip with a smile just for him. It gives Vaht a strange feeling to know that her baby who is due to be born any moment will never know their father but rather will call the king Daddy just as their older brother just has. But after the years she spent with her husband ever since they were teenagers, she saw enough to know that her late husband would gladly step aside so that his family would be the king's. It is no secret how much he loved his lord, and he taught Vaht to as well, even as neither of them had ever met him, even as neither of them understood why Owner was permitted to do what he did without the king's intervention. Vaht now wonders whether Pari was giving Owner time to fall into so great a debt that he now has no hope of paying and thus will never be free again to torment anyone? She doesn't know, but she trusts Pari. Vaht glances at Siohtion and Nicaia, neither of whom seem as enthusiastic as their little brother. Do they see this as a betrayal of their father? She expected it from Nicaia, but Siohtion?

Vaht turns her eyes back to her bridegroom's face, just to get a fresh glimpse of his smile as he finds flowers– "You planted…" Vaht whispers. He planted this patch of diverse flowers during his second visit and now that they are in full bloom this last day of the harvest, he is making a bridal garland according to tradition. He had this in mind all along. He loved her first. *Yadmin*, the word echoes in her heart again as Pari shows her his finished work of art. A crown, the queen's crown with her bridal garland wound around it. He places it on her head, and she takes note of his corresponding headwear. It is a glittering and glorious crown.

The wedding music has grown in strength. How long has it been since he removed the leather bag from her shoulders? Pari has replaced the ring of iron for a crown of precious metal and gems, smothering leather for the most comfortable and beautiful garments she and her sons have ever worn. And they too wear the crowns of princes. They mount up onto the pure white horses reserved for royalty alone. The coats of the six horses that carry them are brilliant, their manes and tails braided and adorned with strands of beaten gold, silver and bronze studded with jewels. The bridles are white as are the saddles to match the coats of the horses, but the fringes of the saddles are dyed a purple only used for royalty.

The music and the singing of the growing crowd of citizens matches its beat to the rhythm of the company's movement. More and more citizens join as they pass through the villages. Hundreds of thousands of horses with coats of all descriptions carry both the royal entourage and citizens from all settlements throughout King Les Pariablues realm.

"Aiwa! Aiwa! Tebal! Tebal, lelal granel canel. Thues ete phumile yada. Eses yareh!" they all sing.

Or, as we would understand, "Make way! Make way! Rejoice! Rejoice, behold the bridegroom comes. Peace on them and their family. Blessed for generations."

As their procession trots forward, flower petals are shaken loose from their places in baskets on the sides of the saddles of several of the attendants. And so the road to the wedding feast is marked out for all who wish to attend.

"Aiwa! Aiwa! Tebal! Tebal, lelal granel canel. Thues ete phumile yada. Eses yareh!"

Nicaia rides with chin up, shoulders as straight as always. But while he keeps up his customary appearance, he is in inner turmoil. As he was dressing, he tied a strip of cloth from one of his old shirts around the parchment King Pariablues handed him and then he tied the ends together in a loop large enough to go around his left bicep. He intends to keep the document there, to test whether the man is sincere. "We'll see, we'll see," he said to Siohtion.

"Aiwa! Aiwa! Tebal! Tebal, lelal granel canel. Thues ete phumile yada. Eses yareh!"

Yes, he will see whether the king is like Owner, willing to burn an agreement at any time or whether he will truly give a share of Owner's vineyards as well as 10,000 years' worth of wages to Nicaia and each of his siblings. For now, he will uphold his end of the bargain, work in the vineyard as he has always done so that the produce can be distributed to the citizens of the kingdom as the king wrote on the inheritance deed. And he will see whether the king will do as he has written.

"Aiwa! Aiwa! Tebal! Tebal, lelal granel canel. Thues ete phumile yada. Eses yareh!"

Chapter 7

"*A*gain!"

Even as thousands celebrate with their king, singing as they tread out the last of the grapes from the harvest, all is not well back at the house of King Les Pariablues. The king left Jeko and his older cousin Koje to oversee his house in his absence for his wedding. He instructed the two of them to oversee the harvest, ensure that his other servants are cared for, as well as see that all tasks assigned to his servants are accomplished according to his will.

In his heart, Jeko wondered what his king's reason was for putting Koje in charge once more, but he has been in his king's service for too long to question his wisdom. He has seldom known him to act foolishly during his reign. Crown Prince Azaryada either.

For years, the boy has been beaten and sworn that he would never turn around and do the same to another person, unless it would be to punish those masters who torment so many. But here, the boy finds himself doing just that under Koje's direction. The chief servant has told him that this is expected of him, and he has found himself too cowardly to rise above the threats of torture and death not to do exactly as Koje instructs. With every stroke he inflicts unjustly on another, he feels his very will to live shrinking and dying within him. And to think that all of his resolve has evaporated in less than the amount of time it has taken for the full moon to pass through the sky again. Less than a month.

"Back to work!" Koje shoves the woman that has hunkered down to shield herself from the rod in the boy's hand.

The boy turns his face away only to have Koje jerked it back.

"Look sharp. Just one look should tell them you are not to be trifled with. Pariablues will not be pleased if he sees you shirk your duty."

And there it is again, that sense that he likes the feeling of power, to be picked out by the king's chief servant and trained by him in such a high position. The truth is that the boy is disgusted by his own heart now that it is out in the open for him to see. The boy has not even noticed that Koje has not yet asked him his name. Most of the time he does not think about how he does not have a name when most do.

"Koje!"

"Ah, Jeko, what are you doing here?"

The boy takes in the sight of the other chief servant. Thus far, he has only heard of him, since Jeko has been elsewhere attending his duties, or not attending according to Koje.

"What are you doing here?" Jeko demands.

"The king himself put me in charge just as well as you."

"And I see that you have only proven your incompetence and pride. Did you think that you would not be found out?"

"And who are you? You have no rank over me." Koje laughs in Jeko's face.

"And what are you doing with this young man? You found someone just like you?"

The boy locks his jaw before he protests. The truth stings.

"Let the king deal with me *when* he comes back."

"He will return. Heitii, Koje, heitii."

Watch, the word echoes through the boy.

Koje gives another laugh. "Then I suggest you attend to your duties."

"Heitii, Koje. You don't know when he will return from afar."

"Heitii," Koje mimics, and the boy finds a larger part of him than he is comfortable admitting is cheering Koje on in his mocking. "You don't know when he'll return, whether at evening, at midnight, when the rooster crows, or in the morning."

Jeko's eyes burst into flame, but he does not step forward, just looks at Koje and the boy. The boy cannot stand the gaze. "Heitii, unless you want him to find you sleeping when he comes suddenly."

"Attend to your duties," Koje says, waving him off.

"And so I will."

The boy averts his eyes from the second scalding look from the other chief servant.

Koje turns to the boy. "Just as I told you. Unreasonable. The king will deal with him. You'll see. He won't be pleased with the disarray Jeko has wrought."

As Jeko continues to walk away, the boy takes a closer look at how glad he is that Koje put Jeko to shame and wonders whether that really is the case. Is Koje really in the right?

"What are you staring at?"

"Nothing, my lord."

"Come, the sun is going down, blow the trumpet." The boy does so to signal the end of the day to the workers and now follows his master. Once away from the field, Koje does as he has for many nights past. But tonight, the boy does not join in with his glutinous, drunken feast. He only does enough to give Koje the impression that he is once more joining in with him as Koje demands.

All the while what Jeko said rings in the boy's ears. But why should he be concerned if he's done just as instructed? He wraps both of his hands tightly around his rod. It must be because the king is like so many other masters who, whether obeyed or disobeyed, whether fault is or is not found, punish slaves. From everything the boy has heard, King Les Pariablues is the worst of that sort. And there is that one word in particular that Jeko repeated that haunts the boy, *Heitii...heitii...heitii...* But now a cry cuts through Koje's stupor and the boy's tortured cycle of thoughts.

"Aiwa! Aiwa! Tebal! Tebal, lelal granel canel. Thues ete phumile yada. Eses yareh!"

Bridegroom? the boy wonders. Jeko bursts into the room and grips his shoulder, commanding him with the rest of the servants. "Make sure the lamps are lit! He'll be knocking any moment." The boy scrambles to do as Jeko says in hopes of minimizing the punishment the king will inflict on him.

Of course, the king is the bridegroom.

"Aiwa! Aiwa! Tebal! Tebal, lelal granel canel. Thues ete phumile yada. Eses yareh!"

The music of celebration continues to reach his ears. By the moment, it gets louder, and by the moment, the boy's chest tightens. He should've known that no matter what he did, it would never be enough for this master who is the cruelest of all. Whatever Koje has had him do to the other servants will be nothing compared to what the king will do to him to express his displeasure. Why did Koje have to purchase him just to put him in this position? But Koje didn't seem concerned for himself...

"To your feet. Serves you right to face your lord looking fully the fool you are," the boy hears Jeko say to Koje as he pulls him up.

The vibration of the knock on the palace door nearly brings the boy to his knees.

"To the door, the king is here!"

The boy cowers, but Jeko has pulled him in right next to Koje in the courtyard. They will be judged together. The gates swing open, and the boy's eyes catch the king's. It is in this moment that he realizes that he has been sorely mistaken about the king and has more reason to fear him than he ever could've imagined. He wishes this ragged breath could be his last so he doesn't have to face his master's judgement. Koje deceived him and he fell for it! He can't remember being angrier in his life than at this moment. This king...no one told him how good he is, but he can see it. If he was a mile away, he could still spot the difference between King Pariablues and all of the other masters he has known.

The procession of celebrants are not dancing and singing out of compulsion. Theirs is a genuine celebration. And the way his servants greet him now with not just bows, but also embracing him as a highly respected friend, and the cheers, the way they are all smiling...

The boy slips down to his knees, knowing that any punishment the king will inflict will be just. The king dismounts and so do his bride and three boys. Princes. And there is another older prince too. Jeko smiles the widest as he grips the king's arm in a handshake while also taking a knee. King Pariablues pulls his middle-aged servant back to his feet. The chief servant also bows before the new queen and the princes.

"And, tell me, Jeko, what is the state of things here?"

"My lord can see and judge for himself." Jeko turns to Koje and the boy. The boy stays on his knees.

"All is not well, Jeko?"

"These two have been beating the servants, Your Majesty."

The boy keeps his head down while Koje laughs stupidly.

"And you can see that they have squandered your stores of food and drink as well, my lord."

"I can see that, and who is this boy?"

"Koje purchased him from the market while you were gone and taught him his ways. Lied about you." The fury in the chief servant's voice makes the boy tremble even more. He'll be tortured, killed...or– worse– be left to suffer.

"Let us go to the throne room. Bring the two of them to stand before me. You will stand before me as well, Jeko."

The boy's legs are nearly too weak to carry him as a firm hand grips each of his shoulders. Koje bumbles along, seemingly too drunk to care what is going on.

"Be seated," King Les Pariablues says once he, his queen and princes have all taken their seats at the far end of the room. The boy keeps his eyes and knees on the floor. All the while, Koje scoffs. The boy clenches his fists. How did he fall for this? As the moments have passed, he has only become more certain of the king's good character. It is too obvious, too stark a contrast to all the evil characters to be in doubt.

"To those much is given, much is also required. Those who know what I ask and do not do it will be punished severely, but for those who don't know and go against my will, they will be punished less severely. Take heed to what you witness here today, and remember that there is mercy.

"Now, Jeko, give me a full report."

And the chief servant does. The king also calls on others of his servants, all by name, from children to seasoned workers. Through it, a full account is laid out of what Koje and the boy have done. And the boy only trembles more by the moment and continues to bow lower until his face is to the ground under the weight of what he has done. He is in awe too. For the first time in his life, he is seeing pure and genuine indignation. Acting as Koje directed him has given him a glimpse of his own heart, but being in King Les Pariablues' presence is pulling back the curtain entirely. All his life, he has wished for the downfall of his and others' tormentors, but who is he to take vengeance on the bands when his heart is no different than theirs?

But something else, a new glimmer of hope burns in his heart. This king is good, truly good. So, if any judge is to have mercy, it will be him.

"Mercy," the boy hears himself whisper the plea, but he quickly clamps his mouth shut and lets the desperation silently grow within him. The king has every right to do as he pleases with him for what he has done to his servants. So, he will remain silent and bear whatever is to come knowing that for once his suffering will be just.

At last, the king pronounces his verdicts, starting with, "Blessed are you, Jeko, for you have been faithful. As for you, Koje, you have disgraced me in your unfaithfulness time and time again. Take him away. He is to be put to death." And with a wave of his hand, the king's servant is taken away, still in his rebellious drunken stupor. "As for this boy: five lashes with your rod, Jeko, will do for him."

The boy does not move.

"Rise," the king says.

But the boy cannot. His eyes stay on the floor. That cannot be all, he barely felt the rod. He doubts that he will even have a bruise.

"Rise, Reydeyn," the king commands.

The boy's head jerks up, eyes wide. Before instinct can pull his eyes away from the king's, he sees a smile that keeps his gaze on King Les Pariablues. For the first time in years, he lets his tears go. "Comostasia?" He struggles to catch his breath. "How do you know my name?" He thought he lost it long ago, yet hearing it has brought it back to him from a place he could never retrieve it himself.

"I call all who are mine by name."

"I am yours," he whispers in agreement with his master.

King Pariablues stands from his throne, steps forward and takes Reydeyn's hands, pulling him to his feet in order to embrace him. "Then come and join us at my table. I will serve you myself." He looks in Jeko's direction, giving him the same invitation.

The boy starts to obey, only to turn his face aside and weep into his master's shoulder. How can he talk about serving him alongside Jeko? His faithful servant of so many years, while he has just arrived and caused nothing but trouble.

Jeko puts a hand on the boy's shoulder from behind as all gathered in the throne room take in the scene. "Mercy, Reydeyn, your king is generous with his mercy. Do not forget that."

The king holds the boy close to his heart as he sobs. "Welcome home, Reydeyn. Welcome home."

Chapter 8

*"N*icaia, welcome home."

"Your Majesty." The echo of the closing of the heavy palace door off the ornate stone walls in the entryway has barely faded.

Pari doesn't comment on how his stepson stubbornly avoids any insinuation of the king as his father. "What are you doing?"

"I thought that no one would need the light anymore." So why burn the fuel through the night?

King Les Pariablues takes the lamp from his hand. "After a lamp is lit, no one puts it under a basket or a bed or in the cellar. It's put on a stand." He replaces the lamp, and Nicaia watches the flames as they flicker. "So that all in the house can see by it. Nothing will stay hidden forever, son. Someday it will all be out in the open."

Nicaia feels his jaw tense. He does not like feeling so exposed.

"And your eye, Nicaia, your eye is the lamp of your body. When your eye is healthy, your whole body is full of light, but when it is bad, your body is full of darkness. Therefore, be careful that the light in you isn't darkness. If then your whole body is full of light, having no part dark, it will be wholly bright, as when a lamp with its rays gives you light." The king pauses.

Nicaia feels somewhat confused by Pari's words, but he stands in place all the same. He's not about to be rude, not about to have fault found in him. However, he can't help but tense as Pari puts his arm around his shoulders. "And then there is that city." He raises a hand as though he can brush it across the dark horizon that lies beyond the walls of the palace.

Nicaia stiffens anew. "The one you can only become a citizen of if you're born again." He says it to keep the king pleased. He will obey as he has always done and then the king will have no excuse to break the promises of the inheritance deed. It is not as though there is anyone to keep him accountable, but Nicaia will know in his heart that when he does break it that the king will be the one in the wrong while he will be blameless.

"Yes, that city. The citizens let their light shine for all to see, and so all who see their good works glorify their Father who dwells there. It truly is a glorious city, son."

The boy squirms. *If anyone deserves to be a citizen, it is me*, the boy thinks, mentally tallying up his list of perceived good works, forgetting what his father said about being born again.

"And what were you doing out there so late?"

"Things needed to be tended. Sowing season is coming soon."

"It is, but there is no need for you to work all hours of the night, son. It's late, come and eat with me and then get a good rest tonight."

"I'm not hungry...Goodnight," the boy mutters.

"I love you, son."

The boy squirms once again. His mother may be married to this king, but he is not his son, and he will not call him father, no matter how many times it is insinuated that he should. Siohtion and Onxwade certainly have no misgivings, and then there's Reydeyn. If anyone should be the king's son it is him, but he is still a servant, a lot like Jeko, really.

In an attempt to make his months of the resting season here bearable, Nicaia has kept himself busy in the stables, grudgingly learning from Reydeyn about caring for the horses and just generally trying to avoid everyone. He is glad that sowing is almost here, not because he'll be with Jeko or anyone else but because he'll get to work. And be away from this place and the people found here, including his overbearing mother who says she is just concerned.

And what does he really want? To put the king in his debt by working for him? As the boy lies down to sleep, he doesn't really know. He just knows that he will never be able to call King Les Pariablues his father. He'll always be Pari, the stranger who, with his son, Azar, interrupted their lives and put him and his family in their debt. If he's really the king, Pari could've just dealt with Owner right away instead of waiting until harvest to arrest him and his servants and then trying them so publicly in the throne room before sentencing them to the mines to work for the rest of their lives, among other sentences that he saw as appropriate for each individual.

There's a knock on his door. "Nicaia? Are you awake? It's Mom."

He closes his eyes and doesn't move.

"Goodnight. Try not to stay out so late again. I love you," she whispers the same words she has for many nights before kissing him on the forehead. With the door shut behind her again,

Nicaia slowly opens his eyes. She thought he was sleeping already. Convenient. He didn't want to talk.

    Nicaia's mind drifts to his brothers. Siohtion and Onxwade wanted to share a room here in the palace, and now the twins sleep in there too. Despite insisting on a little sister, Onxwade has very much warmed up to the idea of two little brothers. Siohtion too has taken to Lazarus and Lumin. Nicaia rolls over onto his side. Is he the only one who cares that the two of them will never know their father? And then there's Onxwade who seems to have forgotten him already, despite knowing him for five years.

    Nicaia keeps on tossing and turning. Why does the light bother him so much every night when he comes in? Why does Pari have to act like he knows...knows things that he just can't? Things about Nicaia that the boy is ignorant of about himself.

    The boy clenches his fists and wishes with all his might for the sowing to come so that he can leave this place that is supposed to be home but can never be.

    Votol trots with head up, gleeful in his enjoyment of the open road. Jeko smiles and pats his mount on the side of his long black neck. He looks over at Reydeyn just behind him and to his left. The former slave looks even more thrilled than the beast. His smile and bright eyes say it all. Jeko looks back at Nicaia who rides to his right. The boy's jaw is set and his shoulders as straight as ever. The sower wonders at the look of determination on the boy's face, wonders what lies underneath.

    "How were the sheep when you left?" Jeko asks Reydeyn. The young man has been spending all of his time that he isn't in the stable or with the king with the crown prince and his flock.

"Azaryada is a good shepherd. He's taught me a lot."

"How's Siohtion?"

Reydeyn smiles. "He's just another sheep we have to keep an eye on. And when Onxwade is out there, well..." He keeps smiling.

"Just think, Lumin and Lazarus might join you one day."

"If they're gonna be anything like their brothers, that will add a whole other dynamic."

"Do you think you're going to be a shepherd?"

"Yeah, I'd like to be, but I have a lot to learn."

"I'm glad you have both come along with me for sowing this year." Jeko glances in Nicaia's direction again, but he gets no response. Typical. No, Jeko does not understand the prince and his resentment. He should be grateful for the king's generosity, but the servant has lived to serve his lord long enough to see the grateful and ungrateful recipients of his goodness and be reminded time and time again that King Les Pariablues and his crown prince son Azaryada are kind to even the unthankful and evil.

"Stop here a moment," he instructs his two companions. "Woah!" Votol neighs and stamps his feet in protest. At the moment, the wind in his mane is far more inviting than the shade of this budding tree.

"What is it, Jeko?" Reydeyn asks, always the eager pupil, while Nicaia just sits there in the saddle, ever compliant, obedient. On the surface.

Jeko looks back and forth at his two pupils. Such a contrast. Wide-eyed wonder to dull-eyed boredom. Gratitude to resentment. Willing servant with his ears bearing the royal purple sapphire studs in his ears to ungrateful son given the crown and signet ring of a beloved prince.

The Sower reaches into a pouch at his heart and pulls out a tiny seed for his two traveling companions to see. "See how those birds are nesting in the branches of this tree?" He motions to the source of the shade. Votol stamps again, and Jeko places a hand on the creature's neck, patting it, silently telling his mount to hold on just a moment more.

"What about them?" Reydeyn asks with genuine curiosity. "Is that the kind of seed the tree grew from?"

Nicaia gives him a look. "You don't know what a mustard seed looks like?"

"No, Your Highness." There is no sarcasm in the young man's response. Jeko admires him for it. The prince is at least ten years younger than him and treats him like ground he has every right to walk on, all the while maintaining a cold front of politeness.

Jeko hands the seed to Reydeyn, and the young man carefully receives it. He borders on being overly cautious with the tiny item. His fascination reminds Jeko of himself.

"I'm listening. Please, continue with what you were saying, my lord," he says.

Jeko smiles. He feels the difference interacting with the two so starkly. One is like a soft field that has just been rained on, worked up as easily as butter and yielding a harvest many times the initial sowing. The other is rocky, making every step behind the plow hard labour, only yielding sprouts that quickly wither away with the first rising of the sun upon them, only springing up long enough to sow false hope of a return on the sweat that salted the ground.

"What do you notice about the seed, Nicaia?"

The boy tensely sets his jaw. In his mind, Jeko hears the grinding of an ungreased millstone. "It's small," he says.

Les Pariablues

Jeko watches as Reydeyn's eyes travel from the tiny golden ball in his hand. "It's so small and yet...The tree is huge. Bigger than any other herb plant."

"Exactly."

"Sounds like that glorious city," Reydeyn says, searching Jeko's eyes for confirmation.

Jeko nods, smiling. "Go on," he encourages after he sees Reydeyn's eyes dart over to Nicaia.

"Tiny and insignificant isn't a problem for the greater King. That's how his kingdom works. It grows."

"Exactly." The middle-aged servant grips the young man's shoulder. He knows that underneath his garment, his skin is scarred by a thousand beatings given by men who knew nothing of this Kingdom that this former slave is now a citizen of.

Being a slave may have preserved his life during many battles, but it is also through being a slave that the young man knows that he was brought to an understanding of his need for the saving of his soul. It was through the evil of a fellow servant reflected in his own heart, through the goodness and justice and mercy of the Koingsung– "King of the Samaritans"– that reflected the light of the truth about the one true greater King, who is the good King of that glorious city, the King who paints the sunsets, through Reydeyn's downcast eyes and into his weary heart.

There, it pierced him. He was confronted by his own evil heart, and he was confronted by the Saviour who paid his debt. It was after his meal with the king, during which he was told about the greater King, that he bowed his knee to him. He savours the memory of that moment, when the queen embraced him, now his sister. She told him about the visits that the king and his crown prince son paid her and her boys and how she too bowed the knee. He savours the lessons since then that have given him the chance to know his greater Lord better.

Reydeyn starts to hand the seed back, but Jeko pushes his hand away and closes his hand around it.

"Keep it until you find a place to sow it. I have one for you, too, Prince Nicaia." He reaches into his pouch and pulls out another seed. The boy takes it mechanically. Without his past experience, Jeko would withhold the gift, seeing no reason to give a seed away when it will not be put to good use. Jeko nudges Votol on, but only at a walk so that he can continue talking to his two companions.

"The Kingdom is like seeds in another way too. When a seed is sown, its sower doesn't really know how it grows, but they see that it does. First it sprouts, and then it grows until it produces a crop that is then harvested." Jeko looks over at Reydeyn and sees his bright-eyed enthusiasm has been dimmed. "Are you alright, Reydeyn?"

He shakes his head. "I'm fine, thank you. What other lessons did you have, sir?"

"Just one more for the moment, then we'll let these horses run free." Jeko takes a breath. "Just as we can now see the signs of spring, we must keep watch for the signs of the greater King's coming."

"After great tribulation," Reydeyn says, still subdued.

"Right."

The young servant nods. Jeko meets eyes for a brief moment with Nicaia, and upon seeing that the lesson is done, the boy prince spurs his horse forward. Jeko watches for a moment and sighs before rewarding Votol's patience. He glances back to ensure that Reydeyn follows.

As he rides, he wishes that his heart was not so heavy for the prince, but even the spring air rushing into his nostrils and through his never shorn hair cannot clear the dark storm clouds from the horizon of his mind's eye. Trouble with Prince Nicaia is coming.

Chapter 9

"What are you doing?" Nicaia demands, stirring where he sits on the ground several paces away.

Startled, Reydeyn tenses. The prince is even more ornery than usual after that last village. The young servant clears his throat, the familiar apprehension has risen as it always does when he is addressed by a superior. Over the months, it has faded a little with the king and queen, Prince Azaryada, Jeko and others he knows he can trust, but he can't imagine that his instinctual fear of those in authority will ever cease. He has to clear his throat again, the delay only adding to his nervousness. "Just mending my garment, Your Highness."

As many times as he has been told and shown that he is not required to avert his eyes when speaking to those in authority, he cannot help it, not with Nicaia. His inability to obey in that respect only worsens his state. For one, he's cowering before a boy half his age, but, more than that, he feels as though he's displeasing his king. The thought of the king's first embrace comes to comfort him as it has many times. So sweet.

"I can see that. And I might have had you mend mine as well, but it looks like you don't know much of anything."

"What are you talking about, my lord?"

"You don't use new cloth to mend an old garment! It doesn't work, the new cloth just pulls at the old and makes it worse." The boy shakes his head and glares at Reydeyn.

The young man shifts backward.

"What?" Nicaia demands and then realizes. "I'm not going to strike you. Don't you know anything?"

"Perhaps not, my prince." Reydeyn swallows and leaves their camp, retreating to the river bank, gripping the cloth hard in his hands with his needle, thread and the new cloth.

"What are you doing?" Nicaia inquires bitterly when Jeko comes over from the horses to where the prince sits stewing on the grass a short distance from the road.

"With what, my prince?"

"The seeds," he says miserably. "Why the waste?" *Samaritans. Samaritans! Get out!* Those and other curses ring in the boy's ears. If he ever thought becoming prince was a good thing, that sentiment is now gone.

"I do not enjoy the bruises either, but they are worth it for the harvest."

Nicaia shakes his head. How can the people be so ungrateful for the seeds they bring? "What harvest?"

"There is always a harvest."

"I don't want to talk." The boy gingerly rubs his bruised arms and legs. If Pari really is a king, then he should send his army in.

Just like he should've done with Owner long before he ever had a chance to put a bag over his head or anyone else's. And the boy knows that Owner put bags over many heads before he ever got around to his family. Pari only rescued them to get his mother as a bride. To think that he's supposed to be his son and the king sent him out here to get pummeled! Why doesn't he come out here himself?

"You'll see, there will be a harvest."

Nicaia shakes his head. "Just leave me alone, Sower." The first night Pari and Azar spent at their house, and Pari entertained them with the story of the Sower, Nicaia had no idea that just a year from then he would be traveling with the Samaritan Sower himself, be a Samaritan, and a Samaritan prince at that. When it was just a story and he asked Azar why the sower wasted the seeds, the crown prince answered that the seeds reveal what every soil is made of. However, neither that answer nor what Jeko has said just now has given him a satisfactory answer about the waste of seeds or his injury at the hands of angry villagers in the process of wasting them.

"For now, but we'll be moving on in the morning, my lord."

"Whatever."

Reydeyn sighs, unable to shake the pain emanating from his left cheekbone. Why does Nicaia intimidate him so much? Perhaps it is because he has something that Reydeyn does not. Determination. Backbone. But Reydeyn also knows that he has citizenship that Nicaia does not. And for that reason, the prince is not to be envied.

Reydeyn thinks back on the last two days and the many villages they have passed through. Each one has its own personality as does each citizen who makes their home in it. Some gratefully receive the seed given by the king, while others remind Reydeyn of Nicaia in that they accept the seed with a cold politeness but not with gladness, blind to their own need. Some proudly present the ground that they have tilled, bragging about it. Others shyly approach Jeko, scarcely willing to offer what they have plowed, embarrassed.

Others do not disguise their ingratitude, talking about how they don't really need the seed and are just trying to make space as though they're doing the king some sort of favour. And then there are the others who are the reason why their garments are in need of washing and mending. The ones who don't just use their words to revile them. But then some see the seeds as so precious that they snatch them from the path or some other inhospitable ground before the birds can peck them up. They are the ones who gather up the seeds formerly received with cold indifference in order to sow them in a more suitable place.

He has watched, Jeko– the Samaritan Sower– respond in kind to the attitudes of the villagers. For the humble, there is generosity. For the proud, there is scarcity. For the unresponsive and indifferent, there is little to no response. To the hostile, there is mercy and longsuffering, seeds left on the path, the only ground they allow the Sower to tread, and that for the toll of blows.

Reydeyn sets aside the items in his hands and takes a knee at the river's edge. He fills his palm with the flowing water and then splashes it onto his cheek. It stings a little, but the coolness is just what he needs. He feels like he is doing something wrong, leaving Jeko to tend the horses alone, but the older servant ordered him to take a break. He closes his eyes and lets a handful run over his head and down his neck. It might seem like a simple pleasure to some, but he will never take it for granted. His eyes snap open, heart pounding. He forces himself to take a breath. He unclenches his fist from around his dagger, reminding himself he does not have to be afraid of a master breathing down his neck, whip in hand.

Why can't he seem to break free? He's free, but it seems as though everything turns his thoughts back to his life as a slave. All Jeko had to do was mention harvest in his lesson under the mustard tree, and he was cringing internally because of the crops he has witnessed the bands stealing, and, in all honesty, the crops he stole too. He excused himself at the time because he was just a poor slave who had to survive somehow, but now he's disgusted at himself. He wishes he had a way to pay those villagers back, but they're all either dead or enslaved themselves.

He hears someone behind him and instinctively jumps to his feet. "Jeko," he fumbles to catch his breath. "How are the horses?"

He feels dizzy, and his body aches. As is their duty, he and Jeko did what they could to protect the prince from the assault. Like he even noticed. But why should Reydeyn be angry? He's doing it out of gratitude to the king to whom he owes everything.

"They are fine." The Sower reaches out and grips his arm to keep him from tipping over, but the young man reflexively flinches, causing him to fall anyway. Jeko catches him and has a seat beside him. "How's your head?" He slips off his sandals so that he can soak his feet in the river next to Reydeyn.

"It's fine, sir," Reydeyn mutters.

"How is it really?" Jeko asks.

Though there is not even the slightest hint of rebuke in the Sower's tone, the young man feels it. Not only has he been caught in a lie, but what's worse is that he's acting– once more– like a slave. As such he is showing his ingratitude– again– for his freedom. He's just as bad as the villagers! But the words of the king from his throne come to mind, *Take heed to what you witness here today, and remember that there is mercy.* He clears his throat and takes the second chance Jeko offers. "Throbbing, sir."

"Let me see your wound."

The young man slowly turns his left cheek toward the Sower. It's swelling enough that the bump obstructs his vision. Other than this, he feels he came through the violent villagers alright. He puts a hand to his forehead.

"Go on and lie down."

Once more, he slowly obeys, resting his head in his palms. He exhales slowly and closes his eyes. Jeko can be trusted to care for him, even if he doesn't watch, and the sun is too bright in his eyes.

"Looks broken," Jeko observes about his cheekbone. "Missed your eye, though, that's the important thing. This will sting a little."

Reydeyn wills himself to lie still. As he does, he marvels and nearly breaks down for gratitude. When was the last time someone cared for him like this? He breathes deeply of the spring air as the Sower tends his wound.

"Have a drink of this." Even as Jeko says it, he raises Reydeyn's head up and helps him drink. "You feel sick?"

"A little, I think."

"That should help. We'll rest here and then continue tomorrow if you are well enough."

"You don't need to stop for me."

Jeko laughs. "And you think I'm in the mood to make Nicaia keep moving when all he wants to do is pout? Not today. Besides, it's almost evening anyway, and your head needs all the rest it can get. It wasn't made to take a rock."

"At least I saw it coming," Reydeyn says, using conversation to distract himself from the tenderness of his cheekbone while Jeko tends it. As much as he appreciates the care, he breathes a sigh of relief when Jeko finishes. He opens his eyes and sees that Jeko has taken up his garment. All three of them changed when they camped. Having more than one thing to wear is still very new to Reydeyn.

"What are you doing?" he asks, sitting up instinctively, the question coming out too briskly for his liking. "Sorry," he adds when he is back on the ground and his head has settled down after the sudden movement.

"For what?"

"I, I'm thinking like a slave again. I never liked anyone touching my things, little that I had, but I couldn't..."

Jeko holds his gaze with gentle eyes. "What?"

"I couldn't say anything." Reydeyn's heart pounds in his chest. Since when does he share what he is thinking with anyone? Since he was set free. The thought puts a smile on his face. One small step toward living in light of the truth.

"I didn't mean to upset you."

"You don't need to apologize."

Jeko reaches out and puts a hand on Reydeyn's shoulder. "To answer your question, I was going to see what I could do about mending it."

"Thank you, and, and thank you for looking after my wound."

"My pleasure. Don't let Prince Nicaia trouble you."

"Wait, will he be alright back at the campsite? He's the prince, and we have to protect him." He almost gets up again, but thinks better of it with his head. Jeko is more competent for the task anyway.

"Don't worry. I can see him from here."

"Oh."

"Rest, Reydeyn."

"What were you saying?"

"Don't let the prince trouble you. It is my pleasure to teach you."

"Yes, sir." It's the only response he can think of, but it hurts him because it is the response he uttered so often as a slave. Two words that he wonders whether he will ever wash off of the tip of his tongue for good.

"I heard what he said to you about your garment."

"You did?"

"Yes, and it honestly would not surprise me if all of the surrounding villages did. His rudeness aside, he has a point."

"Go on."

"The old and new..." Jeko pauses to think. "Old covenant and new covenant...Freedom and slavery."

Reydeyn opens his eyes again to look up at the older servant's face. "I don't understand, sir."

"Just like sewing new cloth into old just makes the tear worse, so everything must be thought of in its proper place."

"I can't think the same way now that I'm free?"

"In more than one sense. Under the greater King's old covenant, there was the law that his people were under. Now, we are under grace, grace being the great King's power in us that is how we can obey his law. Everything in its place."

"Yes, sir."

"Is the rejection troubling you like it's troubling Prince Nicaia?"

"I don't know if trouble is the right word," Reydeyn says slowly.

Jeko encourages him with a wave of his hand. "Speak freely, my friend."

"I have been hurt far–" Reydeyn swallows. He knows in his head that he is free, but he is not used to this kind of friendship. And to think that they won't be separated in a battle or by one of them being sold...He wonders whether he will ever wrap his mind around his new way of life.

The Sower has his eyes fixed on him, but the young man struggles to articulate anything more. He clears his throat nervously. "Does it trouble you?"

"I feel joy and sorrow," the king's chief servant says.

"Yeah," Reydeyn says, relieved to have words put to his feelings so that they don't feel so vague.

"Sorrow because they are rejecting my king."

"But joy because we– Sorry, I interrupted you."

Jeko smiles. "Finish what you were saying."

"I, I'm glad that, that...I don't know how to say it."

"It's proof we belong to him because we're being treated the same way as him."

"And to get to stand in the way of what was coming at his son...even though he doesn't see himself as his son..." Reydeyn sighs, frustrated by his inability to master his tongue.

"Bittersweet, indeed. And speaking of the prince, I'm going to build a fire for all of us." He reaches over and gets his arm under the young man's arms to ease him up to his feet.

Reydeyn feels as though he will fall on his face, but Jeko holds him firm until he lays him down next to where he intends to build the fire. "Here, have a little more of this." He puts the skin to the young man's lips. "There, lie down now. You'll be alright, my friend."

Chapter 10

"It's the Sower!!" a woman's voice heralds from a place Nicaia can't discern as the party of three approaches the village.

The prince, a teenager as of this year, braces himself. He takes a sideways glance at Jeko, unsure what to think of this greeting. Will there be citizens in this village who will welcome them or will there only be more stones cast at them. The prince has always known about the Sower for as long as he can remember, but he never thought that he would be traveling with him, much less be forced into taking the same ridicule.

Especially after all that he has been through with Reydeyn and Jeko, Nicaia is glad at the thought of ending this journey at his family's vineyard. And now it is just a few miles off. This morning, Jeko said that they would reach it in time to spend the night.

There is a lot of work to do before harvest, and Nicaia wishes that he would have left the palace sooner, but the king assured him that the property would be well taken care of. Jeko also told him this morning that they would be meeting the people the king charged with the duty and be hosted by them.

Nicaia wonders how he ever agreed to the arrangement, despite how his mother was fine with it. The prince was not comfortable, in truth, with leaving his mother and brothers at the palace, which kept him from the vineyard. He knows he has been dragging his heels this entire time on the journey because he resents the space between him and them. But they all wanted to stay with Pari and Azar.

And so here he is with Reydeyn accompanying him to assist him in overseeing his vineyard and those who work it, whether hired or a servant. Reydeyn. A servant. The servant who acts more like the king's son than him. Reydeyn, rather than any of his brothers who are supposed to inherit the vineyard with Nicaia. Even Siohtion, the next oldest son...But he's chosen to stay with Azar and his flock of sheep.

Unbelievable.

But Nicaia can't convince his family to act as they should. In time they'll see the king's true colours for themselves– and not the purple and white reserved for royalty. When that happens, he won't have to say a word. Then they'll thank him for securing the vineyard...for all the good it will do when the king turns on them. Then again, as prince, he figures he can do something about amassing his own following who will stand behind him when the time comes. Perhaps even the villagers who threw rocks at him because they believed that he belonged to the king will be among his following. Once they see who he really is, then they'll be on his side. And there is a good number of them.

"The Sower is here! He's here!" A young woman around Reydeyn's age comes racing out to meet them. "Jeko!"

"Par yada, Acacia! To you and all the house of your father, Qodei." Jeko dismounts, reaches out and embraces her, laughing. "It's so good to see you." He kisses her hand.

Reydeyn slides out of the saddle while the prince remains in place. He wishes to be back on his feet after sitting for so long, but he must look his regal part.

"Yada ues, Jeko!" She laughs as well. "And this must be His Highness, Prince Nicaia." She gives a graceful bow with a sort of flourish of her robe.

Nicaia clears his throat. "Yes, I'm Prince Nicaia."

"Yada ues, Your Highness."

Nicaia forces himself not to stare at her. It's just that he's unaccustomed to the sight of such brilliant green eyes.

"And you must be Reydeyn," she says, turning to the servant.

"Yes, ma'am."

"Oh, please, don't make me feel like a grandma." She laughs again and grasps his hand in greeting. The scent of her family's anointing oil wafts toward the three visitors on the evening breeze. "Just call me by name. Acacia."

Reydeyn nods. "Alright."

She motions for the travelers to follow her. "Come, come, you look like you need rest after your journey. My entire family has been eager to greet you as soon as the king's messenger arrived to tell us. Oh, it really is good to see all three of you. Are you well?"

While the two servants lead their horses, Nicaia stays in the saddle and silently nudges his horse on at a walk. The creature follows his command flawlessly.

Jeko reaches out and puts his free hand on Reydeyn's closest shoulder. "We are, though I order some special treatment for this young man. As you can see, he took a stone for the prince in a particularly vulnerable spot."

The younger servant turns away, cheeks reddened by more than just the wind.

"Oh, come now, don't blush, son." Jeko laughs. "I'm proud of you." He grips the young man's shoulder and pulls him a little closer.

"Thank you, Jeko."

The Sower slaps him on the back, and it is a pleasant thought to Reydeyn that it is not painful.

"My father is a skilled physician. He will see that you are treated well," Acaia says.

"I'm really alright."

"And he will see that you are better, my friend." Reydeyn glances at her just in time to catch her winking.

Reydeyn dips his chin once in acknowledgement, burying his uncertainty. He is only just starting to become accustomed to friendly jest and tender teasing. But he does not want to appear rude in his caution.

"And how is the vineyard, Acacia?" Nicaia asks with all of the air of a prince that he can conjure up.

"Very well, Your Highness."

"I would like to see it."

"This evening, my lord?"

"Yes, that would be ideal."

"That can be arranged. My lord may even sleep in his house that is there tonight if that is what he prefers. He is certainly most welcome to stay at our home as well. Whatever is your pleasure." She gives him a nod.

"And has anyone been staying in the house since we left?" Nicaia asks.

"No, Your Highness. It has been strictly respected in that regard. It is your family's home, and thus it is up to you whom you entertain therein. However, it has been maintained according to the king's command."

Nicaia swallows and nods. "I see. Good." He has a crawling suspicion that something will be out of place. And even if he finds nothing, he concludes that it is either the case that something is amiss that will escape his notice, or the king is just drawing him into the false assurance of his favour. He holds in a sigh.

"If anything is out of order, my father will personally make it right. That is his duty and his pleasure. He will restore and then some, my lord."

"He sounds honourable." Just as his own father was, but he doesn't trust her assessment. They are the king's servants. He is surrounded by the king's servants.

The bruises and scratches and the thought of his torn garments are frustrating him more and more the longer they dwell in his mind. How dare the villagers treat him like that when he isn't with the king! Jeko and Reydeyn, they can rightly be seen as one with the king, but why should he be forced into the role?

Why couldn't Nicaia have had the brains in his head to ride alone back to his home, drag his family with him if he had to? But no, the king would come after them. The moment he doesn't do as the king wishes, he will be crushed by his wrathful displeasure, just as Koje was. Perhaps there was so-called mercy for Reydeyn, but Nicaia does know what the king asks, so he cannot imagine the king allowing him to live. For now, there is no use in crossing him anyway, since there is not enough evidence to indict the king of misdeeds. The boy sighs. He must be patient.

"We do not have to go tonight if you do not wish. You may rest, Your Highness," Acacia says.

Nicaia slides off of his horse and grips the reins tightly to keep himself on his feet in such a way that no one will notice that he stumbles at all. He leads his horse behind him. "I wish to see the vineyard tonight."

"Alright, my lord. We will go straight from my father's house. You will at least allow us the pleasure to wash your feet and anoint you to make your arrival official, my prince?"

"Yes, that is fine, Acacia. Thank you for your hospitality. Par yada." Now that he is the one speaking to her rather than Jeko or Reydeyn, he can pronounce the greeting of a guest.

"Yada ues. It is my pleasure for the sake of the king. And, Jeko, it will be official, won't it?"

Nicaia is confused for a moment before he remembers what the king said about a ceremony to welcome a daughter of a dear citizen and servant of his into official servitude to His Royal Majesty.

Jeko smiles. "Yes, daughter. It will be. King Pariablues, Prince Azaryada, Queen Vaht and the other five princes themselves are coming soon, and then it will be, as promised."

"They are coming soon, aren't they?" Acacia asks.

"Yes, very soon."

"Why didn't they come with us?" Nicaia asks, put off anew by the thought that they are coming to the same place as them but did not travel with them. It's not like the prince wanted to travel with them. It's just that, that, well, he isn't quite sure what it is. Just one more thing to get under his skin.

"They had a different route they wished to take, Your Highness."

"Of course." And his brothers won't be staying to work in the vineyard either once the ceremony is through.

"The vineyard is beautiful, even in the resting months, great prince," Acacia says.

"Yes, it is beautiful."

"I will gladly work in it throughout the year. My father's entire household will, my lord."

"As you have kept it during these months?"

"Yes, Your Highness."

"Good. And, you may drop the titles, they are rather redundant."

"Of course. May I call you Nicaia, then?"

"Yes, you may."

"If I may, it's hard for me to believe that we only lived a short distance apart until last harvest and yet we never really met."

"At the river. I saw you there a few times." For, that is one of the most common places where citizens from different villages meet one another. How could he forget her with those eyes of hers?

She nods. "I probably saw you too, I guess."

"Jeko! Yada ues, my brother."

"Qodei. You look well." The two men embrace.

"And I see you have brought your apprentice and the prince. Very good." The large man bows, the end of his dark beard scarcely missing the ground. "Your Highness."

Nicaia is not sure whether he finds the man's exaggerated gesture more amusing or annoying. "Greetings. Par yada." The boy thinks back to the many visits that Pari and Azar paid him and his family. Now, he is the royal visitor being hosted. He just wants to go home. But he will endure the customary greeting, the feet washing and anointing only to wipe away the scent and the scent of the royal anointing oil to wear the anointing oil of his family, even if just for a night in bed when only he will smell it before reapplying the royal oil he is expected to wear to go out in the morning. Even if his brothers and his mother forget his father, he never will. He will never be a member of King Les Pariablues' house. He simply cannot be.

And so, he sits and watches as Qodei performs the greeting duties of a host, bears the common courtesy by comforting himself with thoughts of home. Tonight, he will finally lie down in his own bed and then get up to work in his own vineyard. He will prove himself and in the process, prove the king false. He must keep that end goal in mind. Until then, he will be the flawless prince. Flawless, yes, flawless in every way. Not one fault.

"Would you like to come now, Nicaia?" Acacia draws him out of his thoughts.

"What?"

"To the vineyard. Or would you like to dine first?"

"I will see the vineyard." He told her not to call him by anything other than his name, but that does not mean he will lose his commanding demeanor.

"Shall we walk?"

"Yes. I have been riding long enough."

"Jeko, are you coming?" Acacia asks.

"No, you two go on."

"Be back before dark, Acacia."

"Yes, father."

Les Pariablues

Nicaia does not wish to come back to Qodei's house. But then again, he knows that he will have to think his actions through carefully. He cannot insult his host. He can always come back with Acacia for dinner and then go home alone, even if he slips away after everyone else is asleep. Yes, that is what he will do. It feels good to have a plan in mind as he sets out beside the bright-eyed young woman.

Chapter 11

"*A*nd you are Reydeyn," Qodei says now that they have settled into the feast upon his daughter and the prince's return from the vineyard.

"Yes. Yes, sir," the young man says, clearing his throat. Even after these past months, it seems that whenever someone calls him by name, his entire being slips back to the glorious moment when the king first called him by name.

"It's good to see you again. You've grown into a fine young man from all that I can see and what the king wrote in his message."

Reydeyn is thankful that he refrained from partaking of another sip from his cup or another bite off of his fork just now. "He wrote about me?"

"Of course."

"You make it sound like you know me, sir."

"You lived in this village as a boy when it and you were both much smaller."

"What? But where I lived– wasn't it destroyed?" He knows that he remembers destruction, but he doesn't trust his memory enough to be sure what happened in more detail than that.

"Yes, it was destroyed. I remember it well. Very well. Acacia was just a little girl of three, but she remembers too."

"One of the raiders killed my mother and slung me over his shoulder. I was screaming and crying harder than I ever have, and I did have some pretty violent tantrums," she says.

"My little fighter. I killed that vile man with one stroke. I've never held my daughter tighter," Qodei says. "She buried her face in my shoulder and refused to take it out for at least a day. We didn't let each other out of sight for...years. My wife was pregnant when she was killed. I was convinced it would be a boy who would defend his big sister, but if it was a girl I knew that she'd be just as beautiful as Acacia and her mother."

Reydeyn automatically finds himself glancing at the woman named Rittelle who sits at Qodei's side, hand on his arm and laughing with one of the servants who sits beside her. That in itself is an oddity: the fact that hired workers and servants sit with the family at the table without partitions.

"You look confused, Reydeyn. What is it?"

The young man shakes his head.

"Come now," Qodei says, "ask freely."

"You remarried?" His throat tightens. It's too personal of a question. He should have kept his mouth closed. How could he cave under such little pressure? He wishes his face would at least not heat so much.

"Ah, yes...Another story. When I was His Highness' age," he means Nicaia, "I lost my family to a raid. There was a boy who was my friend since as long as I can remember. I mean, we grew up in the same village, but that day when we both lost our families, we became brothers. We helped rebuild the village when the king ordered it to be so. And it was his soldiers who drove the bands out of this area. They haven't returned since.

"But, well, the two of us were married on the same day. His wife was pregnant, just as mine was when she was killed. He was also killed that day, and, well, we knew that if anything happened to either of us, we could count on the other. We were family. So, I took his wife in, and we became family in a whole new way not long after she gave birth to a beautiful girl." He motions down the table at the young woman absorbed in conversation. "She shares her mother's name."

"Since then, we have been blessed with three sons, and," he reaches down and picks up a tot, "a curly haired surprise." He laughs as the little girl hides her face behind his beard. "The reason why I am keeping my beard. I would shave it, but how can I deprive her of such innocent entertainment?" He gives a shrug.

Reydeyn smiles at the little fingers poking through.

"She'll grow out of it," Jeko says.

Qodei laughs too loudly at the pun, and Acacia, sitting on his side that his wife does not occupy, shakes her head, smiling. She glances at Reydeyn, and he attempts to give her an understanding expression in return, but he is not sure what his face does. He takes a breath, unable to feel entirely comfortable in this environment. He holds in a sigh. As hard as he tries, that seems to be his fate. It is the same at the king's table. Will he always feel the chafing of the chains?

"But, Reydeyn, you must have more questions, do you not?"

The young man's stomach tightens even more. With a shaking hand he barely trusts, he takes hold of his clay cup and tips it just enough to drain a small amount of its contents down his throat. On top of his discomfort, he feels memories stirring in a deep reservoir of his being. He slowly sets his cup back down on the table and breathes a long sigh of relief when he is certain that he has not spilled. It feels as though at least an hour has passed since Qodei spoke to him, but when he looks up across the table, he finds the man patiently waiting.

"Did you know my family?" he asks as steadily as he can. How can it be that freedom means he can speak like this with a stranger? That this stranger cares about him? That this stranger knew him as a boy and remembers him after all this time?

"Yes."

Reydeyn feels lightheaded.

"Now, where to start..."

The young man clears his throat and takes another drink. He opens his mouth, but he can't form the words.

"What is it, Reydeyn?"

"I...How...I've been–" He closes his mouth.

"Go on," the man says as though he doesn't even hear Reydeyn's stumblings. Their eyes meet, and the slave turned servant reads something in his host's eyes that gives him confidence. No longer a slave owned by those who care nothing for him. He can finally breathe easily, and he's just beginning to realize how much he has held his breath throughout his years.

Reydeyn finds that he can hold the man's gaze, look at him as an equal, a fellow servant of the king, and as a guest to a host. Now, he feels the jitters of excitement that always come when he thinks anew of the meaning of his freedom. Beautiful. Glorious. "I've been wondering how the king knew my name."

"What do you mean?"

The emotion of the memory tightens his throat. "He called me by name. He knew my name, not even I knew my name."

"You forgot it?"

"Yes. No one cared to ask when I was a slave, so...yeah. I forgot."

"When King Les Pariablues meets someone, he never forgets their face or their name."

"He met me?"

"He came through the village with Jeko many years during sowing season. The last time wasn't long before the bands raided us."

"But I was just, just a little boy!"

"And he loves children. You've seen that, surely."

Reydeyn nods. "He came through with..." He looks to the Sower. "I met you?"

"It's very possible, seeing as he did, but I don't have my king's memory." The look of nostalgia softly frosts over Jeko's face. "That was when the late queen yet lived. Azaryada was...six. She lived to see that year's harvest, and it was a great one," he says to himself.

The young servant exhales. It seems impossible that he could've had an interaction with either Jeko or the king, both of whom he now loves dearly, and forgotten. Desperation to know more has seized him. "Please, tell me about my family. I don't even know how many siblings I had, and my parents– My memory is gone." He swallows and tries to blink enough to clear his vision. "Please, Qodei."

"You've been wondering all these years?"

"I...I guess. I didn't realize how much I lost. Did you know them well?"

"Well enough. Your father and mother were skilled musicians."

"Did they sing?"

"Yes. And so did you."

"I...I don't think I remember that I did."

"Don't despair, Reydeyn."

The young man nods but finds himself hiding his face in his hands, the weight of years of grief bowing his head.

"You had a little drum you would play on. And you loved it."

Even though it is not enough for him to raise his head, Reydeyn feels a little lighter at the thought that he has at least a vague recollection of that.

"And when weddings happened, oh, your family always made the celebrations so incredible."

Reydeyn manages to look up long enough to ask another question. "Did I have any brothers or sisters?"

"Yes, you were the youngest. You had...eight older siblings."

"Really?"

"Yes."

"Where– Are any of them still alive?"

Qodei shakes his head. "I don't know. You, you had three brothers and five sisters. The oldest three were girls, and then there was a boy, another girl, two boys and another girl."

"What were their names?"

The man shakes his head.

"But you knew my name."

"I'm like Jeko, I'm afraid. I don't have the memory of our king. I remember your family, but their names...They escape me like so many we lost that day. I had to be told your name to remember. I'm sorry."

"They escape me too." Reydeyn clears his throat and finds himself getting to his feet. He stops himself and isn't sure what to do. He can't just leave. What is he thinking?!

"It's a beautiful night. Jeko, would you like to join us for a walk?" Acacia invites, also standing.

Reydeyn nearly falls back into his chair in relief. So this is what it means to have friends who care. Friend, exactly what Jeko has called him time and time again, but a word he knows he has yet to grasp the meaning of. Perhaps he is just a little closer in this moment.

"Come now." Jeko grips his shoulders. "Let us walk."

"Where are you going?" Nicaia asks.

"On a walk, my lord. Would you like to join us?"

Reydeyn holds still. As much as the prince's contempt disconcerts him, he tells himself that any service to the king's son is service to the king. For that reason, he will endure his presence. And perhaps someday, the two of them will be able to embrace as brothers and fellow born again citizens of the glorious city that the king, the crown prince and the Sower have told him so much about. He hopes for that day to come soon. He petitions the greater King for it, or at least he knows that he should if he really is grateful to be counted a citizen of his.

"I will walk on my own, thank you," Nicaia says.

Jeko turns to Qodei. "We appreciate your hospitality."

"My pleasure. And what cost can it be to me with all of the gifts the king always sends with you?"

Reydeyn's mind jerks to when Jeko gave Qodei the gifts. There was extra in anticipation of Acacia officially coming into the king's service. The memory of the interaction only makes Reydeyn in more need of the crisp spring night air. It's a good thing that Jeko is still gripping his arm too as they walk with the green-eyed young woman.

"Are you alright to walk, my friend?"

Reydeyn gives a loud exhale. "Good question," he mutters, feeling quite unsure of himself and his footing. And yet somehow, his feet keep on falling one in front of the other as they learned to do at a time beyond where his memory can reach.

"Ah, take a deep breath of that air." Jeko demonstrates, and Reydeyn automatically mirrors him. "Ah," he breathes out. Acacia half walks, half skips with her arm linked with Jeko's left while Jeko's right upholds Reydeyn.

Yes, even though he does not remember learning to walk or talk, both abilities have stayed with him. And so, perhaps even though he has lost so many other memories, he does indeed carry things forward. Good things.

But the memory of the gifts given by Jeko to Qodei come back to the surface of Reydeyn's thoughts. He knows that he should trust the king, but he has so many memories. Moments that he did not allow himself to think about too deeply as they happened...But now he knows that they have indeed left an imprint on his soul. Parents buried in debt selling their children, or simply having them torn away in exchange for money that could never compensate for their loss or as a gloating pardon of debt. Families torn apart. And he could do nothing.

He realizes that he has clenched his fists. How could he have just done nothing? Because he was held back. Because he was a coward. He feels dizzy with the vicious spinning of regrets. The web is closing around his lungs. It's all he can do to just keep on walking.

"So, you were a slave, Reydeyn?" Acacia asks.

Les Pariablues

Reydeyn hears himself give a pained laugh. "Isn't it obvious?" He thought he was alright after these months in the palace, but when Prince Nicaia rebuked him for his mending methods...It seems ridiculous even to him, and yet seeing it as unreasonable does not ease the chains' chafing. "Isn't that what I still am?" He can't believe that he actually says it out loud, but he has to let something out to ease the pressure.

She turns and looks at him as Jeko maintains his steady grip. "No, not at all." She says it so matter-of-factly, and he thought the transition would be so simple too. But it isn't! "The king has given you a new identity, just like his greater King gives, but you already know that. You're free."

But I don't feel free, counters bitterness. *And yet it's true. Your feelings cannot shake the truth*, answers sweetness.

"What made you want to serve him? The king of the Samaritans, Koingsung," he hears himself asks.

She laughs at the title. "Because I have learned to love him. How about you, my friend?"

"I...He chose me. He knew my name."

Jeko looks from one to the other, smiling. "Well said, children. Well said."

Chapter 12

The moment Acacia's laughter sounds in Vaht's ears, and she sees the two young servants together in the vineyard, her eyes well up. She nudges her horse closer to the king, her husband.

"This is where you met your first husband?" Pari asks.

"We were younger than the two of them. And we didn't know... Those two get to serve a much better master." The sower of the vineyard, in fact.

"Yada ues, mother, Your Majesty," comes the greeting from the young Prince Nicaia, "and upon all who are arriving with you."

Vaht slides out of the saddle and embraces her son. "Par yada, my son." She puts an arm around him and kisses him on the forehead.

"Nicaia!" Siohtion and Onxwade crowd their older brother.

"Par yada!" Pari announces over the entire vineyard as heartily as ever. "And how are the preparations, Nicaia?"

"They are going well, Your Majesty. Qodei has everything in order."

"Very good. I look forward to seeing him and his entire family. And how are you?" The king dismounts and clasps his son's shoulder.

"I am well." Nicaia is glad to be home, but he has found himself tossing and turning in his bed ever since the first night he arrived with the Sower and Reydeyn. Somehow his bed is not as comfortable as he remembers it.

"Your Majesty!"

Nicaia cringes as Reydeyn comes racing toward the king's party like a madman, pulling Acacia with him, who looks just as excited. He lets her go as he outruns her. He slides to a stop on his knees, and Acacia uses him to stop herself when she reaches him. She bows before the royalty as well. What a show! Nicaia averts his gaze. The servant is acting just as much like a son as ever, bowing aside. He's even standing in between him and the king! Well, let him, it's not like Nicaia wants to be a part of Pari's household anyway.

Pari laughs and draws the young servants up into an embrace, one that he did not offer to Nicaia, but Nicaia did not want one anyway.

"And Jeko, it seems our young friends have outpaced you," Pari claps him on the back as the older servant comes panting up the path.

Jeko holds up a finger, dramatically asking for a moment to catch his breath before he responds. Nicaia finds that he is annoyed while the others laugh at the Sower's show. If these people would have only done as he did, they wouldn't have had to make a scene running up like this. They could have just waited like him to receive the king and his party like a proper host. But no, everything must be so informal and emotional. Honestly.

"It is good to see you, my lord."

"And it is good to see you, my Sower."

Nicaia gives them all a nod and moves away from the group where he does not belong and toward the kitchen as Qodei blows past him, his youngest child perched on his shoulders. His wife and other children, except for Acacia, are not far behind him.

Nicaia ignores them. It seems that everyone is coming out to meet the new arrivals. Well, that just means that there is room for him to make sure that things are in their proper order. He enters the deserted kitchen only to turn at the sound of footsteps behind him.

"Nicaia, my lord."

He turns stiffly, irritated at the interruption of his inspection before it can properly begin. "Yes, Jeko?"

"How are things?"

"Everything looks to be in order."

"Yes, it does. Qodei and his household are very conscientious." The Sower moves around the counter and draws Nicaia's eyes to a bowl of dough. "Take a moment to look at this."

Nicaia disguises his sigh in a long, silent exhale. It seems that Jeko is always trying to give him some lesson using some sort of menial something or other that doesn't deserve significance. But he must not allow fault to be found in himself by not listening. "What about it?"

"The leaven."

Nicaia quietly clears his throat to give himself something to do while he waits for Jeko to get to the point. Perhaps someday, he will get the hint that he should stick with teaching Reydeyn who actually wants to hear these silly snippets. Why should he, a prince, be given the servant's portion? Isn't he the king's son? A servant tutor should be for servants. Just one more thing to show how Pari really esteems him. Forget all of the hot air about him and his brothers being just as much princes as Azar. The truth is that the king sees him as a threat, and so he should if he thinks he will have Nicaia forget that he is the firstborn and that he should be treated as such simply because his mother married a man who already has a son named Azar who is older than him.

Nicaia only listens to Jeko's words so that he is able to respond and not look like a fool if Jeko asks any questions.

"It's much like the mustard tree I told you about on the way here, the least of seeds growing to surpass all of the herbs in stature and giving a place for birds to rest. The Kingdom, that glorious city, is like leaven that a woman hid in flour." Jeko sinks his knuckles into the dough for a moment before taking his hand out again. Nicaia finds himself watching it. "And the yeast makes the entire loaf rise. And so the greater Lord expands his kingdom, even when it is kneaded."

Nicaia nods and refrains from making any comments. The Sower just returned earlier today from his sowing rounds in other villages while Reydeyn remained with Nicaia here at the vineyard.

"Are you well, my lord?" the chief servant asks.

"Yes, Jeko. I am just fine. Now, please see that everything... continues to be set in order."

"Of course. Everything is in good order. Relax. Enjoy yourself tonight as we celebrate."

Nicaia nods, but he knows that he will not. After all, how can he rejoice as another person comes into the service of the king whom he can neither love nor trust?

"Excuse me."

The sparkling sapphire studs in Acacia's ears cannot outshine the brightness of her green eyes, and Reydeyn finds it difficult to take his eyes away. From the first time he saw her, that unique feature has fascinated him, and his wonder has not faded as he has gotten to know her and allowed her to get to know him.

"What is it?" she asks.

"Uh...What?"

"You keep looking at me."

He clears his throat and laughs. "Uh-huh, but no particular reason." After the hours they have spent working alongside one another and the other members of her father's household, he has begun to feel more sure of himself.

She laughs in response, but there is not even a hint of nervousness in her, unlike in him. Reydeyn admires his friend for it. As he sees it, she is not proud but also not insecure, so she is in no way self-absorbed. All told, he figures that he cannot do anything else besides admire her for such noble character. And to think that she calls him her friend, and he calls her his.

"You'd better find somewhere else to look from time to time," she informs him with one of her playful winks.

"Why?" Reydeyn second guesses his response. The last thing he needs is the embarrassment of giving the wrong impression.

"Unless you're ready to take my hand," she says, teasing. "You see, my father is on the lookout for good men like you."

"But, but we just met."

"He knew you as a boy," she says casually, and Reydeyn feels like she enjoys teasing him too much with her words.

"You've got to be kidding me."

She laughs once more. "Only partially. Like any good father he– and my mother too, they are looking out for my future."

"Me?"

"Sure."

"Well, I don't know if I'm ready for a wife." And children? He massages his forehead as though he can get the cramp out of his brain. It is threatening to implode. He was taken as a slave too young to ever consider having a family of his own.

"So, stop looking at me," she giggles, bringing him back to the present moment as though she never said anything to send him hurtling out of it.

Now that she has told him, though jokingly, to look away, it is only harder for him to find something else to look at. She keeps giggling, and Reydeyn finds himself laughing with her just because it is the only natural thing he can think of. At the same time, he realizes that he is okay with her enjoying seeing him flustered, and he knows that means that he trusts her. And trusting is not something that a slave does.

He startles when she touches his arm.

"Don't look so serious. Relax." She breathes deeply, setting an example for him. "There's no need to be concerned. My father loves you and has been honoured to get to know you. As have I. And if you remain a friend and never become anything else, well, that will not be a problem. Now, if he despised you, you would have great cause for concern."

"I wouldn't have made it through the night if he did, I guess."

Acacia smiles at him and raises her ornate clay goblet. The silver rim reflects the flickering torchlight. Each of the goblets around the table have a slightly different design etched into the clay, but they each have the same basic shape and rim. She nods at him, and he realizes that she expects him to raise his cup too. "To friendship between servants of the king."

"To friendship," he answers, feeling a warmth in his belly.

Reydeyn wonders whether the touching of two drinking vessels ever sounded so sweet to his ears. But he doesn't wonder for long because he knows that it never has.

Chapter 13

"*D*id you find it?"

"No, I'm going searching away from these pastures."

"I'm coming with you."

Azar smiles at his younger brother. "I would be happy to have you, Siohtion."

"So, where do we go first?"

"We'll follow the river," the crown prince says.

"What if we don't find the sheep?"

"We will find it. This is my father's prized flock of a hundred, and I will not return until I find the sheep that is lost. As always."

"Then let's go," Siohtion says eagerly. The nine-year-old's sense of adventure is piqued.

Azar smiles at him. "Yes." And just as surely as he will return his father's sheep to the fold, he will ensure that his brother, the king's son, is safely returned home as well. "Onxwade!" he calls.

The boy comes running through the grass. "Yeah?"

"Tell Father that Siohtion and I are going after the sheep that has strayed."

"Okay."

"Go now," he says with a laugh. He finds great pleasure in calling the young boy his little brother.

And so Onxwade runs, ever wishing to please his big brother who now turns to Siohtion. "C'mon, brother. The lost must be found."

Prince Azaryada has been on this type of journey many times, and he knows that plenty of citizens consider it a fool's errand. The crown prince out in the wilderness with bands and wild creatures and the enemy troops? Searching for a single sheep? But the criticisms come from those who do not understand the heart of his father. Or his greater King. And that is the reason why he continues to search like this for the strays and runaways. It is an object lesson, and he hopes and petitions his greater King that the point will sink in for Siohtion. That he will understand that he can always come home and that open arms and celebration await.

And so the two sons of the king dressed in rather common clothing follow the river for the sake of the one.

"What a waste," Nicaia mutters as he watches Azar and Siohtion walk away from the vineyard and up the mountain. "What a waste," he mutters again. Siohtion should be here, tending their inheritance, but instead, the king's crown prince is taking him away into the wilderness where anything can happen. And since his brother is going willingly– Well, when something does happen, he can store it up as more evidence against the king and his son. What kind of king is Pari supposed to be anyway? What kind of prince is Azar? For one little old dirty sheep.

Siohtion should know better than to follow, but it seems that he is as taken as Onxwade now with the idea of a new family. Nicaia shakes his head. He would've thought that even if his little brother didn't know better, he would've soon gotten bored of traipsing here and there between when they left the palace and when they arrived here. But no, he wants to go up into the hill country and mountains with his "big brother".

No matter how many weeds he pulls at, Nicaia cannot uproot the bitter sense of betrayal. His mother and brothers have left his father, and they've left him too. Lumin and Lazarus won't even know about their real father. They'll just think that they were always princes. And princes don't care about tending their inheritance. They just leave it to servants so that they can keep on being lazy and useless.

His hand clamps around another stalk, and he jerks backward at the thorns. He stares at his palm and grits his teeth, considering whether to take the time to remove the tiny intruders.

"My lord, may I see your hand?"

Nicaia clears his throat. "If you must." It is one of Qodei's sons. The prince isn't interested in which one. As the boy works, the prince finds a bit of comfort in simply breathing in the air of the place, despite all of the work awaiting him.

"There, Your Highness, is that all of them?"

Nicaia glances at his hand. "It's good enough. Thank you," he replies stiffly.

The boy gives him a respectful nod and moves away into the vineyard again while Nicaia stares at his palm, jaw set. What if he never sees Siohtion again? He looks away in the direction his brother went, out of sight now. He closes his eyes, in denial of his own tears. If Siohtion wishes to leave, why should he stop him? And if he dies because of his own choices, then that is not Nicaia's responsibility. Or so he tries to tell himself.

"Are you coming, Siohtion?"

The boy slowly gets up off of his knees and secures the top of his water skin. "The water's so good."

"Yes, the best in the kingdom always comes from the mountains. Other than the water, how do you like it up here?"

"It's great."

"I've always thought that it was so beautiful."

"Do you come up here a lot?"

"This seems to be the place that the sheep always stray to."

"They must like the grass better."

"But they don't understand the danger." The prince grips the hilt of his dagger, a knife for throwing. It is only one of several that he carries. Enough to fend off an entire pack of wolves if necessary. And it has been necessary on many of his journeys into the wilderness. "Often what looks best to our eyes and what we want the most is exactly what is most dangerous." In the process of looking around, Azar glances in Siohtion's direction, but only time will tell whether there will be a harvest from these seeds he has sown.

"I hear something! Is that it?"

"Yes." Prince Azaryada would know that sound anywhere. Now, he must find its wooly source.

Queen Vaht wraps her fingers around King Pariablues' arm and leans her head on his shoulder as the two of them stand side by side on the roof, looking away toward the mountains. Waiting for their two boys to return with the lost sheep.

"Is something wrong, my love?"

"I'm concerned about Nicaia." She sighs. "I've known for a while that he doesn't acknowledge you as his father– or even perhaps as his king." Vaht knows that she would not say such a thing if she did not trust Pari. How could she, if she knew him to be a ruler so insecure in his position that he would crush anyone at even the slightest hint of treason and thus endanger her son? But she knows Pari to be a ruler who is just as much as he is merciful, as much as any man can be. And what is more, he does not see Nicaia as merely another citizen or the son of his wife but his own son. His very flesh and bone.

"But?"

"But now I wonder whether he even acknowledges me as his mother."

Their eyes meet.

"You know the way he greeted us when we arrived." Her eyes drift out to look into and beyond the vineyard to where Onxwade runs, having coaxed Reydeyn, Acacia and some other servants into a game of tag and then back into the vineyard to where her oldest son– no, second oldest now that Azar is also her son– works with back bent.

"Yes, I know," the king says soberly, joining Vaht in watching the young man in his toil. "I know." He moves to go back into the house.

"Where are you going?"

"To work beside my son."

"And I am coming with you."

On the way, Vaht gets a sense of just how busy a place the vineyard has become. So many faithful citizens are coming to await the return of the princes, just as she and her husband have. What a celebration it will be when they do arrive with the lost sheep. And they will, won't they? Just as Prince Azaryada has returned so many times before.

Nicaia barely looks at his mother and stepfather as they approach. The boy shuffles into a different part of the vineyard. Vaht feels a pang in her heart. What should she say? How can she reconnect with her own son when his perception is so skewed and biased against this king who is so generous?

Meanwhile, Nicaia keeps his head down and tries to focus on his work, even if he has to make something up to occupy his hands. Just anything will do so long as he does not have to think about how the growing crowd reminds him of his mother and the king's wedding, which is the last thing he wishes to consider.

The young servant numbly wipes the blood from his mouth. "Reydeyn!"

He doesn't dare turn to face Acacia.

"Reydeyn, what's wrong?"

He still doesn't turn, but she easily overcomes that wall of defense by walking around him so that she is facing him anyway.

"What happened?"

He shakes his head. If he says it is nothing, that will be a lie, but if he avoids talking about it, that will not be a lie. It will be honesty because what is troubling him is the last thing he wishes to talk about. He just wishes that he could rest assured that no one saw, or heard or otherwise witnessed what just happened. The young prince is simply stressed about the coming harvest and determined to prove himself.

"Reydeyn, I'll admit to having lived a sheltered life, but there is only one explanation for how your lip looks that I can think of."

"My lip is fine. It's not...hing." There he went and lied anyway. He averts his gaze.

"Who did it?"

"And, what? Are you gonna fight for me, woman?"

She smiles. "Again, I have lived a sheltered life, but I have wrestled with my younger brothers enough to know who I shouldn't pick a fight with."

Reydeyn swallows. There she did it yet again: proved herself noble, this time by deflecting a blatant and entirely undeserved insult with grace and poise. "I...I shouldn't have said that."

"So why don't you tell me what's wrong so you don't say more things you don't mean while you hold it inside."

He bites his tongue before it can snap back with all of the things he never was allowed to say while a slave.

You're not resting in his love, he told Prince Nicaia. *He doesn't accept you based on your works. You're not a slave to cruel creditor anymore!!*

You don't know anything! The prince snapped back, but passion had carried the young servant on past when he should've stopped speaking.

You're stewarding this place for your father who's giving you an inheritance. Nothing you did brought you into his household in the first place, and what you do is not how you stay!

And that is when Nicaia struck him on the mouth, hitting at the very source of his words that were so out of place with his station. What was he thinking to chide the prince like that? Has he gotten so caught up in his freedom that he has lost all sense of decency? But the realization just struck him with such force that it dragged the words right out of him. (As though that is an excuse.)

And the realization he made is that both he and Nicaia, while one of them is a prince and the other a servant, are in the same boat. As in, Reydeyn knows where the prince is coming from. He's thinking like a slave. Always in fear of punishment and rejection, always thinking that his own sweat and blood is his only scant chance at security.

But that is not how either of them have to live anymore, not since King Les Pariablues brought them into his household. And yet both of them are struggling with their own tendencies to live as just that: Slaves. Slaves, while they physically could not be more free. Then again, Reydeyn knows he has a major one up on Prince Nicaia. He knows what it is to be free spiritually, as well as physically, and loved by his Father the King, who dwells in that glorious city, rather than just King Pariablues on earth. And Reydeyn has found a father in Jeko.

"They're back!" someone calls. "The lost is found! The lost is found!"

Reydeyn clears his throat and tries to see who is calling. It does him good to see that it is the very Sower he was just thinking about.

"They're back!!" The call is taken up by what sounds like hundreds of voices, quickly turning into a cacophony of celebration.

"The lost is found!"

Les Pariablues

"Found!"

Reydeyn turns away from Acacia so that she does not see the look on his face. He should run with everyone else to greet the two princes, but his heart is too heavy. He startles and staggers back at Acacia's touch before he remembers where he is, in a place where he does not have to fear human contact.

"Reydeyn, what is it?" she patiently asks once more.

The young servant feels a strong hand on his scarred shoulder. "I saw what happened, my son."

Reydeyn's ears tingle, and he spins around. "Don't say anything! Please, Jeko, please."

"What? I don't understand. Who did this to you?" Acacia sounds as close to exasperated with him as Reydeyn can remember her ever sounding during these months they have known one another.

"This is not a house where you will be abused," Jeko sounds calmer, but the firmness of his tone agitates Reydeyn. He knows that he should know that they both love him and care about him, but all he can hear are the voices of his former masters. All he can feel is the all-too-familiar pressure of being backed into a corner. The Sower grips one of his shoulders in each hand. "Reydeyn, the king will not stand for it."

"Jeko...please, let me sit down."

Jeko has a seat beside him on the rock, and Acacia sits on his other side. He puts his elbows on his knees and his head in his hands. Amid everything else he feels, he identifies one thing as being compassion. "Nicaia needs time, Jeko. It's like you said with the seeds." He keeps his eyes on the ground in front of him in an attempt not to seem arrogant in the way he retells the lesson the Sower gave him. "It takes time for a harvest.

Sometimes— Sometimes the seeds lie dormant for years. Or a citizen, they don't know what to do with them, so they keep them stored away until you show them how to plant them." He gets to his feet. "Please, I...I wish to greet Prince Azarzada and Prince Siohtion with the rest."

"Then let's go," Jeko says. It feels good to have him agree with his decision, to be assured that he is not entirely clueless.

Reydeyn catches Acacia looking at him for an answer to her question that he has continued to avoid. Perhaps he will fill her in later and perhaps not. Perhaps he will wait until the harvest comes in and tell her how Nicaia has changed. But by then, why should the past be brought back up? It would be like tilling the soil at harvest, turning the crop back into the ground from which it grew without partaking of it. No, Nicaia's misdeeds need not be brought up any more than Reydeyn wishes for his to be.

Chapter 14

*N*icaia finds himself caught up in the frenzy with everyone else before he checks himself. It is enough that his brother has come back safely from the fool's errand. There is no point in him getting worked up with everyone else. If only the boy could be sure that Siohtion has learned his lesson and will not do such a thing again. To think, two princes going after one sheep out of a hundred, leaving the rest. Ludicrous! He groans inwardly as his mother rushes to embrace and kiss Siohtion. It's understandable, but he wishes that she would still embrace him, her firstborn son, too. Sort of. He isn't sure whether he knows what he wants. Except for things to go back to how they were when she needed him.

He feels sick when his mother turns to Azaryada and embraces him in the same way she did Siohtion, as though he is just as much her son as Nicaia's brother. He turns away and rushes from the crowd. How can she treat both of them like her sons? How can she make no distinction between them? Treat Azar as her firstborn?

Nicaia glances backward and sees the sheep over the heads of the crowd as Azar brings the creature off of his shoulders to present to his father. Nicaia puts his back to the scene once more, thrusts his fingers into his ears and wades through the jostling celebrants.

But a call from Pari to his friends and neighbours breaks through. He holds up the sheep as he shouts, "Rejoice with me, for I have found my sheep that was lost. Rejoice! Rejoice! The lost is found!!"

Nicaia stumbles all the way through the crowd, but he doesn't care. At last, he walks straight into someone and finds the ground suddenly hurtling toward him. He thrusts out his hands to break his fall but is caught first.

"Are you alright, Your Highness?"

Nicaia struggles to find his footing again, and it does not help that he resists the assistance given. After a few tense moments, he straightens up and looks the man in the eyes.

"Qodei," he says.

"Yes. Are you well, my lord?"

Nicaia shakes his head. "I think I'll retire for the night."

"Then I will see you there, my lord. This crowd is joyful, but not so mindful of where they are stepping."

"I noticed," the boy mutters. He casts a thoughtless glance away from Qodei only to catch sight of Jeko with Reydeyn and to quickly look away. He had a father once too.

"What a wonderful celebration," Qodei says.

The prince tenses, unwilling to share his true feelings.

"Ninety-nine left to find the one. And so there will be more joy in that glorious city over the repentance of one sinner than over ninety-nine who have no need to repent," the boy hears Jeko call, drawing Nicaia's eyes back to where he stands with Reydeyn.

The younger servant takes up the call, and so it spreads with the first one, the call to rejoice over the lost sheep being found.

"What is it, Your Highness?"

"I do not feel well," Nicaia says stiffly. "There is nothing else to say."

"Rejoice with me, for I have found my sheep that was lost. Rejoice! Rejoice! The lost is found!!"

I have no need to repent, he tells himself, pushing away the mental picture he has of Reydeyn and his bloody lip. He just needs to go to bed. He will wake in the morning and get back to work. All of the celebrants will be gone. Yes, all will be well. All must be well...And it truly will be once he has broken free of King Pariablues. Someday, he will no longer be called his son by anyone.

"Reydeyn, will you wash my son's feet?" King Pariablues looks the young man straight in the eye.

He starts to reply but quickly stops himself before he can start stammering. Instead, he falls to his knees, overwhelmed. Wash the crown prince's feet? When he is only a servant? Even though it is upon the king's own request, it feels very presumptuous. The young man clears his throat. "I am not the host, my lord." Everything in him heats up, embarrassed by his own words, and he is grateful he did not say them louder. "I will do as you ask."

King Les Pariablues lays a hand on his servant's shoulder and smiles at him. "Thank you."

Reydeyn nods and kneels to perform his duty for the crown prince. He keeps his head down. How could he protest like that? Deny a direct command from the king whom he loves? Does he honestly believe that his wisdom is greater than his master's? His hands tremble.

"Don't be afraid, Reydeyn."

The servant startles and looks up to see who has touched him now. It is Prince Azaryada. He quickly breaks direct eye contact and gets back to washing the crown prince's feet. "My father will do the honours of anointing myself and Siohtion."

Reydeyn finds that he can breathe more easily when he says that. He looks over and sees that the king has knelt before Siohtion to wash his feet. He swallows. He's serving beside his king. He finds a smile forming on his lips. This is the kind of master he belongs to.

Just when he is about to get back to his feet, the crown prince lifts his chin. Reydeyn holds still, now feeling more able to look his master in the eye again.

"What is this blood on your face?" Prince Azaryada asks quietly.

Reydeyn's stomach clenches. He dares not lie, but how can he accuse Prince Nicaia of anything? He just went through this with Jeko. "I would rather not discuss it, Your Highness," he says quietly, hoping that he communicates no defiance. He finds himself unable to look the king or the prince in the eye once more.

"You need not be afraid of us, Reydeyn. Have you done something wrong, my friend?"

The servant's heart pounds. All eyes are turned in this direction. Who all is hearing this? His anxiety growing, he scans the crowd for Nicaia. He takes a second to think about it. He figures that Nicaia is staying as far away from the celebration as possible, probably slaving away in the kitchen or something, anything but celebrating with the father he cannot acknowledge as such.

"Reydeyn," King Pariablues gently pulls him to his feet, "have you done something wrong?"

The servant wishes that he could think straight, but his heart is going at too furious a rate for that. The question is simple enough, or it should be. He can answer it without incriminating anyone by name. But after living being punished often and rewarded rarely, he feels as though he has lost something very precious: all sense of right and wrong.

"Reydeyn, tell us," Prince Azaryada says.

"I don't know, my lords." He swallows. A young woman steps forward out from the crowd. Acacia. And here is Jeko. He takes another breath. It is good to have them at his side, but he must answer the question. And so, knowing despite what he feels that he has been set free to serve a master he can look in the eye, he meets eyes with Prince Azaryada and tries to answer, but his voice is stunted.

The crown prince reaches out and embraces him more like he would his own brother than most would embrace a mere common servant under their command. "There is no need to hide your tears. Now, tell us, what is it that troubles you?"

He focuses on telling the prince, knowing that the others will hear as well. Queen Vaht is also among the group; he is not sure when she joined them. Perhaps she was always here. Most likely. She did greet her two sons, after all. He's just not thinking.

"It is your brother," Reydeyn says. "He acts like a slave when he is a son like you. How can't he see his freedom?" Even as he asks it, what he thought was a simple question comes jabbing back at him relentlessly.

"Did he strike you?" Prince Azaryada asks.

Reydeyn clears his throat and speaks slowly. "He does not understand what being a lord means because he thinks himself a slave, so he doesn't know how to act."

"Is that a yes?"

Reydeyn only nods. "Please, I know what it's like to struggle with being free. He needs time. Mercy." He looks away. "I don't mean to step out of place, my lord. This is your decision."

The crown prince smiles at him.

"Your judgement is sound," King Pariablues says.

Azaryada still has an arm around Reydeyn.

Reydeyn nods. "Thank you, Your Majesty." He wishes he could fade into the ground right about now. And yet, he has just been given the chance to freely share his heart with those he serves. That thought excites him. Yet, he just must learn to control his tongue and not step out of place because the last thing he should be doing is trying to be an advisor. That is why Nicaia struck him in the first place, he just went ahead and spoke up without thinking. He holds in a sigh and watches as the king anoints his two sons.

"And where is Nicaia?" the king asks.

Reydeyn cannot figure out whether the king is directing the question at him, and he does not wish to speak out of turn again. If he does not speak at all he will be alright. Won't he?

He breathes a sigh of relief as Jeko speaks up to answer the question at the same time as Acacia puts an arm around Reydeyn's shoulders.

"I last saw him walking with Qodei away from the celebrations. I believe he was retiring for the night," the Sower says quietly enough that only those in this inner ring can hear what he says.

"He does not wish to celebrate then?" the king asks.

"I do not know, Your Majesty. But Reydeyn is correct. He is deeply troubled."

"I should speak with him."

"Perhaps after everyone is seated for the feast, Your Majesty?"

Reydeyn starts to mentally take notes on how the chief servant advises the king, but that is just it: Jeko is the chief servant. And what is Reydeyn? Just a servant the king has had mercy on. Another servant whom the king loves. And that is enough.

Nicaia stirs at the sound of a knock. "Who's there?"

"Pari."

Nicaia lies still and considers his options. He cannot pretend that he is sleeping, since he has already answered. And to not open to the king, well, a good son would not do that. And so he comes to the door and opens it.

"Were you asleep, son?"

Nicaia cringes. He was more willing to open the door since the king identified himself through the door by the name that he first introduced himself by to Nicaia and his family, but here he goes again calling himself Nicaia's father. "What time is it?"

"Still evening."

Still evening? Was he asleep for only a few minutes? A crawling feeling of disorientation sets him on edge.

"Qodei said that you were not well. We are ready to eat, my son. Won't you join us?"

"I'm not well," the boy says simply, not knowing what else to say. Why would the king mention that he knew he wasn't well and then right afterward ask if he wished to come out to where everyone else is? What kind of logic is that? But Nicaia keeps his face neutral.

"Is it sickness or something else?" Pari asks as though he believes himself to know the answer.

"I don't know what you mean."

"Is it really sickness that keeps you from the celebration?"

How dare he accuse him of lying! And with a face filled with such false compassion yet too. "Yes, it is, Father," he mutters, head in his palm. He leans his head against the doorway. He has a better chance of succeeding in his lie and getting the king away from him if he does not look him in the eye. He cringes, feeling even more like his stomach will return his last meal now that Pari is touching him. It was bad enough that he called him "Father". Worse still, it was probably too quiet for Pari to hear and so his pain is for nothing.

The king helps him back into bed, leaves him for a moment and returns with a tray. He sets it on the small table next his bed. Nicaia keeps his eyes shut as he lies still.

"In case you get hungry," Pari explains. "You are welcome to join us. Your mother and brothers would love to see you, especially Azaryada and Siohtion."

"I know," Nicaia says numbly, not truly believing it.

The king stoops and kisses him on the forehead. "I will make sure that I check on you throughout the night. Rest well."

Nicaia wonders why he doesn't feel better with the sound of the door closing behind his enemy.

"How is he?" Reydeyn asks, having waited outside the door after he handed the king the tray.

"Trying to sleep, I suppose."

There is a silence that feels very long to the servant. He keeps his eyes forward as they walk.

The king now takes him by the shoulders and turns him to face himself. "Petition to the greater King with me for him."

The command instantly turns the servant's throat into a desert, but he nods and reminds himself of who this is. "Of course, my lord." He can't help but smile. What an honour, what a privilege to come before the throne of that glorious city and find that he and the king he serves are brothers, bought by the same blood.

Chapter 15

"Tell me about Reydeyn, how is he?"

"He's fine," Nicaia says, trying to find the words to answer a question he was not prepared for. "Why do you ask, Father?" Now that it is not the first time he has forced himself to say it for the sake of his persona, calling the king father is not as difficult. At least, he is more numb to it now. Nicaia has also become numbly impatient with how the king has stayed here at the vineyard long past the end of the celebration. He is leaving in a few days to return to the palace with Vaht and the other princes besides Nicaia. Siohtion better not go off into the wilderness again. Nicaia knows he needs to talk to is brother. He should be staying here to work the vineyard.

"It is a master's duty to know the well-being of all of those in his household, whether wife or sons or daughters or servants." Pari hands Nicaia a honey spread wafer, and he takes it with a nod.

"Of course. You are a good master in that way. I don't know if any other master has the memory that you do to keep track of everyone." Nicaia studies the man's face, smug in his realization that, no matter what his reputation is to the contrary, the

Koingsung is not above flattery. The trick is getting him to not see it as flattery, and the perfect cover is an adoring son. Yes, perfect.

"And I hope that you learn to follow in my footsteps."

"Of course," he says. "Father?" He stoops to pull another weed, sinking his nails into the stalk to help himself stand calling the king by the title that he only acknowledges one man to rightly hold the honour of in relation to him.

"Yes, son?" The warm glow in the king's tone assures Nicaia that the man believes his act. That fact softens the edge of sourness of hearing himself called "son" by a man who has no claim to him.

"Is Siohtion staying?"

"Where?"

"Here. To help with the vineyard."

"You can ask him. He's planning to go back out into the fields with Azaryada and the flocks."

"Shouldn't he stay here?'

"You would like him to?"

Nicaia nods. This is where his brother belongs.

"Would you like anyone else to stay?"

"I suppose if they wish to, but Siohtion...I'd like him here." Can his words be called a lie if he only says them as the closest description of what he feels? No, it is not a lie. It is just that he and the king are both using the word "want", but they mean two different things by it. The king believes that Nicaia wants his brother here because he loves him. Nicaia wants him here because this is where he should be. And he's not about to let his younger brother hinder him from getting the upper hand over Pari. They must work together to break free.

But will their mother agree to leave, even if given the chance? Even if shown the king's true colours? Nicaia has his doubts. After all, she is the one who has tried to lead her sons in betrayal of her dead husband. Nicaia feels anger rising in his throat and tugs furiously at the weeds. Weed after weed after weed. How dare she betray him! He didn't choose to die. How can she blame him? How can she act like he never existed just because she buried her braid with his body?

He cries out as his shoulder jerks out of its socket. The king catches him, and Nicaia forces himself not to struggle as a good son who trusts and looks to his father to make things better wouldn't. It takes a will of steel, at least in his perception, and the satisfaction that his will is that strong gives him the ability to do as expected.

Nicaia feels his shoulder go back into place at a single touch from the king, despite how long it felt like he holds him. The pain is gone. It's as if nothing was ever amiss in a way that makes the boy feel like there is something amiss, some sort of hidden power to this king. As foolish as he thinks it might be, the suspicion hangs on that Pari somehow put his shoulder out just to intimidate him with this show...Nicaia isn't sure what to think.

"Thanks," he says as clearly as he can manage and returns to the weeds until Pari bids him drink from the water he carries at his waist. And then he works again until he draws him inside to eat.

Reydeyn stumbles from a blow to the side of his head. The damage is done in startling him more than with the actual force. He scrambles to turn to face the one who did it. Nicaia.

"It's just like I told you about using new cloth to mend an old garment! It doesn't work. You'll spoil the wine if you don't use new skins!"

He backs away. "I'm sorry, my lord. I didn't know!"

"That's obvious. How many have you done?"

"I will fix it, my lord."

The prince grabs a fist full of the front of his garment. Reydeyn's heart pounds. "That is not what I asked. How many?"

"Maybe fifty."

"I will do it." The prince shoves Reydeyn away and settles down to inspect the skins. "You're dismissed!" Reydeyn hurries out the door. Of all things! A slave nearly gave the king a reason to cancel the inheritance deed! Pari probably roped Reydeyn into his scheme–

Nicaia cries out, his ear ringing, and jumps to his feet. "Curse you!" It's Acacia.

"How dare you! Next time I will not be so merciful."

"You just hit the king's son. It is you who should be pleading for mercy."

"The king's son is not permitted to strike anyone without cause."

"I had cause."

"No, you didn't, and your father will agree with me. Think twice next time." And with that, she is gone, clasping her throbbing hand.

"You hit him," Reydeyn rasps, pulling her aside as she rounds the corner of the storage house.

"He should know what it's like!" Acacia retorts, keeping her voice down because he started the conversation in hushed tones.

"Don't you get it? He already does know what it's like!" Reydeyn says in a strained whisper.

"I will not let him beat you back into– into your shell of being a slave."

"You had no right to defend me like that. Your place is to petition for him with me. Your place is to turn the other cheek, but you can't understand."

"Understand what? That he's beating you? I can't just stand by–"

"It's not your place," he says evenly. "Hitting him back isn't right. He is the king's son, but he doesn't understand that, and you don't understand the fear he lives under."

"That doesn't give him an excuse!"

"You don't understand, Acaia. I do."

"I know what fear is, or have you forgotten that I watched my pregnant mother die when I was just a baby myself!"

"This is a different kind of fear. He thinks that if he fails with this harvest, he will be disowned, that he somehow has to prove himself worthy. You've always had a father who loves you, and you've never served a master other than the King Pariablues. No, you don't understand, but you can try, and a good place to start is an apology to the prince."

Acacia's blood boils even as cold sweat runs down her back. Go back in there and face the prince? "And what good will letting him get away with this do? He enjoys mocking you. Don't you see that? He's just a boy, but he can send you, a full grown man, cowering."

"I am not cowering."

"That is what it looks like."

"But it isn't."

"Sometimes, it's looks that matter. You can't let him get away with this."

"I will make a decision about that, but I'll tell you this. I'm not going to let you get away with this."

"What? Get away with what?"

"I'm not going to let you go around slapping princes and say nothing."

"Who would you tell?"

"Your father. Jeko. But I won't have to do anything if you do."

"You're threatening me? What kind of friend does that? He's a prince, so he should be held to a higher standard."

"He also needs mercy, and if we don't show him, who will?" He turns and starts walking away.

"Where are you going?" Anger and a sense of betrayal twist around her heart.

"There is work to be done," he calls without turning back.

Acacia balls her fists. She is called to forgive. She knows that. She also knows that it is childish to try and excuse herself from that duty by saying that the prince does not deserve it. Forgiveness is by definition undeserved. And as an authority over her, Nicaia does deserve her respect.

She finds her head bowing a little, ashamed at the resistance she finds in her own heart. She realizes that it shows just how ungrateful she really is. And so, in the afternoon sunlight, she slowly finds her way to her knees. Her petition is brief, but it is sincere, and the sincerity evidences itself as she stands to her feet and reenters the storage house with only a brief glance over to the winepress where she and Reydeyn were taking their turn stomping the grapes just a short while ago.

Acacia swallows and reserves any feelings of distance from the man she considers her best friend to be felt later. For now, she needs to do as he says, and not just because she is scared of him telling her father or the Sower what she has done. As she steps over the threshold, she must push aside the feeling that her friend is being unfair in his treatment of her– calling her to such a higher standard than the prince– in order to concentrate on making this apology.

She takes a deep breath and kneels once more. "My lord?"

No answer.

She is unsure of how much time passes as he continues working. "My lord?"

More silence.

Secretly as he shuffles over the stone floor of the semi-underground storage house to do his work, Nicaia savours a smug feeling. There is something about keeping her on her knees before him that is proving quite satisfying. After all, a servant is not permitted to stand until bidden by their master. Besides that, he is in no mood to talk to her. His ear is still ringing. Ignoring her is a sweeter revenge than any violence. Unlike Reydeyn, she will not hesitate to bring word back to where it will bring it trouble on his head. He must be cunning.

"My lord, I am here to beg your pardon. It was wrong of me to strike you."

Nicaia savours more silence; how fascinating that she is staying there without him saying a word, such power. And why should he interrupt his work for her? He keeps her there until he is certain that all of the wine is in suitable containers. He turns slowly and sees that her head is bowed. Her knees are probably getting quite sore. Pain, and he didn't have to lay a finger on a single tip of a single hair on her head. Now that is power.

"Don't you have work to do?" he brushes her off.

"Yes, my lord."

"Then go."

She struggles to get to her feet.

"You went back?" Reydeyn asks.

Acacia doesn't turn from the kitchen trough. Let someone else get the silent treatment. It's his fault anyway for threatening her into going back to Nicaia. She keeps scrubbing away at the pan, glad that it is layered with something burnt and thus gives her an excuse to stay with it while she makes Reydeyn wait.

"Are you mad at me?"

"What do you think?"

"I don't know. That's why I asked. What happened?" He sets down his bucket and scrubs at the floor.

"He humiliated me."

Reydeyn startles. "What do you mean?" he asks with forced steadiness. He also restrains himself from getting to his feet. He knows what her words might indicate back in his life as a slave. But he knows that his life as a servant under King Les Pariablues is different. He also knows that Nicaia is only a boy, capable of cruelty, yes, but limited in his imagination. "Acacia, did he hurt you?"

"He left me kneeling on the ground in front of him! He wouldn't even speak to me for...I don't know how long it was, but my knees are going to ache for the rest of the week."

"But he didn't touch you?"

"He wouldn't even look me in the eye!"

"That's all you're upset about? Trust me, that's nothing."

"Oh, so I'm just supposed to take it? I'm not keeping my mouth shut about this to the king."

"And if he's punished, it'll just be confirmed to him that–"

"That what?" She spins to face him.

"That he has to prove himself, and his father will punish him if he doesn't."

"There need to be consequences. Even for a prince."

"Consequences, like being struck by a servant?"

"If he's going to stoop as low as he did, he deserves it."

"And what do you deserve, Acacia?"

"What?"

He turns back to the floor and doesn't look up again. She just doesn't get it.

"What do you mean, Reydeyn? C'mon, you can't just say something like that and not explain."

But he doesn't look up from the floor. She'll figure it out. Eventually. Maybe. Maybe she'll eventually remember how she's been forgiven by the King greater than any king in this world, yes, greater even than the one they both wear the purple sapphire studs for. However, there is more. He wonders whether she's right about consequences, and he does feel differently about the prince's mistreatment of someone else than that of himself.

As for Acacia, she chips a nail while she scrubs the pan in her frustration over once more being given the silent treatment. Boys! And what does he expect to prove by telling her that she doesn't understand? Just a stupid and ignorant girl, is that all he sees her as?

Chapter 16

"When can I go looking for a sheep with you, Azar?" Onxwade looks up and asks his big brother.

"You want to?"

"Yeah. Can Siohtion come too?"

"If he wants to."

"I can do it, really." The little boy of six is feeling quite big and strong, being a big brother and all to two babies.

Azar leans down so that he is looking his little brother in the eye. He smiles. The little boy has brought him so much joy ever since they met. "Tell you what, next time a sheep goes missing, you, Siohtion, Reydeyn and I will go and bring it back. How does that sound?"

"What about Nicaia?"

"And if Nicaia wants to come he can too."

"But what if he doesn't want to?"

"Don't you want him to come?"

"He doesn't like me."

"You're wrong, Onxwade. He does love you. He's just struggling with how to show it."

"Does he love you?"

Azar shakes his head. "I don't think he knows what to do with me."

"He doesn't like you."

"He's afraid."

"Why?"

"Because he doesn't understand that the king is now his father, and nothing is going to change that. And...he thinks that because I'm older I'll get treated better than him. Or something."

"That's silly."

"Not really."

"But it's not true."

"No, it's not true, but he misses his father. Don't you still miss your daddy?"

"Yeah, but I have a daddy too."

"Yes, you do. It's just harder for Nicaia to accept that."

"Why?"

"Well, he knew your daddy longer than you did. So, it's harder for him to get used to things being different. You can understand that, I think."

"I guess. But I still think it's silly."

"Maybe you'll understand a little better when you're older."

Onxwade sticks out his tongue.

Azar smiles. "You might be surprised."

The boy crosses his arms. "It's not fair. Just because I'm six, everyone thinks I don't know anything."

Azar laughs and puts his arm around his brother. "Well, I know something that you do know how to do."

"What's that?"

"Throw daggers. That's something we'll need to be good at if we're going to search for a lost sheep. We should practise."

"Yeah!"

The rest of the royal family is set to arrive tomorrow, as in the king, queen and the four princes. Acacia finds it difficult to believe that it is once more time for the harvest. Has she really officially been in the king's service for all of the months between sowing to reaping? It would seem so. It's a wonderful feeling.

Yet the young woman is frustrated because she believes she should be happier. But her happiness has been tainted by conflict. Reydeyn. She thought they were friends, but do friends struggle to deal with things between them? Acacia is not even sure what is between them. Ever since he reprimanded her for defending him against Prince Nicaia and they had that conversation after she apologized, she has kept silent around him, avoided eye contact. And it is not as though he has made much of an effort either. How long has it been? Maybe a week.

She hasn't wanted to talk to him because she feels as though, if they speak to one another, she will feel the lack of connection between them. Does he feel the distance too? Does he even care? Did he ever count her as his best friend as she counted him? Maybe not. Maybe it was all one way, and he's moving on now that he's seen how silly of a girl she really is. Figures. He's found out what she already knew and doesn't see her as worth his time anymore.

Acacia tries to look at it objectively and think of what she would tell someone else if they came to her for advice in this situation– as if. She would probably suggest a conversation, but what is she going to say to Reydeyn? Maybe she should just try and see what happens. It's not like she's tried particularly hard lately. And, before the conflict, conversation between them came easily. So, it may come again. Maybe he doesn't care anymore about how she acted, or at least doesn't hold it against her. She doesn't know what to think. Maybe he just hasn't talked to her because he needs a little break. That's reasonable. It's not like they need to spend every waking moment together.

She needs to do some laundry, and she is glad when she finds Reydeyn already at it. Her heart picks up its pace in anticipation of the words she must say. But she waits until she is set up to work so that she has an excuse to cast her gaze elsewhere besides him. Less awkward for him. Less awkward for her.

She enjoys the satisfaction of taking risks, and so she opens her mouth and forces the words out. "Reydeyn, are we okay?"

"Yeah, why?"

His response deflates her. So matter-of-fact. Like nothing ever happened. Like he has no concept of what it felt like to hear the words he said to her. He seemed so passionate!

She brushes aside a stray strand of hair. Water slips off her fingers and down her face. She clears her throat. She feels even more silly now, but she decides to be on the safe side and say, "Look, Reydeyn, about...last week. With Nicaia–" Why does she even have to explain this? Does this mean that he hasn't thought about it at all and she's been worked up for nothing? "If I need to say I'm sorry for anything, I'm sorry."

"Are you sorry?"

"You do know what I mean with Nicaia?"

"Yeah," he says. "So, are you sorry?"

Sorry for defending him and calling Nicaia's actions for what they were? "I don't know." She feels so insecure in what she doesn't understand about his life as a slave. That's what it is, it feels like there is a place where the two of them can't connect as friends. "Reydeyn, I know I want us to be friends."

"We are friends," he says, once more matter-of-factly.

"Good," Acacia says quietly. She shakes her head and tries to focus on scrubbing the garments. He keeps working too. The young woman is glad for the laundry as an avenue to work out her frustrations. It's like he sees nothing wrong between them. It seems like he should be bothered but maybe he is bothered and he's just not saying anything. If only she knew. *Am I making a big deal over nothing?* she wonders.

Acacia feels the nerves in her back tingle with awkwardness as she works next to Reydeyn. She wishes that the two of them could just talk to each other freely. The tears come uninvited, and she tries to wipe them away unnoticed.

"Are you okay?" he asks.

She shrugs and shakes out the cloth in her hands, wishing for the thousandth time she knew what to say. She turns at the sound of someone entering the room. It is her father.

"Qodei," Reydeyn says, rising to his feet, bowing, if only slightly. Or maybe it is just her imagination.

"Mind if I take over that laundry?"

"No, sir," Reydeyn stammers. "Was I not doing it well?"

Qodei puts a hand on the young man's shoulder with a smile. "Calm down. I just want to talk to my daughter. That's all."

Reydeyn exhales, and Acacia finds it difficult not to stare, trying to understand why he is so nervous all of a sudden. "Oh, right."

"Go on," her father squeezes his shoulder. "See you at the meal."

"Alright."

Acacia watches him go and turns back to the laundry where it is safe to look. She does not need to cry.

"Is there something between you and Reydeyn?"

"More like someone," she says reluctantly. After failing to have a proper conversation with Reydeyn, she is less willing to try with her father. Has she lost her friend? Why should she expect their relationship to continue when that is simply not how life works? Friendships ebb and flow, and that is just how life is.

"Nicaia?" he says.

"What?"

"Is that the someone between you?"

She slowly turns to look back at him. At least her father seems to understand what is going on. "He'll let Nicaia kill him before he ever says anything."

"I know, and I'm going to talk to the king about it."

"What if he– Reydeyn thinks it was me who told?"

"Someone has to."

"Does that mean you think he's wrong too?"

"There is a need for both mercy and justice, and I believe that Nicaia's father should be able to administer both to his own son."

Acacia looks back at her laundry. "I wish he'd just be punished. It's not right what he's doing."

"No, it's not right, but it's the king's business to deal with him. He is a prince."

"He hasn't been for long."

"And? He's still a prince."

She focuses on scrubbing. She doesn't agree, but she doesn't know how to argue, and she doesn't particularly feel like arguing either. It's not like she's going to change her father's mind.

"Acacia. Acacia, look at me."

She slowly obeys. "Yes?"

"What is he to you?"

"What do you mean?" She sighs.

"What is Reydeyn to you?"

"Again, what do you mean?"

"A friend?"

"Yes."

"More than that?"

Acacia clears her throat. "It's more like what am I to him?" she says, thinking that she knows what her father is getting at.

"Perhaps more than you think."

Once again, she doesn't bother with an argument. *I'm not getting my hopes up*, she tells herself. She is glad for the silence as the two of them continue in their work, and she is also glad that she doesn't feel as awkward working next to him as she did to Reydeyn moments ago.

"Father," she breaks the silence, knowing the one subject that her father never tires of and that she also enjoys hearing about, "was it you or Mother who loved the other first?" It seems strange to her that after all these years of her father regaling her with so many tales of her mother and answering so many of her questions that she has never asked this specific question, but she supposes that there must be a first time for everything sometime.

Qodei laughs aloud. "Oh, definitely me." He keeps on laughing.

Acacia looks back and forth between him and the laundry, waiting for an explanation. Today is not one of those days when she gladly joins him in his laughter. Her heart is heavy, and she is frustrated with its heaviness. This shouldn't be this complicated. Why can't she just understand the world better like the rest of adults, the demographic that she is supposedly a part of? Why can't she at least be on par with Reydeyn? Why has she had to be so sheltered all her life? Maybe if she had been captured the day her mother was killed, she would understand better.

Her father breaks into her thoughts, finally catching his breath. Acacia doesn't understand what could possibly be so hilarious. "It was me, and when I told her, she hit me smack on the side of the head."

"What? Why? How could she do that?" Her own mother? How hasn't she heard anything about this before?

"The same reason you hit Nicaia."

Acacia looks away and keeps looking away even as her father's hand comes to rest on her shoulder. "You're a lot like her."

Of course she was found out! But it's not just that frustration, the frustration of still being a little kid who can't get away with anything. She's ill at ease because she knows that the anger she harbours toward the prince is wrong. The greater King has given her a call to forgive as she has been forgiven by him. And yet it seems she can only offer resistance. Worse, there is the frustration that Nicaia of all people– an ungrateful boy who the king adopted and thus made a prince– is the one...the greater King is using to reveal this blight of ingratitude in her heart.

But her father releases her and starts laughing again. "I was a regular old nuisance. I behaved the worst to her little brother."

"Are you saying Nicaia wants to marry me?" She means it to be a somewhat rhetorical question because she is not sure what else to say.

The twinkling in his eyes and the teasing smile on his face feels patronizing, like he isn't taking her seriously. "You would be marrying a prince," he says.

She pushes aside the unreasonable feelings she has toward him and decides to be honest. This is her father, after all, the man who has been here for her during her entire life. "Or I could marry a servant." She has a seat and puts her knees to her chest.

"So you do love him."

She shrugs. "I think I could learn to at least. But I think he wants me to understand him more first, and I don't think that will ever happen. I've always had it easy, always had you." She stares out the window, hoping that he knows she's glad to have him and not blaming him for her inability to connect with Reydeyn. No, that is not anyone's fault but hers, and she can't fix it.

"Don't lose heart." He kisses her on the forehead. "I love you. Always."

She exhales slowly. At least she's worth something to someone, and she knows that her father...and mother are just two of those people, no matter how silly she feels.

Chapter 17

King Les Pariablues steps out into the afternoon sunlight through the doorway of the storage house with one hand laid on Nicaia's shoulder and the other laid on Siohtion's shoulder. He looks around and addresses the entire group who has gathered for the feast. "Well done. It is a bountiful harvest this year." He smiles at both of his sons.

While Nicaia smugly congratulates himself for keeping everyone in line and bringing this moment of praise about as a result of the harvest. Siohtion is smugly satisfied that after all of the reprimanding and demanding he got from his older brother, their father thinks he did a good job. *So, there, Nicaia.* If their father was not present, he would stick out his tongue at his brother... or not. He just did, but not where anyone else can see. Nicaia is included in those who miss it.

"I'm so proud of both of you," Vaht adds, hugging her boys.

"And I commend you, all of my many faithful servants who were right with them. Jeko, Qodei, Acacia, Reydeyn..." the king says warmly. The group bows. "Yada ues," he blesses them.

"It is our honour to serve you, my lord," Jeko says on behalf of them all.

Nicaia cringes inwardly but does not flinch outwardly.

"And it is an honour to have you all in my service. Shall we feast, everyone?" He laughs as cheers rise up from the assembly. "Yes, that is what I am talking about! The greater King has blessed us with a harvest, so we have reason to rejoice, and rejoice we will! Come, my family, my friends." He draws them along to the tables. He slaps Jeko on the back.

Jeko smiles back. In their younger days, it would be on these sorts of occasions when the two of them would wrestle like the boys they were. Now that they are older...well, perhaps later. Tomorrow when they have had the chance to digest their meal. The king smiles at the sight of Azaryada and Reydeyn with their arms over each other's shoulders. That is what he and Jeko once looked like. Young. Not so much anymore. But they still have some years left in them.

And there is the song of the harvest, "Tebal, tebal, yaney pethala!!" It is a shorter chant than the one assigned to wedding processions, but it is fitting and glorious. "Rejoice, rejoice, the ground has sprung!!" Indeed, once more the seeds have proven their worth. For, their purpose is not simply to reveal what the ground into which they are sown is made of, they also prove to change it as they grow. Many times, the Sower himself has been astounded to see the harvest that is gathered from ground he was sure would be infertile when he sowed it, only to find at the reaping that it yielded ten times more than another plot he assumed would bring a bountiful harvest. That is one of the reasons why Jeko loves being the Sower; he gets the privilege of being surprised.

The chief servant's eyes land on Nicaia with his set jaw, working his way toward age fourteen. He turns to look at Siohtion, Onxwade, Lumin on Azar's shoulders and Lazarus on Reydeyn's. He looks over Qodei's children one by one and then back to the princes before his eyes can drift any farther off track. He again rests his gaze on Nicaia. Yes, he does enjoy being surprised. Though, not all the time, especially when he judges a plot to be fertile only to find that it yields nothing in the end.

No, he is not the Lord of the harvest, so he must not worry. But he does intend to watch and do what he can for the plots near him.

"Nicaia, I have heard some things, and they grieve me."

"What have you heard, Father?" Nicaia tries not to sound tense, but he is always tense in his so-called father's presence.

"I have heard of your treatment of one servant in particular."

"Which servant, Father?"

"Reydeyn."

"What have you heard that I have done to him?"

"Tell me first whether you have done anything that you believe someone would be upset with. I know that even when the right thing is done, there will be criticism."

"I do not know what has been reported to you, but I assure you that I was only trying to do what was necessary to ensure a suitable harvest."

"My son, look at me."

Nicaia does as steadily as he can, wishing that Pari would not insist on putting his hands on his shoulders. "Yes, Father?" He nearly has to say it through gritted teeth. He better not have to call this man by that title again any time soon.

"One servant is more valuable than any harvest."

"Yes, Father."

"Do you understand?"

Nicaia nods.

"Then you understand that there is no reason for you to punish a servant for a mistake made in ignorance, especially when that punishment comes out of a wrongful fear of my displeasure?"

Nicaia nods again.

"Follow me in this. A master must show mercy."

"Yes, Father." Nicaia wants nothing more than to bolt, but he must be patient. Leave only when dismissed.

"But I have a question, do you understand what mercy is?"

Nicaia clears his throat. "Who does not?"

"Many. Because there are a relative few who truly understand what it is to be shown mercy. Tell me, have you experienced mercy?"

Nicaia hesitates, strategizing how far he is going to take his act. Flattery is one of his better weapons, but can he bear thanking the king for what he has done for his family? He must. But his mouth sticks.

"I don't mean in the human sense. I am asking you to answer in your own heart whether you have truly experienced the mercy of the greater King in the person of his princely Son. That is what I mean. The answer to that question...it makes all the difference in the world, my son."

Nicaia allows him to hold his gaze and nods compliantly. "I know." And he is numb to the lie. It comes out of his mouth easily.

"If you wish to go, you may."

Nicaia nods. "I will not disappoint you."

Pari nods back and releases him. What the teenage boy does not see when he turns away is the glistening in the king's eyes because he sees himself in the boy. His heart aches for the boy's story to take as happy of a turn as his own did many years ago. Yet he knows the same thing as Jeko, that, though a king, he is not the Lord of the harvest.

"How is our red looking, Acacia?"

"We have a lot still."

"Good. Hand me the brightest spool."

She takes a moment to decide which thread fits her mother's description. "How's this?"

"Just fine. Thank you. Oh, hand me a bunch of blue and purple too while you're in there."

"Okay." She grabs a handful of each and goes back to her own work.

The needle pricks Acacia's finger, but she sucks in her breath, concealing her frustration a little longer. She usually enjoys embroidery, but she's finding it hard to enjoy much of anything, and the fact that her mother is embroidering material to be used for her wedding garment...She doesn't want to think about it. Everyone acts as though her marriage is inevitable. Maybe it is inevitable. Maybe she's just having a mood. Yes, that is all it is. A mood that has her susceptible to annoyance from absolutely anything and a mood that will pass, especially once she gets used to being at the palace rather than the place she has always called home. She might also feel better once Reydeyn returns with the princes from searching for the lost sheep. A celebration in the midst of this cold resting season will be refreshing.

The queen comes through the door, bringing Acacia and her mother to their feet. The woman smiles. "No need to get up, ladies. But you honour me as always. May I join you?"

"Yes, please do," Acacia's mother, Rittelle, says. Acacia smiles. She feels her mood lightening a little. She always enjoys the queen's company.

"Oh, these look lovely." She fingers first Rittelle's work and then Acacia's. "Oh, this purple...Acacia...It's lovely! And...Oh, my, you're doing this bird all freehand." She gasps at the intricate creature that fills the entire panel of textile. "Those flowers and vines in the wings." She laughs with pleasure. "It's beautiful."

"She's very skilled," Rittelle says proudly.

"As if you had to tell me! How did you learn to do this?"

Acacia shrugs. "I just do it."

"Ah, natural gifting. That's wonderful. What are you going to use this piece here for?"

"A curtain, I think." This is one of those moments when Acacia once again second guesses whether she should be using a title to address the queen, but after all of this time and Vaht insisting that in informal settings they may refer to her as they would any other friend, well, Acacia knows that she has nothing to worry about.

"Yes, that would be lovely. You are talented."

"Thank you."

"Do you wish to join us, Vaht? We have extra material and needles and everything. You have generously–"

She laughs. "My husband has provided them. Thank you." She starts to go about the business of selecting what she needs.

"What are you going to make?" Rittelle asks.

"I think I'll try to make some quilt squares."

"Oh, those are good colours," Rittelle says.

Vaht measures, marks and then takes up a knife to cut the cloth, holding the material in place. "Where is your sister, Acacia? She doesn't like to embroider?"

"No, Rittelle has no interest in these kinds of things. She's too much of a tomboy, and I don't blame her." She's always enjoyed romping around with their three younger brothers more than Acacia.

Vaht smile. "Lumin and Lazarus love her."

"Yes, she does well with children."

"And Siohtion and Onxwade love her too." Vaht smiles. "Though I think she tends to help them get into too much trouble." And Acacia knows that her three little brothers are right there with them, while her youngest sister is very much a daddy's girl. And so, she, as the oldest of the family, is with Mother; the youngest is with Father, and the ones in the middle run wild... though not without discipline.

"It is the resting season," Rittelle says, meaning that there is less to do.

"Yes, and I'm glad that the boys could go with Azar, even if it was into the mountains. He'll take care of them."

"But I think that my daughter and Nicaia are getting along pretty well."

"And I'm glad, considering..." Vaht sighs. "He just needs more time, I suppose."

"But how much time?" Acacia's mom asks, and Acacia knows that there is no doubt that they have reached a certain level of openness if she can say something like that to the queen.

"How am I supposed to know? I can't even find the words to speak with him anymore." She sighs again. "My own son."

"Would you like us to petition with you for him?"

Acacia concentrates on where she is putting her needle. Whenever Nicaia comes up in her thoughts or conversation, she second guesses whether she truly forgives him. She petitions once again for strength but wonders whether she really means it. She should care about the boy. She should, but does she? He just grates on her. But that doesn't mean she is excused from loving him. She knows that she can be fairly unlovable herself at times, certainly undeserving of the love of her greater King who has saved her. So, is she really not grateful enough to pass on the love she has been shown?

Acacia realizes that her mother and the queen are holding each other's hands. She figures that she must have missed the queen's response to her mother's offer. It's not like she expected the queen to decline it. She also finds her mind drifting to the mountains and the search for the lost sheep. It is a spontaneous festival in King Pariablues' kingdom: a time of solemn rejoicing that most miss the point of. She wishes that she and her sister, Rittelle, could have gone with them, even that Nicaia would have agreed to go too. Maybe he wouldn't be so miserable out there. After all, he would have something to do, and he wouldn't be under any pressure to ensure a harvest. She is not looking forward to that hassle beginning all over again, but the time for sowing will come as it always does.

And where is Reydeyn right now? Is he staring into the flames of a campfire as she is into the flames of this palace fireplace? Has he thought of her as she has thought of him? No, not as a future wife or anything of that nature, but just as a friend. She just wishes that she knew what he thought of her, whether or how much he cared about her. But she doubts that she will ever know.

"Acacia, are you alright?" Vaht asks.

Acacia looks up from her embroidery and blinks. The deep purple of the cloth throws off her colour perception for the first few moments as she looks up at the rest of the room. She must have been lost in thought longer than she guessed. Or, the two women just spent a shorter amount of time petitioning the greater King than she expected. "Uh...I'm alright, thanks." She gives the queen a smile.

"Really? You aren't just saying that?" she says it teasingly, but Acacia feels like she is being treated like a child, forced to talk when she has no desire to.

"I'm fine, thank you," she says evenly.

"Alright, just checking...Because I don't mind listening to a little gushing about Reydeyn, if that's who you're thinking of."

She blushes despite herself, and that irritates her because the sight will no doubt give the wrong impression. "We're not... pledged to each other."

"But you could be," Vaht whispers.

"But we're not." She turns her eyes back to her stitching and is grateful that Vaht says nothing more. She doesn't need Reydeyn to be her husband, just a friend. Yes, she will be satisfied if she can simply be assured that he really considers her that.

Chapter 18

The night wind glances off of the stretched metal canvas that shelters the three princes and their servant from the winter elements and any predators that roam these mountains. The tent is designed with a cylinder in the center to accommodate a fire. It is around this that Azar and Reydeyn sit across from each other, while Onxwade and Siohtion sleep curled up under thick blankets.

"I never thought that a tent could be this warm," Reydeyn comments quietly in order not to wake the two sleeping princes and thus keep the conversation between himself and the crown prince. He tries not to think about the privilege this is because he might descend into shock and thereby miss out on the honour. To think...Not that long ago, he never could have imagined calling the crown prince of the Samaritans his friend, much less such a good friend. But it is so.

"Yeah, it's Jeko's own design."

"I can believe that," Reydeyn says sleepily. He has learned that his father is a man of many admirable skills.

"Before you drop off to sleep, I've been meaning to talk to you about something." Azar picks up another dagger. The servant is fascinated that, instead of sharpening it as he has all of the others up until now, he turns to cleaning his nails, as though he's nervous. But how can the prince possibly be nervous about talking to him when he is the crown prince and Reydeyn is merely a servant?

"I am listening, my lord," he says when his master does not continue.

"Yes, well, when we get back, I was thinking to get to know Acacia better." He clears his throat then alternates between tending his daggers and using them to clean his nails or trim his beard.

"My lord?"

"Reydeyn, call me by name, especially when we are discussing something like this."

Reydeyn clears his throat. "You mean, call you Azar?"

"Yes. Call me Azar, brother."

He nods. "So what is it?"

"When we return, you know, once the sheep is found and for sure when the festival dies down, well, I mean to see whether she could be my wife."

"Very good. I wish you all the best."

Azar holds up his pointer. "Thing is, you know her far better than I do—"

"Hold on a minute, I thought you were just going to go ahead."

"I am. *If* you do not object."

"Me?"

"Yes, you. As I said, you know her better, and I want what is best for her."

Reydeyn shakes his head and exhales.

The prince continues. "And I asked her about it just before we left. I asked her how she would feel if you would propose marriage, and she said that she would happily agree to it. I asked her father as well, and he was even more enthusiastic."

The memory of the man's firm grip on his shoulder comes automatically to Reydeyn. The servant thinks that he feels about Qodei as he would a big bear: furry, apparent cuddliness but also a creature to keep a sharp eye on. And yet, he knows Acacia's father is just fine to get close to. He just makes Reydeyn nervous, and the young man is not quite sure why.

"Reydeyn?"

The servant clears his throat. "Sorry, did I miss something, Azar?" He has to get used to calling him by that name, but practising will help with that.

"No, no."

"Remind me where we are in the conversation."

"Both Acacia and her father– and mother for that matter– are agreeable to marriage between you and Acacia if you are willing."

"Right."

"She simply believes that you have no intentions in that regard. Is she correct?"

"Perhaps...Just give me a minute."

"Of course."

Reydeyn takes a deep breath. Marriage. Family. For him? He was first introduced to the idea back at the table with Acacia. He has mostly brushed it off as too difficult to fathom; he's barely thought about it since then, in fact. That has been easier since no one else has brought the subject up in serious conversation again. Until now.

"And you think Qodei's serious? That he'd be alright with..."

"Definitely. Rittelle– her mother– she would love it too."

The servant shakes his head. "What about her siblings?"

"You know her brothers love you, and Sariet too."

A smile comes automatically to Reydeyn's lips at the mention of Acacia's little curly-haired sister, but it is only a small one, crowded out by the consternation of other thoughts. "But that would mean I would be a part of the family."

"And? Don't you want that?"

Reydeyn shakes his head again, avoiding Azar's gaze, how can the prince be assuring him like this when he wants Acacia's hand? Why would he– the crown prince– step aside for a servant in his search for a future queen? Because that is who he is. "Azar, you're a better man than me."

The prince laughs. "And yet we both need the same greater King to save us." He laughs a little more. "You know it's true, Reydeyn."

"Yes," he says quietly, staring into the flames of their tent campfire. Even though he doesn't use a title to address the prince after his expression of agreement, he still uses a tone meant to communicate a bowing to authority. How can he convin– Why does he have to try so hard to convince the prince that if he wishes to get to know Acacia better for the purpose of potentially marrying her that he should just go ahead?

"Reydeyn, she is a rare jewel, and she will not be there forever. Is there a reason for you to pass her by and leave her for another?"

He keeps staring into the flickering orange light, the mystery of what fire is made of dancing in the back of his mind like the light on the the canvas. He doesn't know how to answer the prince's question.

"Answer that for yourself. I will not make my move until you make your intentions clear. You have my word on that. May I have yours that you will carefully consider this?"

He starts to nod, but cuts himself off. "Azar, you should just take her. Give the kingdom an excellent future queen."

"There is no guarantee that I will take the throne."

Reydeyn shakes his head. How can he say something like that so calmly?

"You know how fragile life is. Things can change rapidly. But even if she will be queen, what is best for her? I asked her and her parents about what they would think of *you* and her being joined."

"You should've asked about yourself. She would be royalty, if nothing else."

"Tell me, do you wish you were royalty? Answer me honestly."

"I...I don't think so," Reydeyn says.

"What if the king offered to adopt you?"

Reydeyn's mouth sticks open. "Adopt me? After all he's already done?"

"So you are satisfied with being a servant."

"Yes, and I suppose if he made such an offer– How could I refuse such generosity? The king's son?" Reydeyn's mind spins.

"But you are satisfied with the place you are in? As a servant of the king?"

Tears come to Reydeyn's eyes. "Satisfied? More than satisfied." He thinks back to the day when he met the Koingsung. King of the Samaritans, indeed. That day, the word Samaritan that had always left the taste of a curse in his mouth changed entirely to fill him with awed gratitude, pointing him to look even higher.

"And if I am crowned king, or any of my brothers in my stead should I die before that day, you will stand next to the throne as Jeko has, won't you?"

"I...How can I?"

"Because I have asked."

"And I agreed. I agreed to be your right hand as Jeko is the king's. I just have to get used to the idea. I do love you, Azar."

"And I you, my dear friend. So, please, as my dear friend, consider whether there is any reason for you to pass by that rare jewel. Won't you?"

Reydeyn takes a breath. "Yes, of course."

"Not as your master. As your friend."

"Like Jeko."

"Yes."

"I will think about it."

"Azar, if you marry Acacia, will she be my sister?" Onxwade turns over to ask.

The crown prince laughs quietly.

"She would be your sister, yes, but I'm not marrying her yet. Reydeyn gets first priority. Now, go back to sleep."

"What does pie-ority mean?"

"It means that he gets to see whether she should be his wife before I do anything."

"But he's had time."

"It takes a long time sometimes. Go back to sleep before you wake Siohtion up."

"Okay," Onxwade sighs and turns back over.

The crown prince looks over at Reydeyn, who stares into the flames. "Goodnight, my friend." The prince rises to stretch before slipping under the covers.

Reydeyn nods absentmindedly, suddenly determined to think about what Azar has told him very carefully.

The four travelers make their way down the mountain and into a village, headed for the well. The resting season sun has not yet risen, but life has begun for the day, unwilling to wait until light begins to show in the east. Myriads of lanterns and torches illuminate the small settlement.

"Is that you, Commander?" comes a call while they are still some way off. A man is coming out to greet them, lantern in hand. The flame glints dimly off of his distinguished metallic apparel.

"Par yada, Yaren! It is I, Prince Azaryada. I and my companions search for the lost sheep of my father, King Les Pariablues."

"Yada ues, Commander, and, please, introduce me to your companions, my lord," the armor-clad man bows at the waist. His request for the prince to introduce those with him does not necessarily mean that the man does not know who the others are but rather is a part of formal meeting and greeting. The soberness of the man's face does not escape either Azar or Reydeyn. The armor sets them both on edge, though slightly differently based on their individual experiences, and the sight of it in the lantern light, not to mention the presence of other soldiers in full armor openly patrolling the village...

Siohtion and Onxwade are less aware of what is going on, never having had war in their village in their lifetimes of nine and six years. However, they are familiar with the guards, small detachments of soldiers assigned to each village for the express duty of watching over it for the king.

Azar lays a hand on each one's shoulder as he refers to them. "My brothers: Prince Siohtion, Prince Onxwade, and my right hand: Reydeyn."

"Ah, it is an honour to meet the one you chose. And always an honour to have princes come to us."

Right hand. Reydeyn still cannot get over how the prince officially put him in this position the day they left to begin this search.

"Why did you call him Commander?" Onxwade asks. If war had been a part of his life, he would've known that calling royalty by that title entails that there is trouble.

"Because, Your Highness, when royalty comes to a village within their kingdom, that is one of their rightful titles, especially the king or crown prince." Yaren now turns to the crown prince, his face losing all lightness that it had when looking at the younger prince. "A word, Commander?"

Azar nods. They are about to hear what the trouble is. "Siohtion, Onxwade, go to the well and fill up our water skins."

Yaren motions to the nearest soldier. "See our princes to the well."

The soldier bows to his commanding officer and then again and lower to the crown prince. "Yada ues, my friend," the prince says before quickly laying a hand on Reydeyn's shoulder to prevent him from going to the well too. He brings his other hand to rest on Reydeyn's other shoulder and looks him in the eye. "My right hand stays by my side, brother."

"Yes, my lord."

"This way, please." The officer motions them through the door of a nearby dwelling and bids them have a seat. Refreshment is quickly set before them on the table.

"There is war then?" Azar asks.

The officer removes his helmet and holds it on his knee. Reydeyn blinks, captivated by a thick tattooed arch that follows the man's hairline. He knows what it means, and his heart fails him. The only thing that anchors him in reality is a strong grip on his arm. His hearing becomes clear again, but he cannot get over what he sees. His strength still eludes him.

"What troubles your right hand?"

"He was once enslaved by the bands, Yaren." Azar gently brings the lip of the cup to touch Reydeyn's. The water does him a little good.

The lack of any scorn or contempt in the man's eyes, toward either Reydeyn himself or his reaction to his tattoo, tells the servant at once that this man no longer belongs to any band. "My friend, as you have been set free. I have been set free. I am now in the service of the Koingsung, as well as that of the King of kings. I know the first is true for you, is the second?"

Reydeyn needs an extra moment to process what the man just asked. Once he has come to an understanding he can only nod in response.

"Then we are brothers," Yaren says.

The servant puts his head in his hands and his elbows on his knees, wishing that his heart would slow its pace. The room is silent. At last, he looks up. "Then perhaps," Reydeyn clears his throat, "perhaps we should shake hands. I…I never thought I would get to do that with a band member."

"I was a leader," he says sadly.

"Much less so, unless it would be in mockery. I never thought I'd want to."

Yaren reaches out his hand, Reydeyn reaches out his, and they clasp the other's arm. They look each other in the eye and then at the same time their eyes drift to look at the other's purple sapphire studs and then back to the other's face. No more words are needed. Yaren gives a nod and releases his fellow servant's arm. Reydeyn slides back in his seat, still feeling weak, but a smile is on his lips. Yaren smiles back.

"And so we are together because of the King and his under king who are kind to the unthankful and evil," he observes.

Reydeyn smiles wider and glances over at the prince.

"But we must discuss what this trouble is and what it means for your search, my prince."

"Say on, Yaren."

Chapter 19

"Green on the hillside yesterday, Commander. That is what we are dealing with."

"And word has been sent?"

"Yes, Commander."

The crown prince turns toward his right hand who still looks dazed. Little wonder. Azar knows that, though he may try, he is not likely to understand what it means for his dearest servant to have shaken the hand of a man who would have formerly made his life a misery.

"Do you understand what we are talking about, Reydeyn?" Azar asks.

"I, I believe so, my lord," he says slowly. "Just tell me what is expected of me. And, what enemy is green?"

Azar nods. "The forces of the enemy king who wear emeralds in their ears."

Reydeyn nods. Now he knows who they are facing. At least, he knows their reputation as he once knew that of the Koingsung and his Samaritan people. Having learned the truth about the Samaritans, well...he has no high hopes that those who bear the emerald studs will prove their reputation wrong. No, he's seen the marks left on prisoners. He's been tormented by fellow slaves captured from that kingdom. How anyone survives there is beyond him. Sometimes he wonders whether they are of an entirely different race than humanity.

Azar turns back to the officer. "Yaren, Reydeyn and my brothers will remain here under your guard."

"And you as well, Commander? We are also able to escort you safely back to the palace."

"I will continue my search."

"Commander, may I be open?"

"Go on, Yaren."

"Commander, your life is worth much more than that of a single sheep."

The prince looks back at him. "Yaren, do you remember the first time that I went on this sort of search?"

"Yes, Commander," he says quietly.

"Please, tell our friend what you remember."

The man leans back in his chair. "I joined a band when I was...about Prince Nicaia's age. I thought I could ensure protection for our village, or so I told everyone. The truth is that I was arrogant, and I wanted to build my own kingdom. I rose in the ranks until, at last, I had the audacity to capture the crown prince as he searched for his father's sheep. I mocked him, but the King of that glorious city had other plans. Prince Azaryada told me why he went, and the truth hit home. I did not see him as a fool anymore for chasing after a single sheep, and, well, soon I was in the king's service, and what mercy it was. So, I have been here ever since."

Yaren's words cause Reydeyn to pause. Yaren, a rebellious band leader; him, a fearful slave. Both needed and received mercy.

"Yes, you understood," Azar says. "I am not merely searching for a single sheep from my father's prized flock."

"Yes, Commander, but few understand."

"Yet some do. And so I will continue to go."

"Commander?"

"Yes, Reydeyn?"

"I understand why you go, and I wish to go with you. If I am your right hand, how can I do less?" Truthfully, he cannot provide more protection for the prince than the prince can for himself, but he can put what Jeko has taught him with the daggers to use. Together, they will have more protection than either of them would have traveling alone.

"Then come," the prince says with a hand on his shoulder.

"Commander," Yaren says, knowing that at the end of the day, the prince's word is law, "your brothers."

"Are among those who have yet to understand and will remain here. Keep your eyes on the hills to guard us, and may the greater King protect us all."

"Commander, I beg you: Do not stay on the mountains after dark, and allow me to come with you in the light."

"Three is a good number, a measure of invisibility; a measure of defensibility," Azar says. "And we will follow you back down into this village for the night where we will gladly partake of your hospitality."

"Thank you, Commander."

"I may be searching for a single sheep on the mountains in the middle of winter and war, but I am not entirely a fool."

"You are not one in the least, my lord," Yaren says.

"Ah, and what of my father who put you– a former band leader– in charge of a village guard?"

Yaren smiles. "And what of you who is about to come up the mountain with me?"

Azar smiles too and slaps his right hand on the back. "And how do you feel about this, Reydeyn?"

Reydeyn clears his throat. "I think I am alright, but will your, uh, will your brothers...How will they feel about being left behind?"

"Let's find out. I'm sure that if they are not frightened and protest to being left behind, they will feel differently at the end of the day after being accepted into the ranks of Yaren's troops."

"I suppose we shall see," the officer says. "I will retrieve them, and we will all sit down to eat together." He motions to the refreshment before them. "Please, continue to help yourselves. I will be back in a moment."

With Yaren gone, Reydeyn empties his lungs slowly.

"Are you well?" Azar holds out a cake of bread topped with a fruit spread to him.

Reydeyn slowly takes what is offered and sinks his teeth in. "I never expected this. Are there more band members...like him?"

Azar nods. "They have proven to be some of our best soldiers."

"Now you tell me?"

"Haven't you heard the accusation that Samaritans are traitors? It is because of the number of band members who have joined us."

Reydeyn nods. "I suppose I may have heard that somewhere along the way." But Samaritan is just one of those words that get used, reused and rarely explained so that its main meaning remains common knowledge while the etymology is mainly lost.

"I suppose you have a lot to think about."

"What do you mean?" The right hand takes another bite of the cake, savouring the flavour, the tang of sour mixed skillfully with sweet.

"Well, Yaren, and what we discussed last night. With Acacia. Have you given it any thought?"

"I..."

"You don't need to give me an answer, I just hoped that you hadn't brushed it off."

Reydeyn shakes his head and then looks straight at Azar. "No, I don't think that I could. You...You've honoured me. I just..." He finishes his pastry.

"Keep thinking. That is all I ask."

"I will try to come to a conclusion by the time of our return. The festival...And what if one of these times, there is no festival, Azar?"

"Meaning?"

"Meaning the king not only loses his sheep but his son."

"Then I suppose Nicaia would be next in line."

"And you..."

"What?"

"You're alright with him taking the throne after you?"

"You aren't?"

"That's not my decision."

"Will you stand by him, no matter what happens?"

"I– What do you mean?"

"Continue to have mercy on him but not stand for his wrong-doing?"

"I– I will try." He tries to grapple with what that might mean. He wonders whether he has done something wrong in not speaking up about how the prince has treated him, the king only coming to hear about it from Qodei.

"I know you care about him."

"Yes."

"Good. Then continue to."

"We're all here," Yaren announces. With him are several soldiers and their wives and children, Onxwade and Siohtion. The two younger princes squeeze in on either side of Azar. Reydeyn does not mind moving aside for the brothers.

"Will you say the blessing, Commander?" Yaren asks once they are all seated.

"Gladly," Azar says.

Reydeyn listens to the short petition of thanks that the prince offers and then gives up listening to the conversation as his mind drifts to the meals he has eaten in the king's service. During many of them, he and Acacia have sat next to each other. They found one another easy to talk to, and it was good to have a friend as he learned to be settled into his new life. The right hand doubts whether he will ever not think of this life as his new life, ever cease finding new strange things about what it means to be the king's servant, the servant of the King of that glorious city, and the right hand of the crown prince himself. Will Azar take the throne? And when? He dreads the thought of King Les Pariablues dying, but he, too, is mortal.

"I wanna go!" Onxwade breaks into the servant's thoughts to protest.

The right hand rightly assumes that the news has just been broken to the two younger princes that they will be staying in the village while the search continues.

Siohtion is quick to agree with his brother. "Yeah."

Les Pariablues

"But you need to stay here," Azar says firmly.

"But I'm a prince, and he's a servant," Onxwade complains jabbing a finger at Reydeyn.

"And he is a man, and you are a boy."

Onxwade straightens up in his chair. "I can throw daggers just as good as him."

"Cannot," Siohtion says. "I can, though."

Onxwade glares at his brother, but Azar breaks back in.

The crown prince looks back and forth between his two younger brothers. "Remember when we wrestled, and I had both of you pinned at once? There are men out there right now who won't just pin you."

"They'll try to do even worse than kill you," Yaren says.

Azar glances at the officer and nods. The man would know. That is why he has insisted on coming with the prince back up the mountain if the search must continue.

"What's worse?" Onxwade asks.

"They will torture you, my lord, just because you are a prince. They will think that your pain is funny. No, you and Prince Siohtion must stay here as your brother has said."

Onxwade turns to pouting. Reydeyn cannot understand why the boys don't seem to be even a little scared.

Meanwhile, Siohtion hasn't quite given up on diplomacy. "But you're the crown prince, Azar. Don't they want you more?"

Onxwade looks up, seeing hope in his brother's argument. "Yeah!"

Reydeyn watches, still fascinated by the interactions of the different players: the crown prince with his younger adopted prince brothers, the support of the former band leader of the crown prince, and his own place as a former slave to the bands now drawn to the side of the crown prince in a world that he knows that he will never understand without the refraction of the lens of the life he used to live.

"Yes," Azar says, "but Father's sheep must be found." He reaches out and puts a hand on Reydeyn's shoulder and then looks down the table at Yaren. "Let's go."

The three of them rise. Onxwade scrambles out of his chair, nearly scrambling some eggs under his feet in his enthusiasm. But all of the food stays on the table, unlike the possibility that their big brother will relent and allow them to come along for the search. Siohtion and Onxwade know that dish is quickly being removed. Onxwade clings to his brother's arm. "Please," he whines.

"Yeah, why can't we?" Siohtion joins in.

"We'll be back this evening, the greater Lord willing," Azar says, hugging Onxwade and then Siohtion. He then hands his brothers off to the soldiers of the guards who stand by. "Take good care of them. They're a delight when they want to be." Azar slaps the soldier's metal shoulder piece.

"It is our honour, Commander."

Azar nods and motions to Yaren and Reydeyn. Unbeknownst to Reydeyn, two eyes a lot like his own follow him as he leaves, fascinated with the way he moves, fascinated by everything about him, desperately wishing she could be sure of his identity.

Once outside, Reydeyn turns to Azar as they walk. "Commander?"

"Yes, Reydeyn."

"My lord, I have seen how the bands treat a Samaritan, and I've seen how they treat royalty. I have never seen how they treat Samaritan royalty..." He looks over at Yaren for affirmation.

"I am aware," Azar says. "But the sheep must be found."

Reydeyn swallows and determines not to leave the prince. No matter what. Yaren's eyes meet his, and understanding passes between them to which words cannot easily be assigned.

"And the green is crueler," Yaren says.

Reydeyn feels chills. He was put through things for years as a slave, captured and recaptured but always with the avey peazuz galley understanding, that as a slave his loyalty was the wind. Not so anymore with the studs firmly established in his ear lobes. His heart hammers against his chest. He told the prince that he understands why he seeks the sheep and that is the reason why he goes with him. With every new revelation of the danger, the living illustration of which he is a part comes more alive to him. And it is gloriously awful. His mind drifts back to King Les Pariablues at the palace, how according to the tradition, the king commissions Azar every time a sheep strays to search for it. The father sending, the son going willingly and finding the sheep at great personal risk, the joyous festival that spreads throughout the kingdom when the son returns with the unimpressive stray. Yes, gloriously awful.

Chapter 20

*O*fficer, right hand and crown prince approach the village, having covered much ground while not having found what they seek. The light of the short winter day has fled, and the same lanterns and torches light up the small settlement as they did this morning.

"Reydeyn!!" a woman calls, racing out of the village as though her never shorn hair has caught one of the open flames along the street. "Reydeyn!!!!"

At first, the right hand thinks that it is Acacia, but, even in the darkness, it only takes him a moment to realize that the woman is too old to be Acacia. She seems shorter too. He doesn't know what to do when she flings her arms around him, weeping.

The servant is stunned. No one has ever run out to meet him. Yes, he has imagined the reception when they return for the festival- if they return- but this is a stranger, a single stranger running out to greet him. His first thought is that she somehow got the news early that they had found what was lost, but that is only a passing thought that he does not truly believe, a suggestion put forth by his own mind as he struggles to comprehend his situation.

She is still weeping. Finally, Reydeyn puts his arms around her too. The way she called his name...Whenever someone uses his name when he least expects it...It always takes him back to that moment when he learned that he belonged to the king he now serves and is called the right hand of his son.

"Who is she?" he asks Yaren.

"Her name is Tres. It was last month. Found her wandering with emerald studs in her ears. Poor creature was mostly starved, mostly crawling, going nowhere. Turns out she's been a slave since she was about ten when her village was attacked. Only in the last year or two was she captured by the emerald kingdom. Come to think of it, she did say that one of her brothers was named Reydeyn."

"What?!"

"Don't you remember me?" Tres asks– pleads. Tears flowing down her cheeks, she reaches up to hold Reydeyn's face.

"You're my sister?" Reydeyn has no clue what to think. He feels numb. It would be bad enough if he had just lost his family, but he has practically lost all memory of them as well. He hates it. He can't even know for sure that this is his sister.

"Yes. Yes, I'm as sure as I can be that I am. You're my little brother."

"But how can you know?" Frustration fills him. He can't even remember any of his siblings' names! Not even now that he's heard Tres' name does it ring any bell. He was young, but not too young to remember something like that. And yet, he doesn't remember. Anger like he has not felt in a long time seizes him.

She reaches up and brushes his segmented left eyebrow with her fingers. "Your name. And you looked about the right age. And what they told me about you while you were on the search today. And that right there." She keeps brushing his scarred eyebrow. "We were playing tag, and you tripped. Do you remember that? You just fell and then you were bleeding, and I was so scared. Mom sewed you right back up, though."

Reydeyn sighs, once more resigned to his lack of recollection. "No, I don't remember at all." He feels himself push her arms off of him. He needs to get away. Be lightheaded somewhere else. "Excuse me." He finds himself running as vague memories of terror come pounding against him. Their nondescript nature just makes them worse.

The darkness crowds in. The fire. The screams. Someone grabs him, but he won't go this time, not this time. He hits the ground with someone on top of him.

"Reydeyn!"

His strength flees, and his arms fall down at his sides. He stares up at the darkening evening sky. Or is it late afternoon? He feels as though he doesn't even know where he is or who he is anymore. He lets out his breath slowly as the facts of his current circumstances and location come back to him. At least he knows that. Is that Tres crying that he hears in the distance? No, he hasn't run that far.

He glances beside him. Azar lies shoulder to shoulder with him, staring up into the night sky. The prince catches his right hand looking at him and grips his shoulder. "You alright?"

"Everything just kinda came back on me all of a sudden. Except, not the everything that I want."

"What do you mean?"

"I mean that I still don't remember my own family. I never will. It's lost." His voice cracks wide open.

"I'm sorry, Reydeyn." He pauses. "Forgive me for asking if I'm out of line..."

The right hand exhales. Here the prince goes again, deferring to him like he doesn't deserve. And he actually ran after him just now. No, he definitely doesn't just see him as a servant, just as King Les does not merely see his right hand as the Sower or his chief servant but as Jeko: his best friend.

"Were you going to say something, Azar?" The right hand wonders whether the king and the Sower ever stargaze together. Jeko does love the outdoors. He feels a pang in his chest, a longing to see Jeko that causes him to both swallow and shift closer to Azar.

"Yeah, I was just wondering what exactly– if anything– it was that made you run away from Tres."

"I have no guarantee that she's my sister. I mean...I don't know."

"A lot of stuff came crashing in on you?"

"Yes. I don't know how I feel about her being my sister."

"Yeah, I can't say that I would know what to do if I ever met a long lost sibling of mine."

"Do you have any long lost siblings?"

"My mother died giving birth to a stillborn. It was a boy."

"You think about him a lot?"

"Yeah, and maybe it's silly, but I think that's one of the reasons why I like having five little brothers now that Vaht is queen."

"I don't think it's silly. I just don't know if...Is it expected that you're supposed to run to meet a long lost family member?"

"It does seem natural."

"But...this scares me. I don't know how I feel about...I don't know, Azar. I don't know."

"What if you just got to know her as a new friend?"

"Like she'll let me."

"What are you afraid of?"

"I don't want her to talk about anything that I've lost. I have a family now. I have you, a brother. Jeko, a father. The greater King, my Father in another way. Rittelle, like Acacia's mom," he hasn't put it into words until now, "she's treated me like she's my mom, and if things go through with Acacia, she will be. And I guess Acacia's my sister for now. I don't know. Maybe more. But I don't want to think about what I've lost."

"But if this is your sister, and it seems she is...Reydeyn, I know it's hard, but I know that I don't know how hard, but this is your sister. I mean, she's got no one."

"She's got the villagers here. Can't she be here, and I be at the vineyard? We have our separate lives now." Even as he says it, he feels his sentiments changing. It was a shock in the moment but now he is thinking more clearly. At least, he is becoming willing to think of what Tres needs rather than only what he wants. "I should go back. Please, help me up, Azar."

The prince gets on one knee and holds out his hand to his right hand who reaches up and grasps his arm. He flashes back to the moment when he clasped arms with Yaren. Just this morning. After spending the day together, it feels as though they have been friends for years. The man is around 30, still fairly young. If they can connect in a day, a moment even, surely he and his...sister can as well.

At least, he's willing to try.

The right hand slips out from under the covers and pulls on his outer garment.

"Reydeyn, where are you going?"

"To walk, Azar."

"After we were out all day?"

"Yes. I need some air. Look at the stars."

The prince nods. His right hand takes after Jeko in so many ways, including with how he chooses the outdoors over something sheltered for sleeping. "You have your daggers?"

"Yes."

It only makes sense that since Jeko has been his teacher that Reydeyn would imitate him in how he uses the weapons, but the crown prince still finds the similarities in their forms and methods absolutely striking.

"Beware." The guard is on duty, but the emerald kingdom is not known as the cloak and dagger horde for nothing; stealth and cruelty are their specialty.

"Of course."

The notion that Jeko might be Reydeyn's biological father has passed through Azar's mind, but he knows that that is impossible. To start, Jeko's hair hangs long and never shorn as the sign of one who has never been married. And he has said himself that he has no family. He was taken into the king's– Pari's father's– house when he was a baby, abandoned, unnoticed until the king's guard came upon the village after the bands ravaged it. He was raised alongside the current king and has never left his side since. Yes, Jeko and Reydeyn have much in common.

Reydeyn inhales deeply as the chilled night air hits his face. It is good to be out of any place indoors, good to be moving, even after doing so all day. Even to him, it seems counterintuitive that he wishes to be out and about to walk off his fear of what is out in the night. He knows that he should be weary and sound asleep, but he is not. He keeps his eyes open and glancing all around, or so he tries to as he stumbles forward. Too many thoughts are going through his mind that he thought he would've thought through during this day, but Yaren told too many stories as they walked for that. And then there is the business with Tres.

It was good to get the chance to sit at the table next to her, even though barely a word passed between them. It was enough to have her arm over his shoulders as they ate and the others at the table surrounded them with a steady hum of conversation.

But now he tries to turn his thoughts back to family. To Acacia and how she might play into that for him. It seems logical. He should at least give it a chance, shouldn't he? It seems ungrateful to brush off the opportunity to marry now that he has it. And yet Jeko hasn't married.

He wanders on, drawn into the study of the lights that illuminate the streets. One member of the guard passes him, and they acknowledge one another with a cross between a wave and a salute. Reydeyn turns his eyes back to the flickering lanterns and torches. Each one unique. Each one with a purpose. From a distance, they don't look so different.

He shakes his head at himself. That seemed like it was leading up to something like one of Jeko's lessons. But back to Acacia. He decides to discuss the matter with her and her parents upon their return. Yes, that will make it all–

Someone has clamped down on his wrist. He's wandered out of the village? Why is it so dark? Why is he having a hard time breathing? Where did all of the light go? What is all of the noise?

He struggles and by some miracle gets his hands in between the shackle neck of the leather sack and his own neck, yanking it off of himself and breaking free. He has no sense of direction. His fingers frantically grab for one of his daggers as he runs. And runs. A small thought cuts through his burning lungs and muscles to tell him that the strain on his body is being caused by an incline, which means that he is going up into the mountains, which means that he is going away from the village and its safety. But he keeps on going, unsure of which noises he is imagining and which noises indicate a flesh and blood pursuer.

All at once he finds himself surrounded. Emerald glints under the light of the full moon. He takes one stab in the dark before it hits him how many of them there really are. The dagger slips from his fingers where a certain member of the emerald horde picks it up as a trophy. The right hand thought he was fully encircled, but now he sees an opening to his left. The edge of a cliff, the only escape from all misery the cloak and dagger horde may have in mind, and he rushes for it.

Chapter 21

"*A*iwa! Aiwa!"

Azar is on his feet. Aiwa is a word used in the chant of celebration for the wedding procession, but in this case it is a war cry.

"Arise! Arise!"

The crown prince doesn't even have to look for his brothers. They've found him like two electrified magnets.

"Aiwa!"

It is still dark, but it is resting season, so the sun will not rise until the morning has had itself a good beginning. But where is Reydeyn?

"Azar!!" Onxwade screams, pointing.

Fire. His eyes find the window.

"C'mon." He pulls his brothers toward their way of escape. He throws open the wooden doors that cover the opening and then thrusts Onxwade through first, Siohtion next and finally himself. All in a few seconds. Onxwade is howling on the ground. "Oww!!"

From the looks of it, the little boy tumbled out onto some rocks outside the house.

"Commander!"

"We are well, Yaren. Where is Reydeyn?" He holds the smaller of his little brothers to his heart while Siohtion stays close.

Yaren pulls them away from the burning building. Several members of the guard surround them in a protective circle. The villagers are efficiently putting out the flames even as weapons clash.

"He was taken prisoner just before the attack."

Siohtion is quivering, crying without a sound. He turns his face into Azar's shoulder. The crown prince's eyes dart in every direction, taking in the hazy battle scene.

"But we outnumber the green, my lord. He will be found and returned if he lives."

"And what of other prisoners?"

"The same is true for them."

"Then the battle is coming to an end?"

"Yes. This battle, Commander."

"Of course." It will take more than one small skirmish to grind the emerald down to dust.

The circle expands to include several other villagers, Tres among them.

"Is he hurt?" she breaks into Azar's passionate hopes for the permanent demise of the cloak and dagger horde.

"More scared than hurt, I think," Azar says as Onxwade wails for his mother.

"Yaren, where is my brother?" she turns to ask, seeming to have forgotten entirely about the young prince. Azar thinks that she just saw Yaren now. Little wonder that she would miss things in this mess and with her eyes as wild as they are.

"A prisoner, but we will get him back. More guard soldiers have come to reinforce us. They will be routed."

Hot tears trail down her cheeks. Her brother captured only a day after they met up again after years of separation. Despair grips her heart. She finds herself back to the old and tired question of whether to raise her fist at the sky or not bother wasting her energy. Indifference to whether he exists or not set in long ago. She clenches her fists at her sides and stands still with eyes closed, willing the time to pass and for her brother to come to her, having never been captured.

Yaren's prediction proves correct, and the attack is short-lived. Onxwade has cried himself to sleep on his big brother's shoulder.

"Commander."

Azar turns as a captured soldier is dragged before him. His face is full of fearsome scars, disfiguring for the very purpose of intimidation. The scars are old, but his damaged ear is new.

"He carried this dagger, Commander," Yaren says, handing it to the prince.

"You bear many scars, soldier," Azar says, putting the dagger with his others.

The soldier goes to spit, but Yaren recognizes it in time to slam his chin to his chest. "You will respect the prince."

"The prince? Well I couldn't recognize him in his bedclothes. Caught you off guard, we did."

"You will mind your tongue," Yaren warns.

"And what are you going to do?"

"Tell me about your ear. That is what you are going to do," Azar says.

"A little skirmish. One of my fellows thought that he could turn his sword on me. A novice. I turned my sword on him, but he ran off a cliff like a scared rabbit."

"You sure it was one of your fellows? Did he have emeralds in his ears?"

"Maybe not."

"How about sapphire?"

"If he did, good riddance."

"And if they were sapphire, I hold you accountable for the life of my servant."

"The life of your slave?" He gives a roar of foul laughter.

"A life is a life in this kingdom. Put him with the other prisoners." The man is taken away cursing. Azar does his best to cover his brother's ears until the noise is over. "Yaren, any progress?"

"We are scouring the area. We will find him."

"I will join you if you don't mind my bedclothes." The humor in his comment is severely flattened.

"You have your daggers. That is enough. Come."

Siohtion walks with Azar while the prince turns to Tres, who stares off into space. He lays a hand on her shoulder, and she startles. "Hold him for me."

She stares at him while he waits patiently for her to comprehend and then takes Onxwade in her arms, holding him tightly. He smiles for a moment and then hurries after Yaren, hand around Siohtion's wrist to keep him close.

"Deyn! Son!!"

Reyden slowly opens his eyes. *Is it morning? Who is that?*

Nimble as a cat, the man comes sailing down a rope and lands on the ledge at Reydeyn's head.

"Father," he realizes, recognizing Jeko, who can still move like someone half his age. He reaches out for him, the one person in the world that he has been wanting to see most.

The Sower is quick to kneel and cradle the young man's head. He wraps him in his own cloak and gives him water. "Are you cold?"

"Only a little."

"Where are you hurt?"

He manages to clear his throat. "I think I'm just bruised, not broken. I don't know. I landed on my back and haven't moved. I didn't want to risk the emeralds seeing me."

"Your head?"

"It didn't hit first, anyway."

"More water?"

"Yeah."

"Can you hold it?"

"Yes."

"Good." Jeko still supports his back but releases the skin into the hands of his honourary son. "We'll come up in a minute!" he calls.

Reydeyn finishes drinking and tries to embrace Jeko, only to find that his movements come stiffly. The Sower puts his arms around him before he can become too frustrated. "It's good to see you, son. I've missed you."

The younger of the two right hands closes his eyes and leans his face into the older right hand's shoulder.

"Tell me, how did it happen?" he asks after some time.

"I took a walk, and I don't know where I was, but they grabbed me, or tried to, and I ran."

"And the cliff? You fell?"

"I jumped."

"Why?"

"I panicked, Jeko. I'd rather die than be a slave ever again." He sobs. "I can't go back, Father. I can't go back."

Jeko tightens his grip around him.

"Jeko! Reydeyn! Are you coming?"

Jeko looks up and meets eyes with the prince as his face appears at the top of the drop to the ridge. "In a moment, my lord."

Siohtion is at Azar's side. The crown prince remains standing where he called from, waiting for his right hand to come back to him.

"Come, Reydeyn, can you stand? I'll tie you into the rope."

The young man inhales deeply and lets it out. "Let's go, but you're not leaving again for another part of the kingdom, are you?"

"No, son, not just yet."

"Almost there, Tres," Reydeyn tells his sister as they approach the capital riding double. Though it is resting season, the colours strung for their welcome are enough to make any spring envious. They ride to Azar's right, and on the prince's shoulders rides the stray that has now been found.

They departed as a company of four. They return with Jeko and ten rescued female prisoners of various ages from the emerald kingdom, including Tres. For now, the war is at a standstill, and the festival of the Lost-Found may freely proceed. Already the chants of rejoicing have begun.

And here it is: the moment Reydeyn has imagined. Here they come, rushing out to greet them. There is the king running to meet them just ahead of the queen. And there is Acacia. They dismount, and their two groups become one.

"Reydeyn, welcome back." She embraces him, and he embraces her back. "I missed you."

He smiles. "It's good to see you too." He releases her and turns behind him. "I'd like you to meet my sister, Tres. Tres, this is Acacia."

Acacia's face blossoms into a smile. "Yes, I heard. You're about to become a princess."

Tres gives what Acacia interprets as the best she can do for a smile after all she has been through.

The king is going around to greet the ten rescued women and girls, his daughters. Tres is the oldest, and the youngest is between Onxwade and the twin princes in age. The king has taken her up in his arms as though he has always been her adoring father, and it seems that she loves him already. She even giggles. "Tebala," the king says, naming her. Right when the news came of the ten who were rescued, the king, together with the queen, made clear his intentions to adopt all of them as his daughters. The group adoption is to be a part of the festivities.

"And Tres. Come, come all of you. Now is a time to celebrate!! Tebal, tebal!! Aiwa tebal!!!"

Indeed, they will rejoice mightily.

Acacia and Reydeyn are caught up with the main throng together. The beat of the music vibrates merrily in Reydeyn's bones, and he cannot stop smiling.

"How are you doing, Tres?" he asks when they are seated.

She shrugs.

"Believe me, I'm still not used to it, but it's wonderful. And the King who King Pariablues serves is even more wonderful."

Tres doesn't react.

Acacia puts a hand on her friend's shoulder. "She'll be alright."

He nods. "Where's your family seated?" His eyes scan around the table.

"Well, there are my parents. And..."

"What?"

She shakes her head. "Nicaia and Rittelle are together again."

Reydeyn nods, assuming from how she states her observation that the adopted prince's relationship with Acacia's sister has only deepened in his absence.

She goes on to point out the rest of her siblings.

"This is incredible," he says, ever in awe of the king's feasts.

"But how many are actually celebrating?" she asks, her eyes meeting his.

"Something wrong?"

"I just never thought that my own sister was so much like the prince."

"Prince Nicaia?"

"Yes."

"I see. Things have..."

"Come to light. Or they're starting to."

Reydeyn nods. He is privileged with the honour of being the crown prince's right hand, and this journey has helped prepare him to understand that he must accept the cost of such an arrangement. "We have things to talk about, my friend."

"Do we?"

"Yeah, let's go down to the river after the meal."

She nods. "Until then, tebal." She raises her silver cup.

He nods back and touches his cup to hers.

It is well into the night by the time Azar insists that his right hand go to talk with Acacia. And so they make their way down to the river. Reydeyn figures that he'd better just say what he needs to say so he doesn't chicken out altogether. Now is the moment. "Did the prince tell you of his intentions?"

"What intentions?"

Breathe, Reydeyn, just breathe. This is Acacia, he tells himself. "Do you remember what he ask– When he asked…" Of course it's now that his tongue gets tied up in knots.

"Who?"

"Azar…Prince Azaryada–"

"You call him Azar?"

"Yes. I guess we've become friends. More than friends."

"You are his right hand, just as Jeko is to the king."

"Yeah, it's unbelievable, but," he doesn't want to get off track, "he asked you about…whether if I asked you, proposed marriage, or however you say it, what you'd say, right?"

She nods. "He told you about that?"

"Yeah. Did you mean it? What you said?"

"Yes."

"But that was when you were under the impression that I had no intentions of pursuing a marriage covenant with you."

"True. Are you saying that I was wrong?"

"I'm saying that things have changed."

"Really?"

"Acacia, I never dreamed that being the man of a family would be possible for me, but Azar told me to think about it."

"What exactly?"

"Think about whether...You're a rare jewel, and he told me that I should consider carefully before I passed you by, let another have you as wife, including him."

"Who?"

"Azar."

"What do you mean?"

"He told me that he intended to get to know you better upon our return for the purpose of seeing whether you might be a good wife for him or whatever, if I didn't object kinda thing." It's only fair that she knows that she could be in line to the queen's throne.

Acacia's mouth drops open. "The crown prince was going– What?"

"Yeah. Like I said, we...both consider you a rare jewel."

"And he let you have first dibs." She smiles. "Just like him."

"First dibs, that sounds rather...You're a person, not something to be bargained over."

"And you thought about it and...What are you saying?"

"I want to know what you think of the two of us seeing whether marriage might work with the two of us. But I'm not about to stand in the way if you want the prince." Still, having thought about it, his heart aches for her to at least give him a chance. However, he is not about to act less honourably than the prince. This is about what is best for her; not what he wants.

"Reydeyn, I'm honoured that the prince would consider me, and I'm even more honoured that he'd step aside to allow you to go ahead, and I'm glad that he did because I want to learn to love you."

Reydeyn exhales, overwhelmed by his own unexpected relief.

"Are you saying you want to learn to love me too?"

He nods. "Yes, that is what I'm saying, but I want what's best for you. I don't want you in danger with anything that's going to happen in the royal house in coming years."

"I will be no matter who I'm married to because I'm King Pariablues' servant. I mean, if things go south with the prince..." She means Nicaia.

Reydeyn nods. "So, I was thinking, how about this: In a year or so from this sowing, we have our decision made and either are wed then, or I step back and let the prince have you?"

Acacia considers. "Yes," she says after a moment. "That sounds prudent."

He exhales. "Good." A realization strikes him all at once. "I guess I should be talking to your father– your parents. I should've done that first, shouldn't I have? I'm already messing this up." He runs his fingers through his long hair that may be shorn for the first time in just over a year. For Acacia. Because he is free.

Acacia giggles. "Look at it this way. It's not like we're going behind his back. We know that he and Mother approve."

"Does he approve of me?" Reydeyn hears himself ask.

"Of course! Haven't you heard how highly he speaks of you? It's like he and my mother both see you as their son already, regardless of what happens between the two of us."

He gives a nervous laugh. "I guess I'm just too jumpy around him to notice."

"And why are you nervous?"

He lets a breath out slowly. The very quandary he posed to himself not all that long ago. "I don't know."

"You do like him, don't you?"

"Yeah," he realizes just how true it is, "I do. I like him a lot, actually."

"So, what makes you nervous? I mean, how can you like someone and also—"

"Fear them? Isn't that kinda how it works with the greater King...Kinda?"

"Not exactly, but I get what you mean. Loving Him but knowing that He's not to be trifled with, right?"

"Yeah, He's so...great. But, well, that's another thing. Maybe Qodei makes me nervous because he's the one person who can just look at Prince Nicaia and he leaves me alone."

"Are you scared of Prince Nicaia?"

"I don't know."

Acacia takes a moment to think, unwilling to fail to understand her friend. "I get showing mercy to him, that that's what you want to do for him as you've been shown or that you want to respect him as the prince." She sighs. She wishes they weren't talking about the prince, the person she feels drives them apart more than anything else, but they need to. They've agreed to give themselves a year, but she feels like they will need a year to get through everything that Reydeyn carries, that she will need a year to just begin to learn how to come alongside him to carry it.

"I mean, I'm just wondering whether you fear him too, and that's another reason you don't stand up for yourself."

"I don't know. Do I have to know?"

"Maybe just as far as motives go, it's good to know why we do things," she says, trying to be honest and wishing her words didn't sound so, so accusatory or uppity or something.

"Do I have to understand myself? Are you telling me that you understand yourself all the time?"

"No, I guess not."

"That's good."

Acacia searches for something to say into the silence. "I'm glad to know we're friends."

"Why wouldn't we be? I told you we were."

"Yeah, but you just…" She trails off in search of a way to express her thoughts in a way that does not place an unwarranted burden of guilt on Reydeyn. "Were you mad at me for what I did to Nicaia? When I hit him? I know it's been a while, but were you?"

"I don't know. I was upset about what you did, that's for sure."

"Well, I understand a little more now. But I can't just sit by and let him hurt you. That's not what friends do." She wishes that she could know how her words sound to him.

"Yeah, I know."

She laughs softly.

"What?"

"You just kept on saying, 'I don't know' and now, well, you do. Sorry, it's silly."

Reydeyn shrugs and changes directions to walk back from whence they have came. "I was going to talk to your parents, though, you wanna come?"

Chapter 22

"And here he is," Azar says, turning Qodei, who is hand in hand with his wife, to see Reydeyn approaching with his firstborn daughter. Sariet is sleeping over Qodei's shoulder.

Qodei greets them both with a smile. "Well, is something going on, Reydeyn?"

Rittelle grins too, just like Azar. As much as the crown prince thinks of Acacia as a good potential wife for himself, he's proud of his right hand for stepping out. This is right.

"I wanted– we wanted, uh, we're gonna see, you know, whether the two of us being family would be workable."

"What do you mean, Reydeyn?" Qodei asks, giving him a second chance to say it with his tongue untied. "Just take a breath."

Reydeyn obeys and his words do come out more smoothly now. "I mean that, with your approval as Acacia's parents, that the two of us would like to see if a marriage between us would work, if that's the way to say it. Make a decision by next sowing."

Qodei's hand suddenly clamps down on Reydeyn's shoulder, nearly springing his heart out of his chest, but the warm laughter of Acacia's father disarms his fear.

"Reydeyn, that would be wonderful, wouldn't it, Rittelle?"

His wife steps forward and embraces the right hand. "Absolutely, but, please, don't act so nervous around my husband." She steps back but still holds his arms. "He'd only hurt you if you hurt his girl, and you've already proven that you can be trusted. Relax."

"Thank you." the young man nods. His heart is still pounding.

"And what did we miss?"

The group turns to see the king and queen approaching with their ten new daughters, as well as Siohtion, Onxwade, Lazarus and Lumin. Jeko attends them, while Acacia's three little brothers are mixed in too.

They bow instinctively to the newcomers, including Azar to his father and stepmother. The crown prince cannot contain his smile. He now has ten sisters! He grips his right hand's shoulder. "My brother here just got up the courage to take a step forward with Acacia. They might just be married next sowing." He now looks his right hand in the eye. "Proud of you."

Reydeyn looks back, his expression caught between speechless and a smile.

Though no one says anything about it out loud, many among the group are all too aware of the two people who are absent. Nicaia and Rittelle, as in the older of Acacia's younger sisters. But the two of them are not in truth absent from the scene, they merely watch from the shadows. At the same time as they do not want to be welcomed into the group, they blame their families for not including them.

Nicaia glances to his right, the flicker of a torch catching his periphery. And all at once he thinks back to the night when he came in from working and the king reprimanded him for putting out the lamp. *Nothing will stay hidden forever, son. Someday it will all be out in the open,* Pari said. And Nicaia shrinks back farther into the shadows, feeling even more exposed in this moment than he did then.

Rittelle pounds the dough angrily with her fists. Curse this cold that turns it to stone so that she must work all the harder. Curse the sun that is about to come up and draw her one day closer to when she is expected to have her ears pierced in the service of the king she despises. And that is to say nothing of the expectation that she will be wed as well, and all the more now that her older sister is set in life, never mind that they set a year's waiting period. No, she will not be forced into marriage per se, but there will be pressure. As though her singleness prevents any of her younger siblings from marrying or something else just as ridiculous.

And curse these celebrations that continue!! The foolishness of the festivities nearly outdo the foolishness of the errand itself. What kind of future king are they supposed to expect when the crown prince keeps running off over every hill and into every valley after a single runaway sheep? An illustration they call it, a picture of redemption the king deems it. Foolishness!

She flips the wad over with another thud on the wooden board only to be startled by the sound of running water.

"Good morning, Nicaia."

"Rittelle." He nods in greeting.

Now that he is here, the work is a little more bearable, and his presence is what keeps her sane as the rest of the servants wake up and get to work, crowding around her, so glad to serve this idiot's whims.

Until she met Nicaia, she never thought that she would be able to find such camaraderie. But it turns out that he despises the king just as much as she does while also being imprisoned in the inner circle of the kingdom's throne. In short, though they would both be called Samaritans by anyone looking on, as the years have worn on and they have grown up and become more aware of themselves, both of them have come to realize that they are not Samaritans.

Being several years apart, at first, neither of them thought much of the other until their paths began to cross at the vineyard and they gradually found things in common. Rittelle has no qualms about considering the boy her peer now that he has proven that he is her equal in maturity. In Nicaia, she sees the opportunity for something more secret and exciting than marriage. Together, they may actually take the kingdom. Together, they will found their own kingdom, replace the thrones that Pari and Vaht now occupy with their own greater ones. For now, they are both compliant on the outside, the most compliant and hardest working of any that the king calls his subjects. No one will suspect the two flawless ones, the ones who always obey and keep every rule.

Nicaia is proud of himself. What better way to impress the king than by being a son who is even more of a servant than his beloved Azar. Wouldn't that be sweet if Pari did the work for him and set him on the throne rather than Azar? And with all of his foolish ventures into the wild, it is not difficult for Nicaia to imagine a day when he will be right in line for the throne anyway.

For Rittelle, she sees the prince as her way to freedom. Worked correctly, and it will take patience and time, they will succeed in their intentions with the heart of the kingdom in their hands. Yes, together; it is a sweet conspiracy.

The prince has the water on and boiling. He glances back at Rittelle and thinks for a moment, trying to answer for himself why the two of them have connected as they have. It only takes him a moment to figure out the answer: She is the one person he likes around here, and she is the one person who understands him. She will be quite useful in days to come.

"Is there anything to eat in here?"

Nicaia glares at his younger brother. Once more back from his fool's errand. Not too loudly, he replies, "Come and help out, will you? You must have learned something about cooking being outdoors."

"It was a simple question." Siohtion takes a pastry from a basket and dips it in a small bowl of honey. "You should eat something. Might make you less cranky. Maybe a freshly killed deer. Add some onions. That's good."

"If you're not going to help, then leave."

"And I thought you'd be glad to see me. Your little brother."

"Yeah, I'm glad the wolf wasn't mad that you stole his dinner."

Rittelle listens without a word, cheering Nicaia on in her mind.

"Siohtion, come to the table, please." It is Queen Vaht coming through the door. "And, Nicaia and Rittelle, we want you both to join us at the table."

"Yes, mother."

"Of course, Your Majesty."

Siohtion follows with a second pastry, not being too careful to watch where the honey drips.

"Rittelle, there you are, good morning," Acacia comes to greet her.

"Good morning, sister. I hear that you have joyous news."

"Yeah, and you should've joined us."

"I was tired. It was late."

"You work too hard."

Rittelle cringes under her older sister's smile. Just a cute little girl, that's all she's ever been to anyone, even as the second oldest in the family.

She endures a morning greeting and embrace from both her mother and Qodei.

Even her younger brothers are treated older and more capable than she is most of the time, and it doesn't matter whether she plays or works. Just another girl stuck in the middle of the favourite only offspring of Qodei's murdered first wife and the baby girl who is doted on. She is the only child in the family who does not have any of Qodei's blood in her veins, and not even her mother sees how she is overlooked because she overlooks her herself.

Qodei merely does what he must to ward off any appearance of favouritism against her and have everyone think that he sees her as fully his daughter. What a lie. Her mother is preoccupied with Qodei and her other children. And of course the fact that she sees Acacia as the flawless specimen of a daughter, looking more and more like the best friend she lost so violently every day, well, that does not help. Meanwhile, though Rittelle bears her mother's name, neither her mother nor Qodei see any particular reason to adore her. Apparently, she favours her mother more than her father, and her mother lives, so Qodei is deprived of glimpses of his best friend, and her mother fails to see much resemblance to her former husband. Even if she did, she's married again. Just as

Nicaia's mother is. Apparently, Nicaia's and her mother have very short memories of the husbands they claim to have loved.

But it will not always be this way. Rittelle does not have it all planned out what she will do once in power, though she knows it will be a great day. To be queen and never ignored again. Never called a Samaritan again either. And proving that she does not need her family or their approval starts now by proving it to herself. She will make her own decisions. Make sure that Nicaia is crowned king like he deserves, not only keeping the vineyard as is his right, but also receiving the entire territory that, once, King Les Pariablues declared to be his own.

Chapter 23

Jeko rises from his bed and takes a breath to help himself concentrate. After sleeping outside in it, the spring air has really gotten into his blood. He glances over at his son and has to smile. The young man is sprawled on the ground face down, wrapped haphazardly in blankets.

"So that's where all the covers went. Give 'em back." He shakes him awake.

"What?" Reydeyn mumbles.

"Now, is that any way to talk to your father? Get up, it's morning." He grips his hand and pulls him to his feet.

Reydeyn blinks and looks around. Jeko laughs. He'll be awake in a moment. And he figures that if any breath is left in either Acacia or Reydeyn this time next year, his honourary son will be waking up next to his bride on a dew spread morning much like this. "Good morning. How about some breakfast? We've got a big day today."

Reydeyn exhales. "Yeah, right. I'm awake."

"And thank you, greater King, for a new day." Jeko stretches. "Indeed."

In a moment, the two of them have their little campsite all packed up, after which Jeko challenges him to a race back to the house. The dwelling has been enlarged, just as the vineyard has been improved, since it became a royal holding. They come flying around the corner of the house, Reydeyn just barely in front thanks to Jeko's constant change of route meant to make him the champion over his son, only to slam into the king and queen, who have stepped out into the morning air.

Jeko trips over Reydeyn's legs and lands on top of him.

"Well, good morning," Pari says.

"Your Majesty," Reydeyn pants, struggling to get out from under Jeko, while the Sower insists on wrestling him, "my apologies!"

"Jeko, get off the boy and get to work." The king hauls his right hand up in a headlock, only to be brought down to the ground.

Vaht smiles and shakes her head at her husband and his right hand who has just pulled his king down on top of himself.

"Father, what are you doing?" Azar playfully chides, but the king is too busy losing to his right hand to hear. "C'mon in, Reydeyn," he gives him a hand up. "Have some breakfast. Jeko manages to eat in just a minute or two, anyway. There's no need to wait." He kisses the queen on the cheek on their way past. "Good morning, mother. Would you like to come in as well?"

"Someone should look out for the king while he wrestles on the front lawn."

Azar laughs. "Perhaps, but I'm too hungry this morning. If Jeko wishes to assassinate him, I guess this is his lucky moment."

In truth, the village guard, as well as guards who have accompanied the king from the capital, are ever on watch. Moments later, the two middle-aged men come in the door. After washing up in the customary way, they enter the house with arms over each other's shoulders, dragging their feet and panting dramatically. Once their act has gained them the laughter they want, they cut it and are seated.

Everyone in place, the king spreads his hands over the table and says a short blessing. Reydeyn smiles. It is like every meal with this king is a feast of celebration. At least, he thinks that until he has occasion to remember what a real feast of celebration is like. Joy upon joy.

He feels something bump up against him. He looks down and realizes that it is someone. Little Princess Tebala. She reaches out to him, and he takes her up into his arms, seating her on his lap. He has no idea why, but the little girl has taken quite the liking to him while shying away from Tres most of the time.

"Hey, and how are you doing?"

"Good," she replies in her little voice.

And just like that, she reaches and takes a piece of egg off of his plate. He glances over at Acacia, another person Tebala shies away from, and wonders whether they will ever have children of their own. It's still a pretty terrifying thought, but maybe it's not as bad as he is working it up to be.

Tebala slides back down and finds the queen, a woman she has taken a liking to. For a former slave...Reydeyn marvels that she, being so small, does not show more signs of all of the suffering she has gone through. He wonders what he was like at that age, what he would've been like had he been rescued at the same point as she has been. *Rescued,* now isn't that an ironic thought when it was Koje who bought him and brought him into King

Les Pariablues' house. Koje, who told him lie upon lie. Koje, who had him abusing the other servants. Koje, who–

"You ready?"

Reydeyn clears his throat and takes in Jeko's face, the one who spoke to him. "Let's go."

"Good, let's find Nicaia." It is a fairly easy task. He sits without moving with an emptied plate before him. "My lord, are you ready to go to the market?"

He nods. "Yes, Jeko, let us depart. Come, Rittelle."

Reydeyn turns when he feels a hand on his shoulder. Acacia gives him a hug. "I'll be waiting for you when you get back on the eastern side of the vineyard," she whispers.

Reydeyn holds her close for a moment and lets her go again. No, it hasn't been long since they agreed to make their decision by the time next sowing season comes, but he's getting the idea that neither of them is going to want to release the other at the end of that time. Perhaps they should just go ahead before a reason for them not to comes up. But, no, he's getting ahead of himself, forgetting how serious of a commitment this is that they are considering. But he can't get distracted by considering how significant it is just now because he will not be able to concentrate on the task at hand. He sighs.

"Are you alright?" Acacia asks.

He shakes his head. Will he ever be able to make a decision? Wouldn't it be alright if they just stayed friends and nothing more? Then Azar could marry her and the three of them could be close, just as Jeko is close with the king and queen. The thought- and this is not the first time he has considered it- puts him at ease. It seems only logical. What does he know about being the man of a family?

"Reydeyn?"

"I'm alright. I'll see you." He turns to follow Jeko, the prince and Rittelle to the market.

"Come, Reydeyn," Jeko calls into the vineyard.

Acacia looks over at the prince's right hand. "You're going again? There has to only be, what? An hour? Left in the day. What could be the point?"

"It is as the prince instructs," the Sower replies, turning Acacia's eyes in his direction.

"Why don't you come along this time? You've been in the field all day," Reydeyn says.

"While you've been traipsing back and forth from here to the market time after time. When the sun rose, three hours after that, at noon, and then again two hours ago. I think I will come and see what this is all about." She gives him a smile.

Nicaia and Rittelle are already on their way and they must catch up with them.

"Here." Reydeyn hands Acacia the skin of diluted wine as they walk, leaving a comfortable space between themselves and the prince. The taste strikes her strangely, and she grimaces. At least it is something to drink.

"What do you think he's doing?" she turns and whispers to Reydeyn.

"Who?"

"Nicaia."

"With what?"

"This whole thing."

"I don't know what you mean."

"This going back again and again to hire more workers at all of these different times."

Reydeyn shrugs. "Sounds like you've got an idea. I don't."

"Hasn't Jeko told you the story of the workers?"

Reydeyn thinks. "Probably, but you might have to remind me."

"It goes just like this: The landowner goes out at different times throughout the day to the market and hires workers each time. At the same times Nicaia has gone."

"Okay?"

"I wanna know what he's going to do at the end of the day."

"Acacia, I don't know what you're getting at," he says, still keeping his voice low so that the prince and Acacia's sister do not hear their conversation.

"Do you remember what happened at the end of the day in that story?"

Reydeyn nods. "They all got paid the same amount, a day's wage. Okay, Acacia, I don't get it. You think the prince has some trick up his sleeve using that?"

"My sister is in on it too."

"You make it sound like they're criminals."

"The seeds of treason are growing in their hearts and now that they are together, they are helping each other tend those shoots. Trouble is coming, I'm telling you."

Reydeyn shakes his head. "That's a harsh accusation."

"I'm just calling it how I see it."

He looks away at the western horizon and the ball of fire that approaches it. Acacia has not hit Nicaia again, but Reydeyn is uncomfortable with her judgement of him. The same temper that goaded her to strike the prince in vengeance is rising up again, but what if she's not wrong? Still, her tone doesn't sit right with him, like she's claiming to know their hearts and can be sure beyond a shadow of a doubt what they will do. Where is mercy? But maybe he should have mercy on Acacia for not understanding...But this isn't just about Nicaia anymore; this is her sister too. Doesn't she know her own sister?

Prince Nicaia, with the rest following, approaches the people who are standing in the market. Around each of their heads is tied a narrow leather sleeve dyed crimson, the ends hanging down past their shoulders. It is the sign of one looking to be hired on a short term basis. They are crimson cords. The sleeve is wide enough to insert a day's pay. The group of them stand hesitantly. What point is there in hoping for anything now that the day is nearly over?

Reydeyn takes in the sight of them, his eyes falling once more on one in particular. Though her downcast eyes are brown and her hair blonde while Acacia's eyes are green and full of life, her hair dark and skin tanned, the young woman looking for any wage somehow reminds him of Acacia.

Avey peazuz galley, is the saying for slaves and a principle that is both a blessing and a curse when applied. However, though there is no saying for crimson cords, the general sentiments toward them are not ambiguous. They are not trusted, seen as disloyal and unwilling to take on responsibility, just looking for someone to take unwarranted pity on them and give them something for a mere day's- and not even a good day's- work. Practically beggars.

Sometimes a crimson cord is the chosen disguise of band members spying out a village before they plunder it. Sometimes the crimson cords are violent and thieving regardless of their loyalties, either along the road or when scouting out the property on which they are supposedly working to come and steal from the owner after sunset. And, since they are not given their wages until the end of the day, some landowners merely refuse to pay, no matter how well the work is done. Many do not see anything wrong with the practise. It is a day of free labour. Few are willing to stand up in defense of the crimson cords. In some ways, the crimson cords are lower than slaves who, though they suffer greatly, at least have a master who has some commitment to them as their financial investment or a war trophy.

"It is strange that he is taking on so many, I'll give you that," Reydeyn says. He wonders what the king will do at the end of the day, for he has the final say and will have to approve of his son's treatment of the workers. "Maybe this is Nicaia's way of making a statement to everyone about whether he'll follow his father or not."

"Exactly. These are the crimson cords we're talking about. These are the kinds of people that the king would be kind to when no one else is."

"Yeah." He is not sure what to make of the look on her face. "What is it?"

"Well, I'd like to think I'd help them out too. It's not that I don't care, I'm just scared of them. I know a lot of them aren't out to hurt everyone they set their eyes on, but how do you help someone like that wisely when enough of them are dangerous?"

"Good question."

"I mean, I know that if I was in their shoes, I'd hope for someone to help, but that's not a fair trade if I'm unwilling to help them now. If I'm ever there, I hope I have enough understanding to not hate people when they pass me by."

"I don't think you'll ever be there."

"You never know."

"Yeah," Reydeyn says.

They turn their attention back to the prince, who is now addressing the crimson cords standing in the marketplace. Reydeyn scans their faces as he has every other time today they have come to the market today. Some of them have been waiting here all day. Others have arrived since the sun rose on their journeys. And that is another reason for them being despised. They are nomadic, and many do not appreciate sharing their property with those who do not have the discipline to have their own. Travelers who are not homeless are a different story, and it is expected that they will be welcomed as guests.

"You've been here and idle all day, why?" Prince Nicaia asks.

"No one has hired us, my lord." The young woman that Reydeyn has noticed steps out from the rest of the group toward Nicaia. She kneels, pleading for work. Any work.

"You've seen the others I have hired, and you know by now that I am Prince Nicaia, here on behalf of my father the king, King Les Pariablues. Go out and work in my vineyard, and at the end of the day I will give you what is right. And, if you do well in this last hour and wish to stay on, you will find that you will continue to be paid what is right every day that you work. Come."

Reydeyn watches as the young woman hurries on ahead of everyone else. She knows the way to the vineyard. He glances at Acacia and sees that she is watching her too. She definitely looks like she needs the money. Just like all of them do, though it may be more correct that some of them need to learn how to manage money more than they need the commodity itself. And yet he watches as some of the crimson cords hang back, unwilling to work for the king, it would seem. He feels an ache in his stomach, longing for all of them to know the freedom of the king's service. And so, he turns around and goes back to those who have chosen to remain.

"Excuse me, if I may, I would like you to reconsider your refusal to come. Come and serve the king and find him to be the best of earthly masters." He looks around at each of them, all of them unmoving. He wants them to come, but he also decides that now is a good time to examine them all one last time for any sign that they belong to a band.

"Don't waste your time," one says.

"But you need work. This is an offer for more than just the last hour of the day."

"I'm not falling for it."

"Alright, then come and see how the king deals with the other crimson cords who have come. See that he indeed is good, and then either accept or refuse his offer for yourselves."

"Go, it's getting dark soon. You don't want to be out in these streets, not with us here."

"The offer remains open," he says, unsure of how much of a threat the man's words actually are, unsure whether he should turn away and confirm their feelings that they are thoroughly unwelcome and unwanted, unsure of whether he should invite them back as guests. None of them seem to be a part of the band, so he figures that they are simply crimson cords unwilling to work for a mere hour. And, honestly, he doesn't blame them. He only hopes they will hear the tale from the other crimson cords of the king's kindness and generosity and change their minds then. Only time will tell.

And since he is unsure about what he should do for them, he turns away and feels uneasy the entire way back to the vineyard.

Chapter 24

Grumbling crowds into Pari's ears, just as he expected that it would. He keeps his hand on his son's shoulder, cherishing this opportunity to stand side by side with him.

From the last hired to the crimson cords who have been working all day, each one has now been paid the same amount. A day's wage. Accustomed to being cheated and taken advantage of, one of the crimson cords who started at dawn speaks up, "These last ones you hired only worked a measly hour, and you've paid them like they worked through the heat of the day. They've been sitting in the market, taking it easy."

"Go on, son, answer them," Pari encourages Nicaia, the boy having told him what his plan was from the beginning.

"Friend, I haven't wronged you. Didn't you agree to work for a day's wage? So, take it and go where you please. Go to the next place to work or come back here. And if every other worker is given the same as you, why should you be upset? Don't I have the right to do as I wish with my money?"

"Indeed, my son speaks the truth," Pari says. "Or are you upset because we are generous to others? In the end, the last will be first and the first last. Those of you who wish to stay on, come to my son, and he will arrange it."

"Many called. Few chosen," Pari overhears Jeko saying to Reydeyn and Acacia as the crimson cords make their decisions. Some walking away. Some remaining.

The contract of a hired worker, a temporary servant, is set out through a simple exchange. The crimson cord is exchanged for another cord that is a sleeve of the same size, but rather than the deep red, it is white. Or, in this case to distinguish them as hired by royalty, the inside of the sleeve is purple while the outside is white. The labourer retains their first pay in their new cord and then receives a day's wage for every day they work after that. In addition, they have the freedom to choose whether they will lodge with their contractual master, paying nothing, or use their wages to provide themselves with other lodging.

Pari looks upon one of the men who has chosen to exchange his crimson for white. "Kulcam, yada ues."

The man drops to one knee, the cord grasped in his right hand, not having had time to yet tie it around his head. "Master, I know I owe you a debt."

"Yes, fifty days' wages."

"I have no way to pay you, my lord. I can only offer to work for you. Here, you may have this day's wage back as a–"

Pari closes the man's hand around the single coin. "Kulcam, it is forgiven. Yada ues."

The man rises to his feet. "Thank you."

"And if your family needs lodging, you know you are welcome here."

He nods. "Now that I have work with you, we will be able to remain in our current dwelling. Thank you, my lord."

Les Pariablues

"But you will all eat with us, will you not?"

"As you wish, my lord."

From master to lord, perhaps that change in address does not strike you, reader. But it is significant. Master is a title used by a debtor to address the one they owed. Lord is used to address the one that a servant serves. Though Kulcam calls Pari lord, an acknowledgement of submission, it is also a declaration of his freedom.

"We will retrieve them together," Pari says.

"As you wish, my lord."

"I'm proud of you, Nicaia," Pari says, gripping his son's shoulder.

"Thank you, Father," he says smoothly, though the king feels the tension in his tone. Young Rittelle stands at his son's side, and the king questions how she looks upon those who are crimson cords no longer.

Pari now purposefully turns to lay eyes on a young female crimson cord. Beside her stands his oldest daughter, Tres, an arm around her as she stands barefoot, staring at the day's wage in her hand. "Artisana," the king says gently.

Tres looks back at her father, surprised that he knows the crimson cord's name.

Startled out of her shock and indecision, Artisana drops to her knees in deep distress. Her hands cup together, the insides of her wrists pressed to her forehead and the day's wage offered back to its giver in her open palms.

"Will you stay and serve me?"

"Master," she cries, "you increase our debt. I worked but one hour for you, and you have given me a day's wage. And my father already owes you so much. We have nothing to repay you. I did not come here just to work. The debt must be settled, and my father..."

"About two years' wages is what your father owes me. It is not your debt."

"He is dying, master. He is old, and will never rise to work another day. I will work to settle his debt."

"Rise, and do not fear. Take me to your father."

"Yes, master."

Tres reaches down and helps Artisana to her feet.

"Come," he looks directly at each one he is calling to join him, "let us go to see Arcan."

And so, Artisana leads the way, Princess Tres still at her side, as she trudges toward what she dreads. Directly behind her Prince Azaryada, Prince Nicaia, Rittelle, Jeko, Reydeyn and Acacia follow the king. Moments later, she brings the king to a tattered tent beyond the dwellings of the village.

"Par yada," the king says over the humble dwelling. His heart is heavy within him.

"Master?" comes the weak voice of a pale man who lies on his back.

Artisana drops to her knees and hurries to give her father a drink he has no strength to lift his own head to receive.

"I have come to forgive your debt and take both you and your daughter in to care for as members of my own household for as long as you wish."

The old man's eyes fill with tears. "Master, I will not live long. My daughter is all I have, and I give her to you."

"You will both lodge with us at the vineyard. You need not worry about repaying me."

"I will work for you, serve you for life," Artisana says.

"But not to pay off any debt," Pari says, stooping to put a hand on her shoulder. Their eyes meet, and he draws her into his embrace. "Jeko, Reydeyn, bring Arcan. And Artisana, gather what you wish from this place. We will wait for you outside."

Kulcam stands outside the tent staring at nothing in particular even though the colour of the fading sunset's is glorious. Pari puts his hand on the man's shoulder. The tails of the new white and purple cord that is tied around the man's head dangle onto the king's hand. "What is it, Kulcam?"

"I am merely thinking, my lord."

Pari nods. "We will gather your family as we return."

The king glances over at Nicaia and Rittelle. There is something going on between them. He sighs inwardly. Nicaia has hidden motives behind this demonstration. Will his son someday openly turn his back on him? What disaster is rumbling just over the horizon? He shakes his head. One day at a time, and perhaps the disaster will never come. There is still time for the seed to work in the cold hard ground.

Upon departure, the labourer takes all earnings as well as both the white and crimson cords. They wear the crimson but keep the white, which always has some sort of distinct identification marker on the ends corresponding to the house in which they served. The white band means that, should they return to the house they were hired by, they will be welcomed as either a labourer or a guest. A white cord is also a general token of credibility that is usually not given out so readily as it was today to these workers. And to offer it even to the ones who worked but a single hour? What foolishness once more.

Nicaia laughs within himself. He is succeeding. Let everyone think that he is growing to be like the king. Step by step, he will take the hearts of the king's people and then the throne. And now for a test of just how much the king is pleased with him as his son.

"Father," he says as they walk back to the vineyard, "I wish to make Rittelle my right hand, and I was wondering whether you approve."

"We will discuss it with Qodei and Rittelle– her mother– tonight as we eat."

"What then?"

"As long as they and Rittelle approve of it, then yes. She may be announced as such at the same time as Artisana is announced as a permanent servant. Though, I do not believe that will be tonight. She needs more time to consider."

Nicaia feels his stomach turn over. *More time to think, right.* The result is inevitable. Yet one more captivated by the king with the purple sapphire in their ears.

"Thank you, Your Majesty," Rittelle says as sweetly as honey.

"Yes, thank you, Father," Nicaia says.

The king smiles at him, and Nicaia smiles back because the king has no idea that he is not his son.

Artisana turns over and repeats the routine she has had every morning since...a long time. Her parents were more than old enough to be grandparents by the time they had her, the joy of their old age, but their old age is the very thing that has been her sorrow. While sickness or accidents or war might take the parents of her peers, it is only a short matter of time that has stolen hers. Her mother was not strong enough to live beyond the day she brought her into the world, and her father's health has been failing catastrophically for as long as she can remember.

For most of her life, she has been the one who has tried to find work from village to village, the constant burden that her father has carried of his debt to the king being her only inheritance. And now, checking on her father as her first duty when she rises, proves to show her that the day she has always known was coming has arrived. The dawn has not yet broken, and everything around her feels still and cold.

She did not expect to have any tears left when her father finally departed, but she does. Her weeping slowly grows louder, despite how the last thing she wants is to wake anyone around her. But they are awake. Tres is the first to comfort her. The crown prince is there as well and so many more, including the king, the dear and gracious king. Embarrassment fades as she accepts their comfort.

Now, after a month here with her father, she makes her final decision, not out of a compulsion or a sense of guilty obligation but out of gratitude. Tonight, after her father is buried, she will pledge herself for life to the king. Once she can speak, she tells the king as much. It is finally coming to that decision that keeps her going through the dark haze of the day.

Though the day drags, at last, the moment to exchange her cords for piercings in her ears is upon her. Her heart begins to pound.

"Your Majesty," she hears someone address the king and turns to listen in hopes of distracting herself from her nervousness.

"Yes, Kulcam?"

"I wish to offer my service for life as well in this moment, my lord."

"And why do you wish to do such a thing?"

"If I may say it with everyone here as my witness, my lord?"

King Les Pariablues turns to Artisana. "This meal is in remembrance of your father, is this acceptable that Kulcam speaks?"

She only manages to nod, fearful that she will break down once more as she did this morning, as she did at the graveside.

"Hear, my people, all you who are gathered around this table, Kulcam has something he would like to say," the king announces from his seat.

What subdued conversation there is now dies away.

Kulcam slowly stands and turns to Artisana. "Will you stand with me?"

She meets eyes with him and accepts his outstretched hand.

He puts an arm around her, and she realizes how good of a friend he has become. Not like a father, but perhaps an uncle. Tres reaches out from where she sits and squeezes Artisana's hand. "Tonight, we solemnly remember Arcan," Kulcam says. "Two men owed the king a debt. One was strong and able to work it off in time he wouldn't even miss once it was over. The other owed ten times as much and had no strength to work a single hour. He had nothing but a single daughter who he considered his greatest treasure.

"You know that I am talking about Arcan as the one debtor and myself as the other. He, his daughter and I came to this vineyard at the same time, and I have learned much from both him and Artisana. That day, the king forgave us both the debt we owed him.

"It is said that one who is forgiven much loves much, while one who is forgiven little loves little. And I tell you what you already are aware of: both Arcan and his daughter have loved much. I, on the other hand, have taken time to realize that I have been forgiven much and thus am just beginning to love in kind. Though my debt seemed smaller than Arcan's, I have come to realize, as he and his daughter already knew, that the forgiveness I received was no less valuable than the forgiveness he did. Through him, I have come to realize my need for greater forgiveness from a greater King of a greater debt. And so it is in honour of both the King of that glorious city and Arcan that I am joining Artisana in lifelong service to King Les Pariablues. On some accounts I may have been forgiven less, but here and now I pledge that I will not love less."

"If I may, I would like to do the same," a girl says into the silence that has fallen.

All heads turn. It is Rittelle.

Silence falls once more and this time is broken by the king, who brings the three servants close to himself. Queen Vaht stands with him.

And so, more quietly than usual, the ceremony takes place. Artisana does not try to wipe the tears away as they fall, and neither does Reydeyn where he stands. Acacia leans her head on his chest with tears falling too. And all the while Tres continues to hold Artisana's hand throughout the entire thing while Azar watches, looking back and forth between Acacia, sitting so close to Reydeyn, and Artisana. He does not know how much Artisana returns his desire to be friends at the least. And how much can he expect from her in her grief? He decides that even if she does not take notice of him, he will be there for her now and for as long as their paths run next to one another.

Nicaia stands by in support of his right hand. Rittelle has officially been recognized as such for nearly a month, unlike the original plan to have it made official at the same time as Artisana's service to the king. He knows that Rittelle is right, as much as he wishes he could outdo Azar in his servant attitude, Nicaia knows that to take the purple sapphire studs would be a step too far. He must successfully have the king believe that, while having a servant attitude, Nicaia still believes himself to be his son. Otherwise, he will be angered by what he perceives as wrongful rejection of his generosity. After all, it is nothing admirable to act as a servant when that is what a person believes themselves to be. It is only admirable if it is someone giving up higher status. So, for now, Nicaia must cater to the king's ego, go along with the story that the king has acted benevolently toward him and his family.

Meanwhile, once the ceremony is over, Queen Vaht puts her hand on her husband's arm, pulling his attention to Nicaia and Rittelle, who have retreated to the shadows. The king simply nods. Once more, they refuse to join in, though they will move where they are told to. The glint of the sapphire studs in the girl's ears are a painful ruse. The king turns away, his heart even heavier, considering what to do with his coldly obedient son and Qodei's equally mechanically compliant daughter.

Chapter 25

"How is it, Artisana?"

"What, my prince?"

Azar smiles at how the young woman now comfortably looks him in the eye. Though she uses royal titles to address him, they are friends. "How is it being a servant of the Koingsung?"

"I would not want to be anywhere else."

Reydeyn rides next to Acacia behind the crown prince with enough space between them that the two of them can talk without being overheard, not that the right hand believes that the prince is more interested in any conversation over the one he is having with Arcan's daughter. "Are you jealous?" Reydeyn teases.

"Jealous?" Acacia shoots him a shocked look. "How dare you accuse me. I should hit you over the head with this very uncomfortable saddle." She laughs. "That wasn't a very clever threat."

"I was just about to say that. You really think you can scare me?"

"You've seen what I'm capable of. I thought you would know better by now than to mess with me."

"Yet another empty threat!" He throws his hands up and then lowers his voice. "But back to what I was saying before you interrupted. Are you jealous?"

"And why would I be jealous?"

"You haven't noticed how the prince has been pining over Artisana?"

"Pining is a very strong word."

"But I have the inside track, so I know when my prince is... involved in something or someone."

"Do you? And you believe he's involved," she searches for her next words, "that he is pursuing Artisana?"

"I think he might be."

"And you think that makes me jealous."

"I think you might be."

"But why?" She isn't smiling back anymore. "I have you. I thought that this is what this is about– this year. You aren't serious?"

"I was just teasing you."

"But sometimes teasing is just a way to secretly say the truth."

"Acacia, what's wrong?" Apparently while he was just trying to let loose, he has stepped on a tender nerve.

"Tell me the truth, Reydeyn. What are your intentions?"

"I..."

"Because if you aren't planning for marriage then...It's fine if we're just friends, more than fine, but I need to know."

"I was just joking around about you being jealous."

"Yes, but I want to know whether you're saying that you don't want to marry me. Or anyone, for that matter. No one is forcing you to, and what are the prospects for a marriage if the husband or wife isn't really committed to it?"

"I wasn't trying to say anything about my own commitment."

"But now I'm asking you to."

Terror grips him. A nervous laugh comes out all on its own. He's ashamed of his own hesitancy. Does she think that he doesn't love her? As much as she says that she is fine if they do not marry, he cannot bring himself to believe her. Why should she continue to invest her time in him if he has no intention to offer her a future? "I thought we settled on a year," he says as evenly as he can, but he cannot manage to look her in the eye. Why did he have to tease her about Artisana? It's so soon after Arcan's death, so what place has laughter? He stares at his hands and watches his knuckles whiten around the reins.

"We did agree on a year, but do I have to wait until it's over to know how you really feel?"

"Honestly, I don't know if I'll even know how I feel by then."

"Meaning what?"

"Meaning I don't know if I'll ever have it settled in my mind if I can be the man of a family." He closes his eyes. If she is going to go, he isn't going to torture himself by watching her leave. He doesn't move as she briefly brings her mount close enough to lay her hand on his shoulder. He doesn't open his eyes either. The horse will not endanger him; it knows the way.

"You're afraid?"

He nods.

"Me too."

He decides to look at her. "Of what?"

"Of being a wife and mother, but marriage is a good and precious thing, and if it is what the King of that glorious city has for us, why should we let fear rob us?"

He lets her question hang in the air.

"Why should we, Reydeyn?"

He clears his throat. He didn't know that she expected him to answer out loud. He takes a deep breath. "I'm still scared."

"But do you love me?"

"That's not the question." The fact that he doesn't want her to leave proves that he has some sort of attachment or even loyalty to her. Whether that is love or not is another matter.

Confusion wrinkles her face. "I don't get it."

"There are different kinds of love. I need to figure out what I have toward you and whether it is the appropriate– Whether it is what a husband has for his wife. Are you saying that you'd be ready to be my wife?" His curiosity and desperation to know is stronger than his embarrassment over asking such a question. By now he's used to stumbling all over himself around this girl. She doesn't seem to mind.

"If you are ready to be my husband," she says.

He sighs. And so it all falls back on him. "Can you be patient a little longer?"

She nods, but the gesture strikes him as an empty promise. And that hurts because he feels as though he has failed her, dashed her hopes. Yet, he is at a loss for how to form an apology. He is only striving to be honest. Surely, she can understand– No, that is just it, she does not understand how his experience as a slave has complicated what should be a simple matter. And he shouldn't expect her to understand just as he cannot expect her to wait on him. Why should she? The prince and Artisana are only friends, so her prospects with him remain, especially if he steps back now. But before he can think himself any farther out of the arrangement, Acacia turns to him just long enough to get his attention and then continues to talk facing forward while he keeps his eyes on her.

"Reydeyn, what if you don't need to worry about figuring out the words to describe how you feel or what you're prepared to commit to? Think about the way you act, the way you've held me, the way we laugh together and can share so openly with one another. I don't know. Maybe that's not what you need, but maybe it'll help you a little while you also consider how we're doing in light the greater King's standards for a husband and wife."

"You really hope this works out between us?"

She nods without turning his way. "I've chosen you, Reydeyn. I'm just waiting to see whether you choose me. If you don't, then that is your choice, and we remain friends and fellow servants of the king."

Reydeyn lets out a long breath and turns his eyes from her to a pouch at his chest. He opens it and draws out several nuts and some dried fruit. He drops them into his mouth all at once and tries to allow the feeling of chewing to calm him. He reaches into another satchel and holds out a small basket of berries picked fresh an hour or two ago. They are the first hints of the coming harvest. After harvest: resting season. After resting season: sowing. In between now and then: perhaps more ventures after strays with Azar. And right now: back to the capital to witness the king settling some accounts.

"You want any?" He holds the basket out to her.

She slowly looks over and takes two or three off the top with a little nod. Reydeyn shakes his head and puts the basket away. He'd better come up with his answer soon, or he may just lose his friend. And that is the last thing he needs.

"Call up the next account," King Les Pariablues commands.

So many thoughts run through Reydeyn's mind. His own trial with Koje, the day he learned who the king was, and there is something else too: his conversation with Azar last night as they lay under the stars together, talking as brothers.

"Azar," he had begun, realizing just how comfortable he had learned to be with his prince, "may I ask you something about Acacia?"

"Of course."

"Do you still have," he searched for the word, crickets and a distant crackling fire filling in the silence, "intentions toward her?"

"What do you mean?"

"I mean that, if I would step back, would you still step forward?"

"Are you stepping back?"

"Please, just tell me whether you would."

"Why in the world would you? I thought things were going well."

"Are you saying you wouldn't?"

"I believe that things are moving along with Artisana."

He felt as though the prince was teasing him a little. "But what about Acacia?"

"She has you, doesn't she? Or are you proposing a swap? You see whether you and Artisana–"

"No, I don't know if I will ever get married." Reydeyn could not afford to be less than clear.

"What holds you back?"

"How can I?"

"You're a free man," came the gentle reminder.

"Yes," the tears, brought on by a burden of guilt, threatened to bind his tongue.

"Reydeyn, what troubles you?" The prince laid with his right arm under his right hand's head.

"I know that I am free, but I feel the chains like they are still there every waking moment, and so I cannot live in the fullness of the freedom that I know is mine. What is that but ingratitude? Selfishness, cowardice!"

Azar rolled onto his side and put his left hand over Reydeyn's heart as though with a touch he could soothe all of the pain embedded there. "Look at me, brother."

The tears blinded him, but the prince wiped them away.

"Why did you ever choose me?"

"Because I love you," he said it without a hint of hesitation. "I petition for you every day before the greater King. As does my father and your father." No qualifier necessary because Jeko is his father. "As does Acacia. Don't be afraid. Don't be afraid. You are loved, and you are free to love. Love firstly the King of that glorious city and then his people. You are also free to love Acacia."

The prince then petitioned aloud for him before kissing him on the forehead. "Yada ues, brother," he said before lying back down beside him. Reydeyn lay awake silently petitioning for some time afterward. Then, just this morning as they approached the capital, he talked with Acacia. They will be alright. And, yes, perhaps in several months they will be wed.

But it is now approaching evening, and the king is continuing to call up accounts.

"Rodraf the merchant!" Jeko announces.

The finely dressed man is brought forward. His extravagant attire causes Reydeyn to wonder what debt he could possibly owe.

"And how much does he owe?" the king inquires of Jeko. The queen sits on her throne beside him.

"200 thousand years' wages."

Jaws drop. Gasps suck the air clean out of the room.

Looking on, Nicaia crosses his arms. It is expected that merchants will incur debt in their work, especially as they start out plying their trade, and more so if they are royal merchants with finer merchandise. By nature, too, merchants are considered wasteful and manipulative...But this debt. Rittelle slips her arm into Nicaia's while he waits with everyone else for the verdict. What foolishness will the king display now? The prince waits with anticipation for Pari to condemn himself before all of his people.

Queen Vaht's eyes are wide and fixed on the king. In fact, that is where most eyes are as he raises his hands, signaling the moment his pronouncement of judgement.

"Have you any means to pay the full amount at this moment, Rodraf?"

"No, master."

"Then it seems that you, your family and all that you own must be sold, at least as a down payment."

Nicaia feels the corners of his mouth lift at the king's words. It's about time a rotten, irresponsible merchant got what was coming to him. But the corners come back down like a drawbridge. Surely, it is not over. If the king is to be true to his character, there is foolishness yet to be revealed.

"No! My lord, master! Have mercy!!" Rodraf is on his knees with his face to the floor, but his desperation cannot be muffled.

"Patience! Have patience with me, and I will pay you everything. I have resources now–!"

"Enough," King Les Pariablues says. "Your debt is forgiven."

No more jaws are left to be dropped. No more air is left to be snatched out of the room. There is only a vacuum of silence.

"Comastasia!!" The merchant suddenly exclaims, jolting everyone as he rises to his knees and raises his arms. "Oh, thank you, my lord."

Jaws snap back into place. The air explodes back into the room.

How can it be, indeed!! Fire courses through Nicaia's veins. In the chaos of the adulation from those gathered in the throne room, he makes his exit. Rittelle with him.

"Comastasia! And this is the kind of king we have ruling us?" He clenches his fists.

"I know, Nicaia. It isn't right. But someday you'll change it. Until then, walk with me." She grips his arm and draws him along in the garden.

Nicaia jerks away. "Don't touch me." He storms off with Rittelle keeping pace.

"Nicaia! Rittelle!" someone calls after several moments.

It is all Nicaia can do to simply stand still and watch him approach. The so-called king himself.

"Where is justice?" The words come out in a low growl, the growl of an animal crouched and ready to strike.

"Azar paid the debt. I believe you left before that was announced."

The prince shakes his head. Rittelle stands by and watches, thinking this situation equally as foolish as does Nicaia.

"Nicaia, he never could have paid that debt. Are you upset because I am generous to others? Your family owed a debt as well–"

"That was different! We were going to pay, and we could have." He bites his tongue before he adds, *without your help*. "Rodraf was irresponsible. We were making an investment and had a plan."

"But you could not pay either at the time."

"And what's the point of it all?"

"To paint a picture."

"Right, I know. I understand," he says as calmly as he can. He knows where this is headed, and he is not about to hear it. "I need to think about some things. Please, excuse me."

"You and Rittelle walk as long as you need, but I do hope to see you both at my table tonight."

"Of course, Father." And with that, the prince turns away.

Chapter 26

"Yaren!" The soldier stirs from his bed. He was up all night for his shift. Not only has the king brought him here as a guest during this time of settling debts, but he has also honoured him with the privilege to stand guard with the rest of the soldiers posted in this city.

"Yaren! Open the door." The heavy fist threatens to break it right off of its hinges. He leaps to his feet. There must be trouble. He scrambles to collect his armor and weapons. It only takes a moment after his long experience using them. However, the man on the other side of the door gets the better of him before he can use them. Even a seasoned warrior gets caught off guard at times, and now is one of those moments since he expected his visitor to be at his door to inform him, not grab him at the throat.

"Rodraf!"

The man is stronger than him, and an even more skilled warrior than merchant, which is perhaps not saying much considering the debts he manages to incur. "Pay up!"

"What?" He struggles to alleviate some of the pressure on his neck. His vision becomes a patchwork.

"You heard me, you good for nothing scum. You owe me! And you'd better pay before the king changes his mind."

"I don't know what you're talking about!" With great effort, he throws off the man's grip, and the merchant satisfies himself with holding his shoulders.

"Yes, you do."

"And how much do you owe the king?"

"Enough."

"And how much do I owe you?"

"The difference is beside the point. Pay me what you owe."

"My debt paid will do nothing to cover what you owe."

Rodraf slams Yaren against the wall and points a blade to his throat. "I told you to pay! Every bit of it."

Yaren knows how much he owes. Four months' worth of wages. He also knows that he doesn't have it on hand but can fairly easily pay him. Furthermore, he knows that he was a fool to ever borrow from this merchant in the first place. Rodraf is liberal with the money of others and stingy with his own. Yaren could've paid off his debt to the merchant long ago if not for the arbitrary interest.

On top of it all, he not only feels a knife at his throat but one in between his armor and his back. It seems that everyone is at the palace and not around this backstreet suburb to assist him.

"Have patience, and I will pay you. Just as I have made every other payment."

"I need it now. Pay up!"

"I cannot," he hisses against the sting of metal.

"Well, then you will know the chafing of cold chains around your wrists and ankles until you work it up."

And all goes dark with the leather bag over Yaren's face. Rodraf looks around, thinking that he is alone, but the king's servants see him.

"Your Majesty! Your Majesty!!" Acacia pulls Reydeyn down beside her before the throne.

The king raises his arms, silencing all other proceedings of the court. "Reydeyn, what is so urgent?" he inquires of his son's right hand, even though it was Acacia who has cried out.

The young man is speechless and can only shake his head.

"Rise, tell me, what is it?"

Reydeyn remains on his knees. It was all he could do to keep up with Acacia as she dragged him here.

"It's Rodraf, my lord," Acacia says. "And Yaren. He's taken him as his slave! He was taking him onto his ship to sail away."

The king rises from his throne. "Guards, find that scoundrel!!"

"Some have already gone after them, my lord," Acacia says. "Reydeyn and I were not the only ones who saw. They're bringing him back here."

"Good, then we will wait on them. All other matters will be postponed until tomorrow, or later if it takes that long to clear up this matter. And ensure that all present earlier are present for this." He takes a seat on his throne once more. The servant he was dealing with when Acacia and Reydeyn burst in bows and moves away, having no intentions of fleeing. The king is reasonable in how he works out the payment of debts, the fairest of creditors with generosity that many take advantage of, only to find themselves ensnared. The room falls silent, and the tension builds. Acacia helps Reydeyn to his feet and the two of them take their places. Others filter into the room to witness the continuation of what happened earlier. Nicaia and Rittelle slip in at the last moment.

"Rodraf the merchant to see His Majesty!"

"Bring him in!" the king commands. "And tell me, Rodraf, where is Yaren?"

"I do not know, my lord. Am I my brother's keeper?"

"You address me as lord after what you have done? But to answer your question, you are your brother's keeper. You are both my servants. Tell me, where is Yaren?"

"I do not know, my lord!"

"Stay on your knees," the king retorts. "Guards, where is my servant?"

"Outside, my lord."

"Bring him in."

The majestic doors open once more, and two guards escort Yaren. Or, more correctly, there is one on each side of him to assist him as he limps.

"Bring him a chair," the king says, standing and walking toward his injured servant. The chair is brought and set near the throne, and King Pariablues assists him into it. "Have you had water?"

Yaren bows his head for a moment. "Yes, my lord."

"Tell me, Yaren, why are you injured?"

"I was recently beaten, my lord."

"And what enemy is it who has done this to you?"

"One to whom I owe a debt, my lord."

"And what is the amount of your debt?"

"Four months' wages, Your Majesty."

"And whom are you indebted to?"

"Rodraf the merchant, my lord."

"This Rodraf who kneels before me trembling?"

"Yes, my lord."

"Did you know that he owed me a debt?"

"I believe so, my lord."

"And do you know how great a debt it was, my friend?"

"I do not know, Your Majesty."

"200 thousand years' wages. Money that he borrowed from me and used wisely and unwisely in his merchant trade on my behalf. This very morning, I forgave him that debt in the presence of many witnesses. And now, you wicked servant!" He turns in fury toward Rodraf.

The king's words chill the entire atmosphere, a cold curse when those present are so accustomed to his warm blessing. Reydeyn trembles. He's been here before. Koje...

Acacia clutches his arm. And who can manage not to fear in the king's presence at such a time as this?

"You pleaded with me to forgive you your debt, and I did. Shouldn't you have known to give the same mercy to your fellow servant?" It is the roar of a lion.

Rodraf's face meets the ground once more, his entire being trembling.

"Well, since you are so interested in accounting for the wage of every minute, you will not be released from the black dungeon until you pay just that to me," he declares. His voice is quiet, but it carries to the far reaches of the deathly silent room.

Rodraf lets out a howl that nearly scares Reydeyn out of his skin. If not for Azar's firm hands on his shoulders, he would lose his mind.

"Take heed, all of you, particularly those who know greater forgiveness than that of a debt of 200 thousand years. Show that you have been forgiven by forgiving others, or you may find yourself suffering an eternal destiny far worse than the black dungeon." And the king leaves the room, leaving his subjects, his close attendants, his family to look at one another and wonder.

It is only when the former merchant is removed that Reydeyn can breathe again, if only shallowly.

"What kind of prison is he going to?" he manages. "The black dungeon," his voice quivers, "what is that?"

"The worst. It is not said that it is run by torturers for nothing," Azar explains soberly.

"Worse than execution!"

"Yes," Azar says.

"If I ever forgot about his justice..." Reydeyn cannot finish. "I need a walk."

Acacia starts to follow him, but he shakes his head.

"I'll be alright."

Nicaia steps into his path. "May I walk with you, right hand of the crown prince?"

"I suppose, my lord." He glances back at Acacia and notices that she is walking off with her sister, Rittelle. "What is this about, Your Highness?"

"I need some air. I miss the vineyard."

He nods. "Of course." It will do him no good to act as though he doesn't trust the prince, no matter how true that is. "I do as well." He realizes that he should add a title. "My lord."

"And what do you think of what just happened here?"

"Perhaps you should speak first, my lord."

"Reydeyn, enough with the my lord's. You call my brother by his first name. Why not address me in like manner? You are in the inner circle."

Was that flattery? "Yes. I do hope you know that I respect you."

"Why wouldn't I? Unlike some servants, you have never talked back to me or struck me."

Reydeyn suddenly feels a need to scratch the back of his neck. "I thought we were talking about what happened here today."

"And is what happened an isolated incident?"

"I'm sorry. I don't understand."

"Everything is connected. One day leads to another."

"Yes."

"So, what we just witnessed is connected to what has preceded this."

Reydeyn feels like he's watching a dog chasing its tail. The itch has moved to his forehead, so he rubs it with the heel of his right hand. "Yes. I'm sorry, Nicaia, I just don't know what to say."

"What are you thinking about what has taken place with Rodraf?"

Reydeyn sighs. "Justice."

"Justice?" Nicaia laughs. "What else are you thinking?"

"I'm thinking of Koje, Your Highness."

"I told you not to use titles."

"Of course." He bristles.

"Of Koje, yes, and how was it justice for him to be punished and you let off."

"It was mercy. I know that. Just as it was mercy for Rodraf's debt to be taken off of his shoulders."

"But it wasn't."

Reydeyn looks away.

"Does it bother you?"

He sighs and doesn't turn to look at the prince.

"I asked you a question."

"A king must use wisdom in his dealings. Your father has done just that. Do I deserve to be where I am–?"

"No, you do not."

Reydeyn closes his mouth, the words stolen from him.

"And yet here you are," he says, tone now lighter.

Reydeyn clenches his fists. "What is your point?"

"I merely wanted your opinion."

Reydeyn nods. "Then you have it."

"Reydeyn!"

He turns, thinking it is Acacia. Instead, it is his sister, Tres. Interesting: he and Nicaia share a sister now, yet they do not share the same father or mother or other siblings. He waits for her to catch up and gives her his arm when she does. "My lady." He smiles and kisses her hand, but any lightheartedness fades when he looks into her tearful eyes.

She only holds his gaze for a moment before falling onto his chest and weeping. Reydeyn puts his arms around her, unable to speak. Terror. That is what he saw in her eyes. Terror that he knows all too well.

He buries his face in her shoulder and wraps his arms more tightly around her. It is a good place to be, overwhelmed as he is.

"Is there mercy for me? Reydeyn, tell me, is there mercy for me?" she cries.

He pulls away just enough to look his sister in the eye. "For what?"

"For everything. I don't mean with Father, with the king. I mean with the King of that glorious city."

"Yes, there is. Because his princely Son steps in to pay the debt, just like Azar stepped in to pay Rodraf's." But since Rodraf rejected it, the offer of payment was withdrawn.

"But what if I cannot forgive?"

"He gives strength."

She slips down to her knees under the weight of the things that she knows she has done. The way she has stolen and manipulated for her own selfish gain, the way she has dishonoured her body, and not simply to survive. And it is not just what she has done. She has become aware of the head of the corrupt stream of her life. "Then may the greater King be merciful to me, a sinner." She drops to her knees and pounds a fist against her heart. Over and over, she cries out with the same words while her brother keeps his arms around her.

Nicaia turns away, his heart smug, counting up all the good things he does. The way he obeys, the way his serving goes above and beyond, the way the people have already praised him for what he does, the way he works hard every day- unlike others- unlike his brothers, unlike Tres who did nothing to deserve her freedom or her adoption by the king, unlike Reydeyn who should have been punished with Koje. He looks up with a conceited smirk. "You know it too, oh King of that glorious city."

As the sun sets, Prince Nicaia and Princess Tres both return to the king's house. Only the latter justified.

Chapter 27

"Well, Reydeyn, sowing starts in less than a month."

The young servant nods.

"Any decision yet?" Tres asks. "I think Acacia's afraid to ask."

Knowing how closely knit his sister has become with both Artisana and Acacia, Reydeyn deduces that Tres has understated her level of certainty. "Why would she be afraid?"

"Because she doesn't want to nag you, but she's desperate to know for sure. You need to talk to her."

He sighs. "Yeah, I know." Oh, for the time when this will be over. "Where is she?"

"C'mon, I'll take you to her." She leads the way and then leaves him outside the door of Acacia's room in Qodei's house.

Reydeyn raises his fist and brings down it against the wood.

"Who is it?"

"Reydeyn."

"Come in." Her words come hesitantly like she's trying to do something else that requires concentration at the same time as answering him.

Reydeyn forces his hand to grip the doorknob, give it a twist and then to enter. She looks up from her thread to greet him with a warm smile. "Hello. And what can I do for you, sir?"

He takes a closer look at the mass of thread. "What happened?"

"Just a small tangle."

He raises his eyebrows. How she has the patience is even more beyond him than how the colourful strands got as mashed together as they have.

"I brought these from the palace, and I wasn't too careful about how I put them in the box. Now, I pay the price. I should've brought them on spools." She shrugs. "Gives me something to do."

He nods, not sure where to look or what to do with his hands or anything. "Do you want the door open?"

"It doesn't need to be."

Since it was closed when he arrived, he closes it again. He starts pacing. There has not been much to do lately. No searches for a sheep. Not much tending of the vineyard. Just the clock ticking down to the time when he must make his decision. And here the moment is.

"So, to what do I owe the honour of your presence?" she asks.

"Tres told me I should talk to you, and she's right."

"She told me she was going to send you my way."

He nods.

"So?"

"What?"

"Are you ready to give your final answer?" She keeps her eyes on the knots as she continues to tear into them.

"I think so. It's just that, all of the same old insecurities are coming up." There isn't enough room for him to pace properly, so he feels dizziness setting in, but he continues because he needs something to do.

"Well, lay them all out and let them die. Because I'm not losing you to them."

"You mean that," he says to himself.

"Of course I do," she says as if his words were a question to her. Exasperation is unmistakable in her tone. "So, lay them out."

"What's the point if we've already been over them?"

"I don't care if we've talked about them a thousand times before now! They're obviously still a problem, and I'm not going to lose you to them. I told you that, and I mean it."

"And what if they don't die today?"

"We come to a place where they are sufficiently put away so that we can deal with them together as husband and wife. Or is that not what you want?"

Reydeyn stops where he is and looks at her only to find that she is looking right back. Time slows to a tenth its customary speed while he considers. "Yes," he whispers at last.

"Then go ahead."

"Being...married," it does him good to actually say it, helps himself accept it, "that would mean that I would be a part of your family."

"You would be my family," she says. She looks back at her threads.

Reydeyn props himself up against where the walls meet. "Yeah, there's that, but I mean that that would make me part of your parents'– of Qodei and Rittelle's family, you know?"

"Their son-in-law. And?"

He shakes his head, unable to figure out how to say what he feels.

"They've been ready to welcome you like that practically from the day they met you."

"But how can I be a part of them?"

She tilts her head. "What would make that inappropriate?"

"I guess..." He sighs, the truth of what he is feeling put into words sounding foolish even to him. "I was a slave."

"Seriously?"

"What do you mean?"

"I mean, does that still hold you back?"

"What do you think this is all about?!" He puts his hand to his head. Does she still not get it after all this time?

She drums her fingers on the table.

"I didn't mean to yell," he says, though he wonders whether that isn't a lie.

"You just startled me, that's all." She pauses and lays the threads aside before standing and stepping towards him.

He lets her wrap her arms around him and then slowly responds in like manner.

"I wish I understood your pain better."

"I don't know if I should say that I wish you did too." Because how can he wish the suffering of his life on her?

"I know the King of that glorious city understands. I know we're equals because of Him. I mean, even in an earthly sense that's way less important." She forgoes any more words and simply touches the sapphire stud in his right ear and then the identical one in her left ear to show what she means.

Reydeyn closes his eyes. It's good to be reminded what it's like to hold her, but he forces himself to release her before he holds her too close and crosses boundaries the two of them have vowed never to, out of respect for one another and their greater King.

Les Pariablues

"Here, I, I made this a few years ago, and maybe I should've given it to you sooner, but I just found it last week." She hands it to him.

He turns the wood over and over in his hands, confusion creeping over his features. "A bone?"

"Yes, carved out of acacia wood."

He nods, now examining the shape of a cross punched out of the middle of the wooden piece.

"Bone of my bone," she says.

He nods.

"And then that in the middle is a reminder that marriage isn't just between the man and woman. There's a picture, and the greater King, as the Creator, is the one who joins them. I made it, thinking I'd give it to my man. Then, I kinda forgot about it until I found it again." She reaches out and pulls the bone apart.

Reydeyn blinks, taking a moment to see how the two pieces join. "This take you a while to make?"

She shrugs. "Maybe a little. Azar helped me when he stopped here on the way back from one of his seeking missions."

He nods.

"Keep that half, and we'll put it back together...?"

Reydeyn meets her steady inquiring gaze. He nods, resolve setting in and baring its teeth against his fear. He smiles. "I'm going to talk to your father to see how soon things can be arranged." Oh, the relief of finally coming to a decision! No turning back now. He takes a deep breath to keep his feet on the ground. He laughs. "It's about time."

"I'll say. You really mean it?"

"Yeah, I do."

She squeals and grabs his entire right arm in both hands. "C'mon, c'mon, c'mon!" She throws open her door and races through the halls. "Mother! Father!! Where are you? It's finally happening!!!"

Reydeyn laughs with her and stumbles forward, trying to keep his balance as her grip pulls him down. When did he start feeling so free? "Oh, Qodei, I might just steal her away if you don't come out," he calls.

"Mother, Father!" Acacia shouts.

Qodie suddenly steps out from a doorway and lifts Reydeyn off the ground by the shoulders. "Now what is this about stealing away my daughter and not becoming my son-in-law?" he demands in a booming voice.

Excitement shields Reydeyn from the full force of the shock of Qodei's unexpected appearance. "It is alright, isn't it?"

"Alright? Alright that you aren't going to become my son-in-law and still take my daughter? Absolutely not. Rittelle!" The man swings Reydeyn into a sort of headlock under his arm. "Just wait until my wife hears about this. She'll–"

"I'm here. Now what is this?"

"The difference between a proper wedding at sowing time and the elopement of our firstborn daughter."

"Oh, put the boy down."

"Does that mean we have your approval?" Reydeyn asks, looking up at Acacia's parents while his toes strive to tickle the floor. The blood rushing to his head only deepens the red tinge that was already creeping into his visage.

Rittelle senior laughs merrily. This isn't her daughter by blood, but no one would ever know looking on, except perhaps by the bright green eyes that Acacia alone has out of the family. "I told you to put the boy down, we have a wedding to plan." She bends down, cupping Reydeyn's face in her hands, even while his feet continue to dangle, and kisses him on the forehead. "Yada ues, my son." Having blessed him, she turns to her daughter, repeating the words and gesture before grabbing Acacia by the hand and pulling her to wherever she has in mind.

Meanwhile, Qodei sets Reydeyn back on his feet. "Women, such excitable characters, aren't they?" And the grizzly of a man embraces him with some of the greatest enthusiasm he has ever put into a single hug. "Well done. You will not find a finer woman."

Reydeyn simply smiles back and continues to hold onto Qodei lest he faint from excitement. He glances up at the face of the solidly built man and catches sight of the sheen of tears in his eyes.

"I'm so proud of you," he whispers, holding him close. "So proud. I know that took courage."

"He did it then?"

Reydeyn glances over his shoulder. "Father."

The Sower draws him into an embrace of his own.

And in some room on the other side of the house, the proud mother is singing over her daughter, "Aiwa! Aiwa! Tabal! Tebal, lela granel canel. Tues ete phumile yada. Eses yareh!"

Reydeyn hears himself laugh for joy. He's the bridegroom. He's actually the bridegroom! And soon, a whole crowd will rejoice as he and his bride come, they will bless them, wishing peace on them and their family, calling down blessing on their line for generations.

Though fear and uncertainty lingers in his heart, he has no regrets about the decision to go ahead with this.

"Tebal!!"

The king, the crown prince and their right hands have returned from yet another search with a sheep borne on the prince's shoulders. Yet another stray brought back into the fold.

Acacia runs to meet Reydeyn, and the crown prince's right hand catches her up in his arms. This time away has made him long for the day they are to be joined all the more. The rest of the bride-to-be's family is here to greet them too.

"So, Qodei, how long before I may call your daughter mine as well?" Jeko inquires with eyes bright.

Qodei the grizzly claps the Sower on the back. "Ah, this celebration will blend into the next in a matter of a day."

"Tomorrow?"

"Unless you need more time to look presentable after your journey."

Acacia, still held in Reydeyn's arms, rests her head on his shoulder and smiles back at her father for a moment before looking her groom in the eyes. "He's quite presentable now."

"Oh, no, you haven't seen anything yet. I have plans," Jeko promises cryptically.

Reydeyn looks back at Jeko. "What do you mean?"

"C'mon, now. A bridegroom must be just as prepared as his bride." He slaps him on the back. "Don't you worry about a thing. You will be ready."

And so it is, as the sun stoops to touch the western horizon the next day, Reydeyn finds himself ready. The festival of the Lost-Found shifts in a moment, and the people take up the wedding chant.

"Aiwa! Aiwa! Tebal! Tebal, lelal granel canel. Thues ete phumile yada. Eses yareh!" they all sing.

Les Pariablues

Generations? Comastasia? Reydeyn wonders as he hands his braid to Jeko and Acacia hands hers to Qodei and Rittelle.

Together, the new couple takes the single seed that Jeko handed to Reydeyn years ago during a lesson under a mustard tree and sows it in the earth that is just beginning to thaw.

"Only fitting that the Sower's son begin the sowing season at his wedding," Jeko explained when he told the couple about his idea to have the sowing of the seed as a part of the ceremony.

Reydeyn lingers on his knees after the seed is planted, looking at the freshly displaced and replaced earth. He looks back at his bride. His bride! And then looks up and smiles. He utters no words, but he knows that the King of that glorious city hears his gratitude.

Acacia gasps in wonder and points to the west. "Look at those colours!!" Disregarding whatever tradition may be next in the ceremony, she grabs his hand and pulls him up to the roof of her childhood dwelling. "It's glorious."

"Like a wedding gift."

"Yarehsus," she says.

Indeed, blessing upon blessing. Cheers ascend as the silhouetted couple seal their commitment with a kiss.

Chapter 28

"*A*iwa! Aiwa! Tebal! Tebal, lelal granel canel. Thues ete phumile yada. Eses yareh!" Jeko cannot get the chant out of his head. He has been singing it to himself since he woke up and now turns to humming it to himself. He reaches into his bag and casts another handful of seeds onto the freshly plowed ground.

There is spring both in the air and in his step once more. And he knows that he has much reason to rejoice. Year after year, he has come to this village as he has to so many others. Just a short time ago, when he came around with Nicaia and Reydeyn, this was one of the villages that harassed them. And how he wishes that the two of them could see this for themselves.

But Nicaia is preoccupied with his vineyard and Reydeyn is on his honeymoon with Acacia. The Sower knows his place in the chain of command; Nicaia is the prince. But, if Jeko talks to Pari, who does have authority over the prince, then Nicaia will come. Grudgingly, no doubt, but the sight may do him good. Yes, Jeko will have to find a way for both Reydeyn and Nicaia to see this year's harvest. No, it does not even have to be quite harvest. It will be enough to wait until the seeds have had time to sprout and their fruit begin to show. Being in the middle of the season, the prince should feel more free to leave the tending of the vineyard in the hands of the servants than he would at either sowing or reaping.

But now, he should shift his thinking away from unpleasant thoughts that dampen his rejoicing. And that includes the ache for how Nicaia once again did not celebrate at the festival of the Lost-Found or with Reydeyn and Acacia. And what will happen in the event that Azar marries Artisana? Will he sit even that out with Rittelle, while at the same time doing his duty as called upon? Jeko shakes his head, laying those thoughts down as he must for the moment. Now is the time for celebration.

Slightly bored of humming, the Sower begins to whistle, and before long he is singing again.

"Aiwa! Aiwa! Tebal! Tebal, lelal granel canel. Thues ete phumile yada. Eses yareh!"

He laughs for joy to himself as he lives it all over again. He has a son. And a daughter for that matter! What joy. He cannot wait until the two of them come back. Will he be holding a grandchild next year?

He laughs again. Perhaps that would not be best if he is to have any hope of concentrating on his work. He must at least pass on his trade before he allows the joy of having this family to consume him. And Qodei thinks that *he* is the proud father. Hah, he has nothing on Jeko. The Sower feels as though this smile has permanently thrust his face into its mold. He does not mind.

Coming to the end of the field, he seats himself in the place they have reserved for him at the supper table, satisfied. Instead of stones, the villagers now offer him bread and other tokens of the last harvest that was brought forth despite their resistance. In addition, he takes part in the portions of the recent hunt that they offer him.

"Yada ues!!" he calls on behalf of the king as he rides out of the village to spend another night under the stars with Votol. He begins singing again as he washes and shines his mount's black coat by the river. The noble beast snorts as though he wishes to sing along and begrudges the fact that his master has a voice while he does not.

"And such an exceptional one at that," Jeko teases the creature as though Votol can understand. The Sower laughs and returns to singing. With his horse cared for, Jeko removes his clothes and bathes, savouring every minute of it. *If anyone has been listening to me singing all day, they may be questioning my sanity*, he laughs once more to himself.

Some might also question his sanity the way he is lying in the river. But, what most would call cold, the Sower deems invigorating, just the thing before hours of admiring the velvet canvas and striving once more to count the tiny diamonds strewn upon it by the most skillful of jewelers. He releases a contented sigh and lets himself fall back into the river, immersing himself entirely for several moments before rising, dressing and making his way to his campsite. His never shorn hair hangs loose and wet.

Once his fire is lit, he pulls the braid that Reydeyn gave him out of his bag. He fingers it. In his estimation, it is made of something more precious than gold. He reclines against his snoring horse and lays the braid across his chest, turning his eyes upward and allowing his mind to wander into thoughts of the future...

Chapter 29

⁓ YEARS LATER ⁓

"*F*ather! Father! I found it, I *found* it!!" Princess Tebala, now ten years of age, races toward the throne room, interrupting all royal daily proceedings with a silver coin held high above her head for all to see. Behind her trail those who are already prepared to celebrate with her.

King Les Pariablues is just as excited as his daughter. He stands to his feet, catches his daughter in his arms and spins her around like he has done since she was little. He laughs and looks around at the servants standing in attendance. "What are you waiting for? What was lost has been found! We must celebrate. Prepare my table."

"Bala!!" Clay meets clay, and the prince and his right hand bring their cups to their lips to taste of the fruit of the vine.

"Lalala-lala-lala–"

"Sit down, Kulcam," Prince Onxwade interrupts and motions to the man into his seat.

"My lord, you wound me. You cut off my songwriting inspiration! Don't you think that was a good idea for the chorus?"

"No, I don't. Now, sit."

"Ah, fine." He takes another sip from his cup, swishing the liquid around to prolong the presence of the taste in his mouth before setting his cup on the arm of his chair. "You have done it, my lord!" Kulcam congratulates Prince Onxwade.

Now an older teenager, the boy beams. "As I have every year since we began this venture. As you remind me." As his right hand, Kulcam has been with the boy every step of the way, doing much as far as stewarding their profits, as well as the king's son for the sake of his father, who can only join his son on some of his voyages.

"Indeed. A merchant you were born to be!"

"Ah, not just any merchant." He shakes his head. "No, not just any merchant." Apple and honey mingle with the taste of the wine that is exceptional all on its own. It is a blend of Prince Nicaia's own design, only one of many beginning to be famous throughout the world, thanks to his younger brother's enterprising ventures.

"No, indeed. You have single handedly redeemed the very term. And to think, you are a Samaritan yet too. It is indeed a miracle of double redemption!!"

Their eyes drift down from the tower built in the middle of the thriving vineyard where they sit and over to the olive grove where the ten princesses pick from the ripe trees to make fresh oil for the upcoming wedding. It will be the largest since Vaht became queen and even larger because of just how beloved of a son Prince

Azaryada is, not to mention how thrilled King Les Pariablues and Queen Vaht are to have Artisana for a daughter-in-law.

The silver coins strung around each of their heads shimmer in the sunlight. Kulcam can almost believe that he can hear their soft jingling carried on the breeze to his ears. There is one for every year that each individual princess has lived. The kingdom has just recently celebrated how Tebala– after much diligent searching by lantern light with broom in hand– found one of her coins after it fell away from the others unnoticed. Now all ten are securely in place. She is the youngest of the princesses.

"Tres, Tengithae, Thuis, Turene, Turst, Thimna, Teakim, Tekoa, Traei and Tebala." Kulcam raises his clay vessel as if to toast the king's daughters. "I think I have them all. And in order. My…they are stunning." He takes yet another sip.

Onxwade turns to him. "Don't get any ideas. You've had too much wine."

"On the contrary, my lord, one can never have enough of what your brother makes. But I think the real problem is that, while I am too old, and you are too related. No need to be sour, my prince."

"Yaren, get your face out of that scroll. Where's your spear? Don't you hear this man's threats against royalty?"

"Calm down." He tilts his cup back and taps the bottom to ensure it is empty before setting it on the table. "I am far too tied up in love with my wife." He smiles. "And the children she has given me. No man could be prouder of his family."

Onxwade rolls his eyes. And people think that boys are immature. Yaren remains silent, eyes open to their surroundings.

"When do we leave on our next venture, my prince?" Kulcam asks.

"As soon as the wedding is over."

"And then to uncharted waters and lands! How glorious." Kulcam spreads the map out on the table.

Yaren sets his scroll aside and leans in too, now that Kulcam seems to be done running his mouth in all the foolish directions that he intends to for one day. However, the guard keeps his eyes open to their surroundings, every once in a while raising the tube of lenses he crafted to his eye. He is still working to make lenses that will show him things at an even greater distance. All in time, but he is not keen to take too much time with the tensions rising as they are. The bands. The cloak and dagger horde, otherwise known as the emerald kingdom.

Now is not a time of peace, not that he would know much about the absence of war.

"And what treasures do you hope to find, Prince Onxwade?" Kulcam asks.

The prince looks off in the direction of his sisters, some of whom may come along for the voyage. However, neither the young women and girls nor the trees around them are where his focus is. It is as though he has built lenses that can carry his eyes to where the waves break on the rocks and sand and even beyond that to where the sea laps a far horizon.

In the silence, Yaren and Kulcam assume that the prince does not intend to answer, yet, after a moment, he comes out of his daydream just enough to whisper, "Treasure worth more than everything I own."

Kulcam looks at Yaren, who fingers his chin. Both of them, as well as Kulcam's family, plan to accompany the prince as they have many times before, so, though they may not understand the prince's answer at the moment, there is at least hope that they may witness the meaning of his words lived out.

The branches of the mustard tree planted years ago overshadows the crown prince and his right hand.

"How does it feel, Reydeyn?"

"What's that, Azar?"

"To be married?"

"Sometimes I still don't believe it, but then she hits me over the head and reminds me." He laughs. "More like she holds onto me and doesn't let go until my senses return to me. Why do you ask?"

"Well, I had a reason in mind, but now I'm wondering about what she's been telling Artisana to prepare her for marrying me."

"All good things, all good things." He smirks at the prince.

"It's a good thing I trust you both."

Reydeyn laughs aloud, something that he has never lost the joy of learning to do more fully. It is one of the many gifts bound up in freedom.

Azar shifts so that his head rests on the chest of his right hand and both of them watch the blue sky through the branches. In many ways, his right hand has become closer to him than any of his brothers. Either of them would give their life for the other without a second thought.

"Azar! Azar, tell him to stop!"

The prince, still a fairly young man, sits up and then rises to his feet to catch his little brother in his arms. "What has he done now, Lumin?" His eyes sparkle as he sees Lazarus coming after his twin. Though they are as old as Nicaia was when he first met him, these boys often act younger than their age.

Lazarus' mischievous smile, razor in hand, put together with the missing strands on the side of Lumin's head tells the story.

"Alright, you've had your fun. Hand it over." Azar holds out his hand.

Lazarus crosses his arms only to be pinned by his older brother. "Hey!"

With ease, Azar takes the razor and matches Lumin's haircut on Lazarus' head.

"There, I think that should do. Now, I suggest that you both take care to keep the hair of your head intact. What will you do if you shave it all off and have none left to braid and give to Father?"

Lazarus sulks, arms still crossed. "I'm not getting married, and neither is he."

"You just might change your mind. But in the meantime, how about some tug of war in the river?"

Lazarus narrows his eyes at Lumin. "I get Reydeyn."

"And I get Azar," Lumin says.

Azar laughs and shakes his head. It is the twins' favourite game, and that does not surprise him one bit considering how they are constantly competing with one another. The teams don't surprise him either. Had Lumin been the offender– which he is fifty percent of the time– Lazarus would've wanted Azar on his team after having his case vindicated. However, the tables are turned today, and Lazarus is looking for an opportunity to plunge Azar's face into the mud. All in good brotherly fun that Azar enjoys even more when Artisana watches.

The crown prince slips the razor into a pouch at his belt. "C'mon." He reaches down, Reydeyn catches his hand, and the four of them make their way to the river.

"Grateful! All you ever do is complain when I come to work with you."

"And tell me, Siohtion, what would become of our inheritance if I did not stay here year after year?"

Siohtion shakes his head and fills the next skin from the large clay jar taken fresh from the press.

"You don't even care, do you?"

"Care about what?"

"You don't care about this vineyard. Siohtion, this was the vineyard our father bought. Our father. Or don't you remember him? You know, the one who cut the deal with Owner?"

"What are you getting at, Nic?" The last thing Siohtion needs is a reminder of the father who died when he'd barely seen eight years of life and especially from his older brother.

"What I'm saying," Prince Nicaia says, the nickname having done its intended work of irritation, "is that you won't get anything if you don't work for it. Not by running off–"

"You know I haven't gone seeking a sheep in years!" The boy's face flushes. He is a man, but his brother refuses to see him as such. He can never please him. He'll never be able to please Father either, not with all of the restrictions on his behaviour. He wants to see the world, and he will. He knows his ticket out.

"And what have you ever done for this vineyard?"

"Enough."

"No, you're wrong. You've done nothing, nothing as far as giving Pari reason to give you your inheritance."

"He'd give it to me if I'd ask just as much as to you." Or so he says to keep off the defensive. It doesn't matter what he does, his brother always turns away with a cold shoulder of disapproval. Every time has added a layer of ice around his heart until it has grown numb to everyone around him.

"Really? And why should either of us have to ask. Look at the girls. They get a piece of their inheritance every year. Don't you see? He's passing us by! He only cared about us as long as we were important to Mother, his so-called queen. Now, what are we but dusty tapestries in his hall? We have to work if we're going to keep what we have or we'll lose what little we have, and you're going to have to start working for real if you expect any part in this place. Even Onxwade gets that."

Siohtion lets out a cross between a laugh and a grunt. He's done caring about what he once thought his brother was. What's the point caring anything about him if he's going to act like this? He has no reason to stay. "You think I'm going to work like a slave when I'm a prince? I'll prove you wrong, I'll get my inheritance while you keep beating away at the ground."

"Go on, ask him for the full sum, see if he gives it to you. See if he even has it!" Nicaia steps in front of his brother. "Unlike me, you're never willing to do anything he asks." If nothing else, he has gained a measure of respect in the eyes of the king. That gives him some leverage. And then there is Rittelle, his marvelous right hand he would trade for nothing and give up anything for– even the vineyard– except perhaps his own life. But what is his life worth without her, the vineyard and the reputation and riches they have built together?

Les Pariablues

Siohtion shoves Nicaia aside with all his strength as he has wanted to do for a long time and savours the short term feeling of release. The beginning of freedom. He'll show him. He'll show them all! He'll make it just as well as Onxwade.

Now where is that boy? His eyes turn to the tower in the vineyard. Of course. That is his favourite place to be, makes him feel all high and mighty, the little brother who made it. The little brother whose dreams all came true. The prince shakes his head. Stuck in between two wildly successful brothers, what does he have to offer as the king's son, not to mention to his mother? But he doesn't want to offer them anything. This is his life.

And as for the younger of his two wildly successful brothers, some résumé he has. He's still working for the king, all of his profits channeled right back into the kingdom. It is time that Siohtion lived it up for himself, founded a life for himself outside of the confines of the borders of King Les Pariablues' realm. He's never really belonged, anyway.

He enters the tower and scales the ladder rungs in a heartbeat.

"Your Highness, welcome." Yaren holds out a hand to the prince only to have it rejected.

"I'm coming with you, Onxwade," Siohtion says. In this moment his set jaw looks much like Nicaia's.

"Where?" And he won't even give him the courtesy of looking his way, always daydreaming about distant lands, far off treasure only to pour it all into the king's pocket. What a waste. And looking down on Siohtion all the while like he's so much better than his older brother. He used to look up to him!

"On your voyage, where else?"

"Since when have you cared?" Onxwade retorts.

"Since I plan to help fund your venture."

Onxwade laughs. "I don't want the hour's wage you have left after squandering the rest."

Anger flares behind Siohtion's eyes. His fists clench, but he forbids them from striking as he would in the shadows. In the shadows, he keeps his identity closely guarded behind a disguise. There, he is only known as one of the rabble and one who comes and goes freely. For years of nights, he has managed to keep his identity a secret. But he wants more. He is tired of slipping away in the night, only to return in the day and only to receive looks of disappointment, disdain and words of disapproval. He wants to be able to enjoy his ventures, so getting away to one of the far lands Onxwade is voyaging to, beyond the borders of the purple sapphire kingdom ruled by the Koingsung, is his best bet. And he knows about bets.

"I have other funds. I offer you the wages of 10,000 years. Paid to you in full once we land."

Onxwade turns to look at him. "Fine." He dismisses him with his hand, indifferent to his offer. "We'll see. Is that all?"

"See you at the table." And with that, he slips back down the ladder and heads to secure his inheritance. He has no reason to wait any longer.

Chapter 30

"Jeko," King Les Pariablues says to his right hand, "you know how these things work: There is no starting to build a tower without first ensuring that there are funds with which to finish it. Or else, what happens when the foundation is laid and no more can be done?"

"The builder is mocked for not acquiring what is necessary to complete the structure."

"Exactly, my Sower. And what of war?"

"A king must know whether he is able to meet his enemy who has 20,000 with his own army of 10,000," Jeko says.

"And so it is with choosing to bow the knee to the King of that glorious city, one must count the cost," Pari adds to himself.

"Indeed. And what is your decision, my king?"

The house that the king took Vaht and her sons from has been renovated over the years, and it is here that she sits next to the king, holding onto his arm and leaning in to listen as the future of their nation is discussed. She is prepared to comment when invited or if she thinks of something she believes relevant, knowing she is just as free to speak as Pari and Jeko. However, she is mostly content to listen to these two close friends, studying how their conversation reveals the bonds that have formed and strengthened between them through the years.

"We must go and take this kingdom," Pari says with his lion-like authority, and it has nothing to do with his volume. "Whether by force or through diplomacy. The emerald kingdom must fall before it destroys everything it can touch. There will be no terms of surrender or peace on our end. Now, Vaht," he turns to her, taking her hand in his, "you will remain in this realm."

"How long?" All she wants to know is when she will see him again.

"Probably a long time. There will be war."

Vaht's throat clenches at the thought of losing yet another husband. She is also not indifferent in the least to whether Jeko lives or dies. And what of all of the servants she has come to know who may or may not return? Surely, even those who do return will not return the same. The thought of that change is nearly worse than the thought of parting with them altogether.

"But you must stay here, help rule this kingdom in my absence, along with our son and his new bride."

"When do you intend to leave?"

"After the wedding." An agitated look comes over his face.

"What is it?"

"I send my servants out with the invitations. Have any of those I invited responded? No. So, I send my servants again, and I am still waiting to receive word from any of them how they fare in their errands." He sighs, the impression that his entire kingdom has turned against him sets in deeper by the day.

Vaht reaches out to smooth the creases in his face. But how can he not be concerned for her? Here he plans to go with his right hand to secure a kingdom for himself in a distant land when those in his own land are turning against him. They will not even celebrate at the marriage of the crown prince!

"There will be word," Vaht reassures him.

"But what word?" He leans back into his cushioned chair and sighs, glistening eyes to the ceiling.

"Father? Mother?"

The king, queen and Jeko turn their eyes to the doorway.

"Siohtion, my son. Welcome." If only he could know that the young man returns his love!

He nods. "I am here to ask for my inheritance," he says without blinking.

The king closes his eyes for a moment and inhales. Not just those of his own citizens but those of his own house. Here his own son– adopted being far beside the point– Siohtion, whom he loves, is asking for what is only to be given to him at the king's death or at another time the king decides, not blatantly demanded in such a way as to cut all ties. Pari exhales and looks in Jeko's direction. "Very well, give out the inheritance to my children, to each their own." Each must choose whom they will love, and whom they love, they will follow. Those who love him will remain. Those who turn away will bear the shame of the consequences.

Vaht rushes toward her son, and the king follows with weary steps and a heavy heart.

"Do you know what you have just asked?"

"Yes, and I will be going with Onxwade. The inheritance money will be more than enough to cover the venture and bring in returns to the kingdom."

Vaht looks into her son's eyes, searching, hoping against hope that this is truly about bringing in profit for the good of their people, rather than the pursuit of Siohtion's own ambitions. "And when do you leave?"

"After the wedding, of course. Why would I miss that?" he asks smoothly.

Pari reaches out and puts a hand on his son's shoulder before drawing him into an embrace. "I love you, son. And may you find treasure on your journeys."

"Thank you, Father." And with that, he leaves.

"Pari," Vaht grips his wrists, "he's not going for you. The only time when he is compliant like that is when he wants something. He's up to no good!" Her own words tear into her. How can she accuse her own son of something so dreadful?

"He's at an age where he must make his own decisions."

"But to just let him go?" The tears are beginning in her eyes.

"Yes," he says sadly. "Just let him go."

Her head bows, ashamed that it is her own son who is causing such trouble in the king's house. But it is not just Siohtion. Nicaia's cold indifference is just as bad, if not worse. And the way Onxwade is so rarely around…And Lazarus is already taking after Siohtion. Perhaps it is better for Siohtion to go so that his influence is cut out of Lazarus' life. Lumin is the one bright spot. As for the ten girls, well, Vaht does not believe that she can be entirely sure how loyal all of them are to the king. Yes, she loves them, but she does not feel as responsible for their choices as she does for those of her boys.

The king lifts her chin so that their eyes meet. "What troubles you?"

"I will do my best for you while you are gone."

"And why? Because you love me? Or is there some other reason?"

"It seems that my boys have done nothing but cause you pain, especially lately."

"Not true, and even if that were true, I would not blame you for their choices." He bows his head just enough to give her a kiss.

"Thank you." But she still feels a weight in her stomach. It seems that more often lately, she has been remembering from whence Pari lifted her and feeling how unworthy that makes her to be where she is now. She is desperate to do well so that he will be pleased– beyond pleased. But isn't that what Nicaia has been trying to do ever since Pari married her? Trying to earn the king's love? No. No, he has been trying to show how much he deserves Pari's love, only to turn away and reject it when it comes his way. But the attitude forming in her and the one she has observed in her son are close enough that she knows that she must beware. She cannot change her son's heart, but she knows where to go for her own to be changed.

The king and queen take their seats once more. "As for preparations for our departure," Pari says, "Jeko, take this down." He goes on to name three of his servants. "The first will be given 100 years' wages, the second forty years' and the third twenty years'. Those amounts suit their respective abilities. While we are gone, they can each trade and increase that amount."

He lists the names of ten more servants. "I will give each of them three months' wages to steward and increase through trade. When we return, these thirteen servants will give an account to me of how they have used what I have given them in the service of the kingdom and then be rewarded accordingly. Have them all appear before me tomorrow morning."

"Very good. They are all already in the city," Jeko says.

The king taps his fingers on the arm of his chair. "And perhaps they will be more prompt in their response than those invited to the wedding," he mutters to himself.

Vaht puts her arm around the king's shoulders. The indifference of those he has invited has inflicted a deep wound. This is his beloved firstborn, his crown prince, the only surviving son of his first wife. Yes, he loves all of his children, he has no favourites, but the rebuff of this invitation is a particularly offensive insult. It speaks of rebellion, revolution even, since Azar is set to be the future king. Pari shakes his head.

"Father!"

"Oh, just in time." He leaps up from his chair and meets his daughter. Once again, he has no favourites among his posterity, but there is a spark in Tebala's eyes that warms his heart every time she comes running to him and has a way of reminding him that life is worth living. He catches her up in his arms and laughs. "Oh, come here, my daughters." The others have come behind her.

He smiles and embraces each one as does Vaht. In a single day, she went from thinking she might only ever have daughters-in-law to not knowing what to think of the blessing of ten girls to call her own.

"What are we just in time for?" Tebala asks eagerly.

Pari starts to open his mouth.

"To judge what do with these scoundrels!" Yaren announces, leading in four rather muddy specimens of humanity that only cause the king's spirits to soar higher. Laughter begins to fill the room.

"Indeed, your hawk, here," Kulcam claps his hand over Yaren's shoulder, "spotted the four of them in the river training to infiltrate your fairest vineyard."

"And so you tied them up with their own rope," the king observes. "Fitting, very fitting."

"I thought so," Yaren says.

"Actually it's pretty tight," Reydeyn says, giving the crown prince a playful scowl.

Lumin and Lazarus are tied up with the same rope as Azar and Reydeyn, and both twins are failing to hold in their laughter. Their snickers only cause everyone else to laugh more.

"Well, I have a question, Yaren. Does not the river run inside the bounds of the vineyard? If you indeed have the eyes of a hawk, how can you explain that you allowed them to pass over the wall before apprehending them if they posed a threat?"

"I have no answer, Your Majesty!" Yaren falls to his knees. "Oh, please, mercy!"

Pari laughs outright. "Mercy? Well, I will pardon you if you tell me whose idea this was in the first place."

"His! Greatness, it was all his!" Yaren points desperately at the crown prince.

"My own son! I should have known you could not keep your garments unstained by mud. Has Artisana seen you in this state?"

"No, but she saw me last time I fell in the river and thought me quite handsome."

The king shakes his head, still smiling. "Go, get cleaned up."

"Aw, I don't want a bath!" Lumin protests.

"Me either," Lazarus agrees.

"Aw, but it is law that all scoundrels who break into my vineyard must be subjected to the purging of the waters. It is the only just punishment."

"Hug first!" Lazarus bolts forward with Lumin picking up the joke, threatening all with clean clothes with the tragedy of mud.

The girls squeal to get away, only to burst into laughter as Azar and Reydeyn are caught off guard and fall on top of the twins, pulled down by the rope that binds them, stopping the boys before Yaren and Kulcam can step in.

"Ah, take them away, and get them clean!" The king swings his arm toward the door. "Aiwa! Aiwa! Make haste."

"Of course, my king," Kulcam says, winking at Yaren. "We shall."

"But, tell me, wasn't Onxwade with you up in the tower?"

"I believe he went to find Siohtion, my lord," Kulcam says.

The king nods, painfully reminded of Siohtion's decision to depart. "Alright, off you go."

"As you wish. Up with you!" Kulcam says, working with Yaren to haul their four prisoners up from the floor and lead them out as they came in. Wisely deciding not to unbind the two young princes until they are properly bathed.

Tebala now turns to look up at Pari. "Daddy, can we play a game, please?"

"Of course." He turns to Jeko. "Make sure that Azar knows I wish to speak with him."

Jeko nods. "Do you wish for me to be there for the conversation?"

"Of course." Which means that Vaht and Reydeyn will be as well. Perhaps Acacia too.

"I will go immediately."

"But come back and join us."

"Oh, don't go." Tebala clings to his arm. "Stay and play with us."

"I'll be back. Just go ahead and start without me," Jeko says.

"Okay."

As the rest of the group goes on their merry way to organize their game, Tres quietly slips away from the group. Her father notices, but so does her mother, who motions to him to continue with the rest of the girls while she goes after her.

"What is it, Tres?"

"I'm a little old for games. I am the oldest princess, so I should be dignified."

Her words sting the queen. It seems as though Vaht is not the only one especially struggling with her past.

"What else?" Vaht asks gently.

"What else can there possibly be?"

Vaht searches her mind, but she stops to avoid any tactics of manipulation. "Won't you tell me?"

"No, I really do not wish to talk about it."

"May I at least walk with you?"

"I would prefer to walk alone," she says stiffly.

Vaht sighs. "One hug first."

Tres clears her throat and turns to face the queen.

"I love you."

"Love you too," she says quickly and then flees back to the olive orchard she never should have left.

Reydeyn looks up into the olive tree where his sister has situated herself. Every once in a while, she absentmindedly picks a single olive to eat, whether or not she cares first to examine its ripeness, her brother cannot tell. He does not bother saying a word, just slips up into the tree beside her. He doubts that he'll ever fully comprehend what it means for her to be his sister after missing most of the first two decades of each others' lives.

He settles down on a branch around the same level as her. This orchard was part of Qodei's property, but Reydeyn's father-in-law does not consider it a loss to have signed over the deed to royalty.

"Did Acacia and Artisana send you?" Tres breaks the silence of her own volition.

"They didn't have the chance because I was already coming."

"And what are you looking for?"

Reydeyn inhales, considering his words carefully. His wife and the crown prince's betrothed said that his sister refused to speak with either of them, whereas Tres has begun the conversation with him, so he considers the interaction to be going in the right direction so far. He breathes a silent petition that it will continue to go in the right direction. "If you don't want to, you don't have to tell me what's wrong, but I'm not going to go anywhere until you come out of this tree."

"Why?"

"Because I'm not leaving you alone in your pain."

"What if you're the cause of it?"

"Then I want to do what I need to make it right."

Silence.

Reydeyn sighs, disappointment setting in. Maybe this is as far as they are going to get and he will be spending tonight in this tree.

"It makes no sense." She runs her fingers all the way down her long strands of hair and shakes her head. Are those tears? "Why is it only me?"

"Tres, what did I do?"

"You were tied up." She stares off in the opposite direction of the tower, to the southwest.

Reydeyn clears his throat. "Go on."

"The others were slaves too, didn't it bother them?"

Silence.

"Tres, I don't understand."

"It didn't bother you either?" As far as she can see, it doesn't, but how does that make sense?

"What?"

"That you were tied up. All dirty...that didn't bother you?"

"Just now? Not at all."

"But how couldn't it? I can't even stand cuffs on my sleeves rubbing my wrists."

Reydeyn sighs. "I just didn't think about it."

"Well, I did."

"I...I'm sorry." He's not quite sure how to apologize for something that was just an opportunity for them all to laugh. But he does understand the weight of memories of bondage stirred up. "I'm sorry, Tres." Should he have known and called the whole thing off before it began? He looks over at her and holds out his hand. He breathes a sigh of relief as she grips his palm.

"Is that all that's bothering you, Tres?"

"Isn't that enough?"

"Sure, but lots of stuff can be going on at once."

"It is."

"What do you mean?"

"With the kingdom. It's slipping away. The people are never going to let Azar be king. And they're just tolerating Father."

Reydeyn nods and takes in the cloud configurations so far above their heads. He needs the perspective, the reminder of his actual size and the size of the greater King too. "And I'd be going crazy if I didn't trust the King of that glorious city. No matter who sits on the throne of our realm, the greater King is in control. His kingdom will stand forever."

He draws his eyes out of the sky and sets them back on his sister. Their eyes meet. What he sees in hers is his own fear and uncertainty mingled with genuine belief that the words that he has just uttered are true. What he feels is her arms wrapping around him in search of comfort, so he gives what he can.

Chapter 31

*R*age courses through Pari's veins. Even he did not expect the report of the treatment of his servants to be as catastrophic as it turned out to be. After years of resistance shown to his Sower, in the back of his mind, he expected there to be some resistance on this occasion, yet why would an invitation to a royal wedding feast– Samaritan or not– be met with such violence? Why?

"Come," was the invitation. Ignored. And so he sent out his servants once more with all the more urgency. "Look," he told his messengers to say to those invited, "I have planned a feast! Oxen and fattened calves prepared. Everything. Everything! is ready. Come, come to the wedding feast, the great supper for the marriage of my beloved son."

His tortured thoughts work their way out of his mouth. "Ignored! 'Oh, I have a farm.' 'I have a business.' 'I have a yoke of oxen I absolutely must try out.' 'I've just bought a piece of land I must secure for myself and prepare for the coming sowing.' 'I just married and must attend to my wife.'" The king shakes his head. "Ignored! Harassed! Even killed!" He sighs and puts his head in his hands, falling back into a chair next to the sickbed at Qodei's.

One of those servants was the youngest of Qodei's three sons. Loyek. The boy scarcely made it back to the house alive and is still recovering from his injuries. Just one more reason for Rittelle- his own son's right hand- to despise him.

"My lord?" Loyek stirs, roused by the king's volume, no doubt.

Pari takes a knee on the floor next to the boy's bed and grips his hand. He places his other hand on the boy's head and a sad smile forms on his lips. "Good and faithful, Loyek. You will indeed share in my joy as you have shared in the despising."

"Thank you, Your Majesty."

He smiles just a little wider.

"Did they ever throw stones at you?"

The king props up his servant's head and helps him drink. "Yes." He sighs. Siohtion has no idea how much the king is aware of his recent activities in the shadows, and it is all the more painful for him because he knows that he himself was worse. He boasted about it. And it is those very choices that are coming back to haunt him now, the reason why his own people despise him. Koingsung. The details have been muddled with time, but the title smears his entire reign as an everlasting curse. Indeed, a curse that has even touched this innocent boy.

Is that why he is letting Siohtion go and perhaps never return? Because he does not wish to face even a glimpse of what he once was?

There is a heavy hand on his shoulder, but it is not a cruel hand. "I do not blame you, Pari," Qodei says. "And neither does Rittelle."

"Which one?" He sighs.

"My wife. And my daughter should not."

The king shakes his head. "And how can I deny what I have done?"

"You are entirely different now. Believe me, I've seen what the King of that glorious city has done with you. Those who know Him understand that your life is not one to be despised but one to be viewed as, as something more magnificent than the greatest piece of creation. It's a work of redemption. No man is perfect, but when the grace of the greater King is applied to a life, well, that person will be made good in the end."

"And what about...what I did to those who rejected the invitation?"

"Those murderers?"

Pari lets the question hang in the air, waiting for his servant to answer it, since he is the one who posed it. Meanwhile, he studies the details of Loyek's features as he lies with eyes closed and chest steadily rising and falling. Yes, the boy is Qodei's son. Just as Azar is his. In appearance and character. He looks from the boy's sapphire studs to Qodei's. Such commitment. Loyalty he could never hope to deserve.

"Just punishment," Qodei finally says.

Pari looks back at Loyek.

"To send your army and have their dwellings burned after how they treated your servants. Absolutely. Had they come out on their knees pleading for mercy and acknowledging their wrong, that would have been a different story, but they came out fully armed to meet you. There is only one just punishment for murder, my lord, and the blood of your servants cried out for vengeance."

"How is he?" a woman's voice carries from the doorway.

Pari doesn't look directly at her, just enough to identify her with certainty as Qodei's wife. "Resting," he answers.

"I meant you." Rittelle puts a hand on his shoulder.

He turns, only to realize that it is Vaht who has touched him and now slips into his lap, while Rittelle sits beside her husband.

"My lord?" Rittelle inquires.

Pari sighs. "I'm not sure. Thank you." How can he leave his kingdom in this state internally to attend to things outside? But he must. Conflict with the emerald kingdom and the bands only intensifies. Onxwade assured him that, as he continues to establish himself as a merchant trading abroad, they are gaining allies as other kingdoms chafe under the direct rule of the cloak and dagger horde or the constant terror of the prospect. He and Jeko must depart soon, but there must first be a celebration for the marriage of his son. The great supper must be held before all preparations for the feast are in vain.

Two more enter the room. Azar and Artisana.

"Father, a simple dinner is more than enough for us," Azar says, kneeling next to his father. Artisana stands at his shoulder.

The king touches his son's cheek and considers. They must act swiftly. And they will. "No, my son," he looks up at Artisana and then stands, "my daughter. Your wedding feast is prepared, but those invited proved themselves unworthy."

He turns to Qodei and Rittelle.

"What is your command, my lord?" Rittelle asks eagerly, seeming to sense a hint of his plan.

"Are we going to have it anyway?" Loyek asks, starting to sit up.

Qodei turns and smiles at his boy, who he could not be more proud of. He puts a hand behind his son's back.

"Yes," the king says.

The air in the room is suddenly less heavy and the lightness begins to filter out into the rest of the kingdom, room by room, house by house, citizen by citizen. "Go. Go into the well-traveled roads and invite all that you find...the poor, the crippled, the blind, the lame! Anyone who will come."

Loyek swings his feet over the side of the bed. "I want to go." His pleading eyes meet the king's. How can he refuse him?

He turns his back toward his servant and squats down. "Then c'mon."

The boy laughs and wraps his arms around the king's neck. "There's a great supper! A great supper!" He cries.

Qodei wraps a belt around the king's chest and then around his son's back, securing his boy to their lord's back.

"Come! Come everyone!!"

And moments later, the first sound of hooves of the heralds' horses pound the earth, calling indiscriminately to any citizen with ears to hear.

"Tebal! Tebal!"

Even Nicaia feels the joy in the air working itself into his bones as the palace fills with guests. He moves among the servants, for once not insisting on trying to gain approval; he has earned respect by now.

He spots Onxwade. He stops at a distance to observe his little brother inspecting the various vessels with the deepest fascination. The two brothers have the other to thank for their success– that is the truth. But neither is keen to admit their indebtedness, especially to each other and even more to themselves. At the same time, they are all too eager to point out to themselves and each other how the other would not be where they are if not for what the other did. The king is burdened by this fact, longing for his family to be knit tightly together rather than always competing.

"My lord." A servant bowing before Pari and momentarily diverts Nicaia's attention from his merchant kin. "As you have commanded, we have done and invited all found on the well-traveled roads. But there is still room at the table."

"Then continue to go out, down every little road you may find. Persuade them to come in and fill up my house and my table. This is the great supper to celebrate the marriage of my beloved son. Let them all come in. But the ones I invited at first, who refused, none of them will take part."

And so the citizens continue to enter in.

Jeko approaches Onxwade. "What fascinates you, my lord?" He waits a moment and then puts his hand on the prince's shoulder.

Startled, Onxwade's wide eyes meet the Sower's smile. The prince clears his throat. "What is it?"

"What fascinates you, my lord?"

"I knew that the king– my father– that he had acquired much treasure, but these, these vessels. They're magnificent. Some are hundreds of years old, some were just made months ago."

The Sower smiles anew. "And each one beautiful and adding to the picture in its own way."

Onxwade nods and looks at the king's right hand expectantly. "What, my lord?"

"Oh, I just thought you might have some sort of lesson like you always seem to." He starts to turn away.

"As a matter of fact, I do. Just as you see that your father has brought out treasure that is both old and new to grace the table for this banquet, so every student of the words of the King of that glorious city is able to draw out truths from every portion, as well as understand how each piece complements the others."

Onxwade nods and stands still to survey the entire table, glittering in the torchlight.

Jeko grips the young man's shoulder for a moment and then moves on.

Nicaia shakes his head. Yet another instance of insignificant things being given undue meaning. He takes the stairs and looks down from the mezzanine. The sight of the guests is overwhelming, both good and bad citizens, but all significant differences seem to dissolve as each one is decked out with a wedding garment. Nicaia's short term reverie is broken by Jeko's hand on his shoulder.

"Well, Your Highness?"

"What, Sower?"

"How does it feel to be a part of today?"

Nicaia considers. His feelings toward his...toward the king have shifted. Sure, he still doesn't trust the ruler, but he at least knows that he values Pari's respect. "It is good. The realm needs reason to rejoice. The king needs as many citizens behind him as possible."

"Indeed, my lord. Indeed. Yet, he does not ultimately trust in men, which is one of the wisest things anyone can do."

Nicaia nods. The Sower may say that, but the prince knows that he has gained himself leverage through his hard work in the vineyard. It has paid off, and the king has entrusted him with more and more of the agriculture of the kingdom. Jeko, with Reydeyn following him, will still be the Sowers, but Nicaia has found his place. And that sense of security has done him good. He has earned his place. And yet, he cannot feel entirely settled.

Jeko, seeming to have finished speaking with Nicaia, raises his voice so that all gathered might hear him. "Friends, friends," he calls. Nicaia now understands why the Sower is speaking up, the citizens are all crowding to what they deem to be the most distinguished of seats, nearly trampling over one another. "Do not seek the high seats, my friends, lest someone more distinguished than you arrive and you are asked by your host to give your seat to them, only to be ashamed as you move to the lowest seat. Instead, my friends, take the lowest seat so that when the one who invited you comes by, he will call you to a higher seat. For, all who exalt themselves will find themselves humbled. However, the one who humbles themselves will find themselves exalted."

Nicaia feels a chill run up and down his back at the silence that has followed Jeko's short speech. Then, there are sounds of shuffling as some act on the lesson given. He startles when someone takes hold of his arm. He turns. "Rittelle," he smiles inwardly, "how is Loyek?"

She shakes her head. "The boy is a fool. The king sends him out to die, and here he is celebrating." She points down to where her brother moves happily among the guests.

Nicaia chews the inside of his cheek, considering her bitter words. They ring true with him in a way. But is it possible that scraps of the king's true character have filtered through the tangle of his bitter prejudice? He sighs and shakes his head, the doubts of the resentment he still harbours washed back out to sea as quickly as they drifted in and leaving the resentment intact. "No, it does not make sense." The prince looks around the table. "But for now, we join them, my right hand."

"For now," she mutters against the strain of her tense being.

Chapter 32

"Where is he?" Princess Thuis grumbles. She casts her torch aside.

"How long does he expect us to wait?" Princess Teakim adds with equal annoyance.

The sun is stooping to kiss the western horizon while the sky blushes purple and pink, red, orange and yellow.

"Why are you so mad?" Princess Tebala pipes up. "Aren't you excited?" She leans back on her hands and allows the waning light to bathe her in its glory.

"Just be quiet," Princess Thimna retorts.

"Hey, leave her alone," Princess Tres says, preempting any coming attacks on her youngest sister who takes more than her share of sororal reprimands. As the oldest sister, it is her duty to protect the rest and especially the youngest.

"Her? The spoiled little favourite?" Thimna shoots back as though she is the innocent one.

"She can take it. And Azar should too," Princess Turene adds.

Tres starts to open her mouth to continue her defense but stops when she sees that Tebala isn't listening. Instead, she's leaning on Princess Traei and watching the sunset. A gentle smile fills her face. Tres wonders whether it is also the way the light evening breeze rustles through their coin garlands like windchimes, as well as the colours that have her smiling. Probably.

She knows that the girl has always done well finding joy in simple things. Tres smiles, her two sisters with their eyes to the west have the right idea, and so she joins them. Tengithae and Tekoa soon catch on, leaving the other five to gripe, something they have learned to do more and more as they have tasted of the world beyond their own realm. Tres regrets not remaining in the throne room that day to join in on the game instead of feeling sorry for herself up in the olive tree; she figures that she probably missed one of the last, if not the last good time they could've had as all ten sisters. At least the rest could have it as nine.

One by one, the stars show themselves in the heavens. Meanwhile, up on the roof of the dwelling behind the princesses, Acacia watches silently with Artisana, anticipation of the crown prince's arrival increasing every moment. One by one, the princesses are overtaken by first drowsiness and then sleep. Until midnight comes. A cry. And the call awakens the princesses, who each scramble for their torch, some having to look farther than others.

And the call comes closer, signaling that Prince Azaryada has come at last to collect his bride and bring her to the palace for the great supper.

"Reydeyn," Jeko turns to him as he comes through the door. "Father, hello."

"You were looking for me? Is the bridegroom ready to go then?"

"Not yet, Azar told me to find you and wait together. The king is going around to make sure that all of the guests and everything else is in order." His eyes trace their way over the various sacks, clay jars, ranging in size from the size of a cup to waist high, and wooden boxes, all containers for seeds. From the ceiling hang countless specimens in preparation for the day they will be buried in the ground only to shoot forth with new life for the benefit of the citizens of King Les Pariablues' realm.

"I see. Good timing."

Reydeyn automatically looks at him.

"I have taught you my trade. In my absence, it will be your responsibility to see that the seeds are sown."

The servant nods.

"What's wrong?"

"I don't want you to go."

The Sower lays a firm grip on his son's shoulder and meets his gaze. "I will miss you as well. Very, very much."

"And it's not only that."

"Yes?"

"I just," he sighs, "I've been thinking...about those that the king had destroyed...that I should've been one of the servants to go...and, really, my main question is why do so many turn away?"

"Narrow is the gate," Jeko says to himself and stares up and out the high window. The sun has been gone for hours. "The way is hard. Few find it."

"But the way is easy and the gate wide that leads to destruction. Many enter by it," Reydeyn says, recognizing the story that Jeko has told him many times before. "So enter by the narrow gate."

"Yes," Jeko says.

Reydeyn watches as his father keeps his eyes out the window, hoping he will continue. After several moments, he does.

"One of these days, the doors will be shut on a greater feast and many will try to enter. 'Lord, Lord,' they'll call, 'didn't we do mighty works in Your name?' They will beg and plead, only to hear Him say, 'I do not know you. Depart, depart, you evildoers.' Deep sorrow and great rage will be their portion."

"What are you saying, Jeko?"

"I'm answering your question."

"Are you saying that even some of those who seem like they're citizens of that glorious city might not be?"

"Isn't that what I just told you that the King himself said?"

"Yeah, I'd just rather not have to think about it. To have lived your whole life deceived?"

"Indeed," he says soberly.

"What?"

"I fear that, even tonight, some we believe to be our own will be revealed as having no part among us."

"Who?"

"I do not know hearts, Reydeyn."

"Yaren!" comes the call from within the palace.

Reydeyn glances at his father only to feel a rush of air. He hurries to follow the Sower. It is the king calling.

"Your Majesty, what is the matter?" Jeko inquires upon his arrival.

Yaren already has a man with his hands pinned behind his back. It takes Reydeyn only a moment to realize why he looks so out of place.

"No wedding garment," King Pariablues tells his right hand.

Anger, echoing the king's, creeps into the Sower's face.

"Seeing this, I approached him. 'Friend, how is that you are not wearing the appropriate clothes for my sons' wedding?'"

"No answer for your king?" Jeko glares at the man who now shrinks away in a way that makes Reydeyn think of both Koje and Rodraf who cared only for their own skins.

"What will you do to him?" Reydeyn asks, grasping the situation. Having been taken in as a guest, the least this man could have done to show respect for his royal host and ruler, not to mention gratitude for the king's generosity, was wear the clothes expected, which the king would have provided him had he cared about showing appropriate regard.

"Yaren, tie him hand and foot and throw him out!"

Deep sorrow and great rage, Reydeyn shudders with the echoing of Jeko's words. No, not the Sower's words. If they originated with him, they would not ring with such power.

Up on the roof above the unmarried princesses, "Is that him?" Artisana raises herself up to her full height.

Acacia grips her arm and smiles. "C'mon." On the way, they are met by Rittelle– the bride's stand-in mother– and her other two stand-in sisters: Rittelle and Sariet. Together they burst out the door. Well, you can guess which of them lagged behind. Rittelle feels as though she can barely breathe with all that she is holding back. Is she honestly expected to celebrate with the crown prince's bride forced into their family? Celebrate as though she is the sister of the bride when Artisana is nothing more than a crimson cord the king has the audacity to raise up to royalty? Some royalty.

"Give me some!" Thuis shouts.

Tres steps in front of Tebala before Thuis lunges and takes more than just Tebala's oil.

"C'mon, just give us some," Turene says.

The wedding call sounds again with more voices. The words can almost be made out as the procession comes toward them through the city streets.

"Our torches won't keep burning without it," Thimna agrees.

"We need it," Teakim says. "You should have brought extra like we did."

"Hand it over, he'll be here any minute!" Thuis demands.

The words of the chant are now clear and still becoming louder with every repetition, adding to the urgency. "Aiwa! Aiwa! Tebal! Tebal, lela granel canel. Tues ete phumile yada. Eses yareh!"

"Then you'd better hurry. We don't have enough to share with you and keep our torches burning," Tres says.

"Yeah, go and buy some for yourselves," Traei says.

"Go on, they don't have any for you," Rittelle says, as the five of them turn away in a huff. She only allows the smallest slice of the bitterness she feels to be heard in her words. Let them miss the wedding! They're a threat to Nicaia's place in the family, anyway. Even if all ten of them cannot be done away with at once, this will take care of five; half. They will never live down the shame of failing to light the procession due to their own foolishness. This reveals who they really are, how they could not care less for the king and the wedding of his son.

She now has reason to smile as the procession moves along with the five wise princesses, leaving the five foolish princesses behind. She smiles wider later on as pounding on the door interrupts the meal and the five of them are turned away at the closed door by the crown prince himself.

"Less competition," she says to Nicaia.

"Indeed," he agrees.

Reydeyn hears himself sniff once again. It's useless to try to hold back the tears. Jeko and King Les Pariablues have left at last for the emerald kingdom. He keeps his arm tightly around his wife, knowing that the two of them will be leaving soon too, though only for a short while, leaving Azar to rule with his new bride– Artisana– and mother– Queen Vaht.

Reydeyn comforts himself by holding fiercely to the memory of the two men he loves so dearly, memories never having been things he has held onto easily. He thinks over the last words that the king spoke from his saddle, addressing the group of them while at the same time cherishing the embraces of his king and father that they gave just moments before.

"Are servants thanked?" Pari asked rhetorically, turning his head slowly to take in their faces. Waves lapping at the shore and the hulls of ships docked filled in what would have been silence. "After his servants have been out plowing or keeping sheep, does their lord invite them to the table?"

Some heads shook as a silent answer to his second rhetorical question.

"No, instead, he calls them to prepare his supper and dress to serve him and only after that to eat and drink themselves. And does he thank his servants for following his commands?"

Again, there are heads shaking.

"So let us, as we serve the King of that glorious city, having done what he commands, acknowledge that we are but his unworthy servants who have done our duty." And with that, the king raised his hands and blessed them. "Yada ues."

"Yada ues," they called as the king and his right hand rode away.

Reydeyn emerges from his thoughts to the sensation of Azar's finger brushing aside his tears.

"Reydeyn," Acacia says, "I need to tell you something."

"Yes?"

She searches for where to begin. "It's more dangerous than ever out there. How will they ever believe that you're coming to bring blessing after what the king has done to those who refused him? His own daughters?"

"What he did was justified. Besides, his daughters left of their own free will." And the five of them have gone with Onxwade on his voyage.

"Yes, but people aren't reasonable, Reydeyn."

"The ones who have known his blessing in the harvest will remember it now in the sowing. But, wait, you were talking about me going. You're coming too."

She looks away. "I was, but how can I endanger two lives?"

"What?"

"You're a father, Reydeyn."

Reydeyn stumbles backward into Azar, who holds him steady.

"Go on, take a walk, it's alright."

Reydeyn needs no more permission to bolt from the room as sickness overtakes him. Why must he be torn between loyalty to his family and loyalty to his king? Why is he inhibited from rejoicing as he should with his wife over this new life?

"Excuse me." Acacia moves away from the prince and his new bride to work out her own fears and frustrations into a ball of dough. Left alone, she punches the raw bread down and watches it, knowing that it will rise up again, just as it has every other time she has made bread. And in the same way, the Kingdom will prevail even when King Les Pariablues' falls, as all earthly kingdoms must. She knows too that she and Reydeyn are a part of that glorious and eternal city, and so they are secure both now and forever.

She is in the midst of preparing her husband's daggers when he returns, wraps his arms around her from behind and kisses her.

"In his will, I will return to the two of you," he whispers in her ear.

"I know. You'll need these." She hands the daggers over to him.

He stares at the instruments of defense wondering how he can possibly kill another person, wondering whether it will come down to that.

Acacia seems to read his thoughts. "To use as you see fit."

He nods. "Thank you."

"Who will go with you?"

"Lazarus and Lumin, my sister and Tebala."

Acacia nods, considering.

"Some guards as well, though with weapons hidden to cut down on the intimidation factor."

"Right. Well, you need to get ready to go."

Reydeyn looks in her eyes, smiles and wraps his arms around her. "I think I know where to start," he whispers. "No way I'm leaving without a proper farewell from my wife and little one."

"Pari?" Jeko stirs from sleep to the rustling of a scroll. He recognizes it all too well. The king has opened it many times since receiving it at the border of his realm.

The words are few but cutting and hard to be forgotten. "You will not rule us," the king recites aloud.

"Pari, you cannot read that in the dark."

"Will there be a kingdom to return to?" comes the tearful voice through the darkness.

"My lord, do not fret. You have done what you can and trusted the greater King with both your efforts and what is beyond your abilities."

"But that does not help me feel less like I have abandoned those we left behind."

"My king, this journey is necessary. It is not just the scroll, is it?" He has been trying to get to the heart of his best friend's burden ever since they left.

"Kulcam and Loyek," Pari says, and Jeko remains silent. "The smile on Loyek's face said it all. He treasures that three months' worth of wages, and I believe him when he said that he will use it wisely. But Kulcam, did you see the look on his face when charged with the same amount?"

"I did, my lord."

"And I fear that his disappointment will only prove to grow into a despising of the gift I have given him."

Jeko is silent. He recalls his conversation with his son in the seed cellar. Kulcam was one of the very ones he had in mind as they discussed the narrow and wide roads. He seemed to do well in the beginning with his grand speech at Arcan's funeral, but it seems that time has shown him to be stony, weedy ground, though the shoots have perhaps taken longer to wither and be choked than in some other pebble ridden fields. Lately, he has shown himself consumed with earthly treasures at the expense of things of greater value. And the way he has indulged the princesses with luxuries from far and wide as though pleasure is all there is to life...

"I don't expect him to do much with it," Pari says.

"We must wait until harvest, my king."

Chapter 33

*O*nxwade holds the ring between his pointer and thumb. If there were light for the purple sapphire to catch, it would shine brilliantly like the ring on his own finger that designates him as a prince. "Kulcam!"

"My lord?"

"Call off the search." He slips the ring into a pouch at his side. "Prince Siohtion is dead."

Kulcam rushes below deck, face riddled with confusion. "How do you know, my prince?"

He is not about to tell Kulcam about the ring lest he takes it to make a profit off of. "I have my ways. He is not coming back. Take my word for it. Now, prepare the boat to go ashore for business."

His right hand nods, noting the belongings that have vanished from Siohtion's quarters and, Onxwade assumes, the literal meaning behind his figurative speech.

"And he didn't even leave us the money he promised," the prince's manager mutters. Yes, he understands what has happened.

"I must send word to Father." Not that this will be news to the king. It is likely a waste of time to attempt to deliver a letter to him, away in the emerald kingdom as he is. They have all known that this day was coming.

Once alone, Onxwade takes the ring back out of his pouch. He swallows. Night after night, he found it left behind as his brother went out to do as he pleased. He pounds his fist into the hull. What a waste. Well, at least there is no more waiting for the inevitable. Prince Siohtion is indeed dead.

And he has more important things to do than send word. He spins around and ascends to the main deck, lungs burning. Once on deck, he gasps for air as if returning from a great depth.

His brother is dead. Dead while he lives. But Onxwade determines that he will not allow his brother's absence to inhibit his quest for riches from beyond the grave. He is all the more determined now to find treasure worth more than all that he owns. Yes, even more than this massive merchant fleet that he has acquired.

Give me justice! Justice from my enemies! Kulcam massages his forehead. At last, his ears can stop ringing with the cries of the widow.

It is a mystery to him. Day after day, and more than once a day, she has been working on breaking his door down with her fist, pleading for justice. Until this morning, when he finally had enough.

Prince Onxwade does not bother knocking to announce his entrance. "Well, Kulcam, you finally gave in?"

"Yes, my lord, and this is making me wish very much that you had never made me judge in this city."

Onxwade shrugs. "Since you don't care about the opinions of the citizens, I doubt your resignation would be lamented."

"Indeed, I fear neither these people nor the greater King."

Onxwade shakes his head, bent over blueprints for new crop storehouses. It is an exceptional harvest this year. "And what of that grand speech you gave at Arcan's departure dinner?"

"Poetry. And at the time I thought that I believed it. Since then...I have found greater pleasure in other things."

The prince sighs and picks up his parchments. "Right. Goodnight," he says to his manager, uncomfortable with the man's apathy.

"Goodnight, my prince."

Alone once more, Kulcam fingers his way through the records on the desk before him. In need of a quill, he begins rummaging through the drawers. Next to the ink, he finds something wrapped up in a cloth. He shakes his head. The king has just returned from the emerald kingdom after seven years' absence and is calling up accounts. Soon, he will know that Kulcam has done nothing with the three months' wages that he was entrusted with. He bristles at the thought of Loyek and his three months' wages. How could the king entrust them with the same amount when Loyek is yet a boy and Kulcam has been with the king's son during his entire journey to becoming a successful merchant?

On some accounts I may have been forgiven less, but here and now I pledge that I will not love less, he once said. Kulcam shakes his head again. The words of another lifetime, spoken in an emotional moment.

Upon Kulcam coming to the king as bidden to give account for what was entrusted to him, the king will receive the three months' wages back, but nothing more. Not after what Kulcam has heard of his dealings in the emerald kingdom. Reaping what he did not sow. The manager shakes his head again. He has accounts to attend to for his prince, who, unlike his stepfather, has made him a rich man...even though he doesn't know how rich or how many luxuries Kulcam has enjoyed because of his funds.

He lets out an exasperated sigh at the sound of another knock on the door. Can he get no peace? The knock sounds again. The right hand shoves the tip of the quill into the ink and rises to answer the door.

"If it is that widow again..." he mutters.

"Son, go and work and in the vineyard," the king told him and then his twin. It was one of the last things that he said to Lazarus and Lumin, calling them to help their older brother in his absence.

"I'll go," Lazarus remembers himself saying so enthusiastically.

"I won't. I'm not working for Nicaia," Lazarus remembers Lumin saying. The cold and hard refusal tainted their entire farewell. But what has become of them since then?

The difference between rock and sand. Lumin did go to work in the vineyard after all, while contrary to his word, Lazarus did not. Lumin has built himself a house on a rock, following architectural directions their father left them, while Lazarus decided to try things his own way. Sand. And he has had nothing but trouble since.

Without a proper foundation for his house, he lost all of his money to endless repairs until he had none left. One great storm brought him down with his house in a great fall. And here he is, back at his rich brother's door. He is not here to ask for bread for guests at midnight, as he did time and time again so that his guests would not know the financial state he was in, calling his brother out of bed. He is here for himself in hopes of just a little mercy, a few crumbs from this rich man, whose every meal is a feast to rival one of their father's.

The door opens, and Lazarus once more feels the glare of his brother's disdain. Once, Onxwade counted him a friend. Now, full of sores and lying at his gate as a common beggar, there is no pity left and no sense of duty to a brother and fellow prince.

"You've brought this on yourself," is the cold pronouncement over his brother and his downcast gaze.

Lazarus does not try to open his mouth. The door slams shut and he slowly turns away. Slowly, with nothing left to go home to and no way to get back to the realm where he is prince, he makes his way back to the gate and lies down again. Perhaps tonight, the dogs will leave him be. Perhaps, tomorrow, Onxwade will have mercy on him.

Siohtion tosses and turns under the stars. His stomach roars like a predator ready to devour him. Feeding pigs for nothing. That is what he has come to! What a fool he's been. Did he really think that his inheritance money would last forever? No, that is just it. He did not think. Now, it is about time that he began to. Time that he thought about how he is ready to eat what he is feeding the pigs. Think about how even the crimson cords who his father hires have more than enough to eat and drink and wear and be sheltered by, while he is starving to death in a famine stricken land.

It's time to go home. If he can even get there. He has to. And now he's heard that his father has returned. But what will he say?

That's it...

"Father, I have sinned against the King of that glorious city and against you. I'm not worthy to be called your son. Make me like one of your hired crimson cords." For, he is indeed a crimson cord.

His own words strike at his heart. He ought to make things right between him and the King of that glorious city first of all, before setting out on his journey. To do that, he knows he must accept that only that King can right what he has wronged. He finds his way to his knees, head bowed. "Have mercy on me, a sinner."

And so the young man begins stumbling toward home, justified because of the great King's Son paying his debt, yet wondering whether the waste he has made of his life can ever be redeemed.

"Lazarus, wake up."

The prince stirs and tries to make out the face of the one who just spoke.

"It's me, Lumin."

"Lumin? What are you–"

"C'mon, brother. Get up." Lumin does not wait for Lazarus to put in any effort. He simply slings his twin's arm over his shoulders and helps him mount up in front of him on his horse.

"But I deserve this. I should've listened to Father. I never should've built my house on sand."

"You're right, but your physical house is not of the greatest concern. Do you remember when Jeko told us that story about the two men and what he said building on the rock and building on sand without a foundation stood for?"

Lazarus thinks hard. "The one on the rock hears and obeys. The one on the sand hears but does not obey."

"You have heard, Lazarus, and there is still time to obey."

He nods. "Why did you come after me?"

"Father sent me."

"Of course...And I start where?"

"Realizing that all you'll ever do without the greater King making you his is build your house on sand. It might look like you have it all together in this life, but when the storm of death comes, it'll all be shown for what a shambles it is. There is no greater fall than into a lost eternity. Acknowledge that. Acknowledge that you've gone your own way, denied the greater King's rightful rule over your life and then bow your knee to him. Trust that he covered the debt you've incurred with his own life given for you. Trust that he lives again and that, through his power, your house will be founded on the rock. You will obey."

Lazarus nods. He knows all this, but being reminded by his brother brings it all back fresh and new. As Lumin tends his sores by the campfire and provides him with water and food, he is suddenly aware that he is richer than Onxwade could ever imagine.

Restless. Desperate. Onxwade cannot sleep.

Two times over through the last seven years, he has sold everything for the sake of a great treasure. Both times his spirits soared. First, it was that treasure he found buried in a field. He buried it again, sold everything, bought the field and rejoiced over having obtained the treasure. Through the treasure, he built his wealth back up until, one day, as he was searching for pearls, he found one of great price. Once more, he sold everything to obtain it. Once more, he built up his belongings. Yet, he has found no lasting satisfaction from his investments.

He has no satisfaction with the person he has become either. Just yesterday, he congratulated Kulcam for using dishonest means to save his own skin. Onxwade should've known that the man was wasting his possessions. Angry that all the things he had worked for were being washed away by his unfaithful right hand, he was ready to cut ties and told Kulcam as much. Well, Kulcam was not about to be left out in the cold, unable to do physical labour and too ashamed to beg. Next Onxwade heard, his manager and right hand had called up those who owed Onxwade and discounted their debts, thus ingratiating himself to them that they may always welcome him into their houses. And Onxwade figured that he could not fire him anymore. How could he turn away such a shrewd man who might use his wits against him? However, Onxwade now wonders about his decision.

Ultimately, the prince finds himself unsettled because, whenever he considers the sum of his life, he immediately thinks of the abundance of his possessions. Is that truly the totality of his life?

He thinks upon the most recent project that has him occupied. This year's harvest is too large for his current storehouses. How it never leaves his mind where the seeds came from. Jeko. Without the Sower's seeds...he would not be where he is. So, he woke up invigorated by the thought of tearing down his old storehouses to raise up new ones in their stead to house the exceptionally bountiful harvest. Larger. More elaborate.

He drew up the blueprints with speed, but having them completed only has him feeling empty. This is not the first time that he has built new storehouses. It's just one more project to give him a sense of purpose. Something slightly different than charting yet another voyage in search of more distant lands.

Even as a dream overtakes him, the restlessness does not relinquish its hold on Prince Onxwade. In his dream, the merchant prince is transported to a beach where his fishing fleet has just docked. Vast nets. Glistening scales as far as his eye can see. So many fishermen with skilled hands sorting the good from the bad. The sight is overwhelming. The good fish into containers for the market. The bad are thrown away. Division. One way or the other. Over and over and over again.

Jeko's voice now breaks in from somewhere unseen, but Onxwade can hear him just as clearly as when he and Onxwade sorted his first catch. "It will be like this at the end of this age. The King of that glorious city will send his herald-warriors to separate the evil from the righteous. The evil will be thrown into a fiery furnace where there will be deep sorrow and great rage."

Ever between waking and sleeping, Onxwade's troubled mind turns again to thoughts of his new storehouses and what he might add to the blueprints. Anything to rid himself of this inward aching void. The void, he has been trying to fill with riches, only to find the pit's bottom made of quicksand, ever lowering, the opening ever widening. What will the herald-warriors of the King of that glorious city do with him in the end?

Thinking of the provisions from the harvest, he keeps telling himself, "Soul, you are amply supplied for years to come! So, relax. Eat, drink, and be merry." Perhaps taking it easy, rather than working, can change how he feels.

But, in his dream, he sees a rich man much like himself with similar ambitions to live it up. There is light too bright to look at and a thundering voice speaking over him, the voice of the greater King himself, "Fool! Tonight your soul is required of you. Who will enjoy all that you have laid up then?"

"You can gain everything in the world, Onxwade, but it will mean nothing without the riches that the greater King has to offer," Jeko once said, but Onxwade has still allowed Kulcam to blind his eyes with dreams of greatness.

Still more troubled, Onxwade rises from his bed to stand at his window and see whether his brother still lies at the gate. He shudders when he does not see him. He clutches the seams of his purple cloak and pulls it closer around him. Faint, he lies back down only to be consumed by another troubling dream.

Lazarus is dead at his gate. He watches as the greater King's herald-warriors take up his brother from the earth to be with the King of that glorious city. But how can it be? What has his brother done differently from him? They have both pursued riches, though Onxwade has been more successful.

But, now, he sees Lazarus enjoying the pleasures of that glorious city, while flames surround him. Onxwade is desperate for water. He thought that he was being tormented by his thoughts, but now he is in anguish.

"Mercy! Mercy! Send Lazarus to dip his finger in water, just enough to cool my tongue. Please! I'm in agony!"

It is Jeko's voice that answers him. "Son, remember, during your life, you enjoyed your good things and Lazarus his evil things. Now, he's comforted, and you are in torment. Besides, there is a great chasm fixed between here and there so that no one can pass between these two places."

"Then, please, send Lazarus back to my family. Let him warn them, lest they come and suffer this agony too!"

"They have the words of the King of this glorious city."

"But if someone would come back from the dead to them, they will turn to the greater King." As he now knows he should have done when he had a chance. He has never felt so desperate for escape and yet also just as sure that there is no way out.

"If they do not heed the words of the King of this glorious city, not even witnessing someone rising from the dead will change their minds."

Onxwade gasps as his eyes fly open. His entire body trembles, rendering him unable to rise from his bed. Dreams, but not merely dreams. He knows what he must do. He must take to heart the very thing that his father said as he departed for his first merchant voyage. There is no gain in obtaining all the world has to offer and forfeiting one's own soul.

Indeed, even Kulcam's behaviour compels him to delay no longer. If his unfaithful manager schemed as he did to ensure he had a place to go in this physical life, surely, Onxwade should be doing something to ensure that he has a place to go in his spiritual life. It is time he began to live for the King of that glorious city.

Chapter 34

If only Loyek could urge his mount on faster. After all these years, the king's children, who have spread far and wide, are coming home! A good number of them, in any case. Onxwade, Lumin, Lazarus, as well as two of the five princesses who departed after Azar's wedding: Thuis and Teakim. There is no word on Siohtion, and Princesses Turene, Turst and Thimna apparently prefer to stay in distant lands as they have since departing on Onxwade's fleet.

There will be tebal in the king's house, and Loyek cannot wait to share in–

He is knocked onto his back, stunned by the rocky ground. Someone has unhorsed him, and now they are on top of him. Crimson cords. Savage blows fall from every direction without the courtesy of a split second to contemplate his defense. All goes dark as his senses fail him.

You really think these celebrations are for you, Siohtion? Nicaia challenged him. *You're so blind. All of these feasts when you come back with the sheep are for Azar, Pari's beloved son. He'd never put one on for any of us.*

Doubts like these, planted by his older brother in years past, plague Siohtion. Yet he trudges on, barely able to see the path in front of him. He doesn't want a feast, just a little bread. Water! There. There's a well up ahead. That will give him the strength to go just a little farther.

"The money!" Loyek gasps only to fall back onto a bed. A bed?
"Your Samaritan is awake!"

A bed? Wasn't he just out on the side of the road? Didn't two men that he thought would help him pass by on the other side of the way? Wasn't the sun beating down on him? Why did he take such a dangerous road to begin with?

"Water," he cries, now having remembered that the money he was thinking of is safe and sound. Onxwade carried his most recent profits from the three months' wages King Pariablues entrusted to him back to his father the king ahead of Loyek, while Loyek traveled back via the most direct land route. So, he set himself up to be robbed, but the thieves got nothing that matters.

"Here, drink, boy."

He laps up all he can, briefly remembering another moment of consciousness when a man stopped to help him. He put something on his wounds. Was it oil and wine? "Thank you," he manages as he falls back onto the pillows. "The king will reward you."

"Do you really think, Samaritan?"

He opens his eyes for a moment and does not know what to do. There are emeralds in the ears of the man who gave him a drink. Fear and confusion have gripped him.

"You? You helped me?"

The man turns away and addresses another man who Loyek assumes owns this place. Probably the one who announced that he woke up. "Take this. It is two days' wages. Use it to care for him, and whatever other expense you incur, I will pay when I return."

"When you return," grumbles the other man.

The man with the emerald studs turns and walks away.

"Wait!" Loyek cries out, but the man does not heed him.

"Don't bother, boy. He's not worth your time."

"He saved my life when others passed me by. Please, make sure he is brought to the king and rewarded."

"He's an emerald!"

"I don't care. He saw the sapphires in my ears and did not turn away. Please!"

But the man simply closes his hand around the two coins he was just given and begins to leave the room. "Go after him yourself, if you wish to be associated with the enemy."

But Loyek lacks the strength. And so the man who saved his life is lost to him for good and his money kept by the man he meant to care for Loyek. The day does not end before he sends Loyek away to the king, having no interest in being burdened any further by a servant of the Koingsung.

However, though the servant never again sees the man who rescued him, he never forgets him or ceases to make petition to the greater King that he will be blessed.

The king grips Onxwade's shoulder and smiles at him. "Your merchant network opened the way for our servants to trade. Let us hear what they have done with what I entrusted to them."

The king begins by calling forward the three entrusted with the greatest amounts.

"Your Majesty," the servant reports with eyes bright, "you entrusted me with 100 years' wages. Through trade, I have doubled the amount."

"Excellent! Well done, good and faithful servant. You have proved reliable in little. You will be set over much. For, we have new territory to ensure the governance of. You will indeed share in my joy."

The servant entrusted with forty years' wages reports next that she has also doubled what was given to her. The king commends her faithfulness with enthusiasm equal to that which he had toward the first servant. Next, the servant entrusted with twenty years' wages...

"My lord, I heard of your severe dealings in the emerald kingdom. You reap where you do not sow. So, being afraid, I took your twenty years' wages and hid it. I kept it safe all this time. So, here it is, what is yours."

Anticipation grips the room. Breath comes less easily as the king's countenance shifts. "You evil and lazy servant," he declares. "You knew that I reaped where I didn't sow, did you? Well, the least you could have done was put my money in a bank to gain interest. Take the twenty years' wages from him and give it to the one with 200 years' wages. Everyone who has will be given more until he has an abundance. But the one who does not have anything, even what little he has will be taken. Cast this worthless servant out!"

Onxwade notices Kulcam fidgeting. The prince turns his face away. Surely...

The studs are removed from the worthless servants' ears and returned to the king while the latent twenty years' wages is endowed to the first servant who proved faithful with the wages of a century. Pari closes his hand around the sapphires and gives them all a moment to breathe before continuing, "Now, for the ten servants to whom I entrusted three months' wages to. Loyek, step forward."

The boy comes out of his daze, as they all must after witnessing the removal of the worthless servant. The eager smile returns to his face. "My lord, the three months' wages you entrusted to me is now 30 months' worth."

King Pariablues' face glows with delight once more. "Well done! Good and faithful, Loyek. You too have been faithful in little. So, you will be set over much. Ten cities in the emerald kingdom."

The young servant's eyes and mouth fall open. He steps backward right into his father who grips his shoulders. "Well done, son. Well done," Qodei congratulates his speechless boy. He draws him over to stand with the rest of his family.

"Acacia," the king says, "I also entrusted you with three months' wages."

"Yes, my lord, and it has multiplied into fifteen months' wages." Two small girls, each holding a hand of their big brother, stand just in front of her and her husband, while a baby boy is strapped to her chest. Reydeyn smiles as the king, once more, commends a faithful servant.

"Five cities, that's my girl," he whispers into her ear and kisses her.

Acacia smiles and glances in Loyek's direction. Her brother is still speechless.

And so the king calls up the next seven servants to whom he entrusted three months' wages, rewarding them according to the pattern he set forth with Loyek and Acacia.

Onxwade takes a deep breath as Kulcam is called forward last of all. Once forgiven by the king for a debt, he pledged that he would not love less. Now, it is harvest time, the time when the soil is revealed for what it is.

The prince's heart sinks as his right hand steps forward and opens up a cloth to reveal twelve silver rimmed copper coins. Three months' wages. He utters the same excuse as the other worthless servant. The king utters the same verdict. And the look of dismay on Kulcam's face as the three months' wages is given to the very boy he despised for being made his equal…He does not even seem to regret what he has done, only to be sorry that the king does not see it from his point of view.

"…even what he has will be taken away," the king declares for the second time. Kulcam is cast out, his sapphire studs returned to the king. Artisana turns her face into Azar's shoulder, weeping for the man who took his studs the same hour as she took hers, only to prove himself a fraud.

"And as for the citizens who wrote this," the king displays a scroll, "who refused my rule, have them executed."

Today is a day of justice. It is a sober occasion. Yet, as the faithful are revealed, brilliant light is cast upon the scene. And there is tebal for those who love Pari, as all become aware that the king has returned to his throne.

Jeko raises the ax and brings it down on the trunk. The entire fig tree shudders. After several more skillful swings, the entire plant falls.

"Good riddance," Nicaia says. "It should have come down three years ago."

The Sower lays his hand on the prince's work-hardened shoulder. He is more determined than ever since the king's return to show that he has earned his place.

"Patience, my lord," Jeko says. "It was worth the year of special attention, fertilizer..." He says no more, deciding not to speak without an engaged audience.

Nicaia shakes his head, grips the trunk and starts pulling it away. It should have been firewood long ago, rather than using up the ground. Jeko reaches out and, together, he and the prince haul the felled fruitless plant away. Having thrown it on the pile to be burned, their ears catch wind of music.

What now, Nicaia groans inwardly. Earlier, the king went tearing out of the palace. Now, it sounds as though he is throwing another one of his foolish feasts.

"Tebal," the telltale cry grates against the prince's ear while lifting Jeko's heart to sing. The Sower races on ahead while Nicaia drags his heels. Approaching the palace, Nicaia spots the crown prince's right hand.

"Reydeyn!" he calls, diverting Reydeyn's course to one of the palace wine storehouses.

"What's going on?"

"Your brother has come home, Nicaia!"

"What brother? Siohtion?" *That foolish wretch?*

"Yes, he's come home to your father, and the king has killed the fattened calf!" The under-Sower laughs. "He's put his princely ring back on his finger, clothed him in a robe, put sandals on his feet."

Nicaia's fists clench. He wishes he could strike that stupid smile right off of Reydeyn's face, but he is too drunk with tebal to feel it.

"He washed his feet, anointed his head. All because he was dead and is now alive, lost and now found. So, we celebrate."

"I don't believe this!" He storms away. It would be one thing if his father would receive Siohtion as the crimson cord he has always been. But, no, he's celebrating him as the lost sheep who has wandered on home and reinstating him as a prince! And to think that the king is going to use the wine Nicaia has provided, that he is about to waste it on Siohtion's welcome. The very nerve.

"Son!!"

Prince Nicaia halts in his tracks, every part of his being rigid. He knows that voice.

"Son, please, come and rejoice with us. Your brother has come home."

He spins around to face his adversary. "Years! Day after day I have served you. I never once disobeyed a single command that you gave me. Yet, yet, you never once gave me even a goat to celebrate with my friends. But now, now that this son of yours has returned, this son of yours who has absolutely devoured his inheritance with prostitutes, *now* you kill the fattened calf for *him*!!"

Pari reaches out to hold him by the shoulders, but the prince shakes him off.

Les Pariablues

"What? What could you possibly have to say? All these years while you were gone, *I* increased the wealth of *your* kingdom while *he* wasted it, and for what?"

"Son, you have worked hard, and all that is mine is yours. But it was fitting that we celebrate over your brother. He was lost and is now found, dead and now alive!"

"Fine, have your son!" He jerks his princely ring off of his finger, settings rife with dirt from years of wasted labour, and throws it to the ground.

And with that, Nicaia takes what is his and departs, plotting how he will begin to destroy his father at sowing and then entirely at reaping. Seven years, he was gone securing his kingdom. Now, he will lose it all in one.

Chapter 35

Kulcam surveys his work, running his hand up and down the strap of his sower's satchel. He thinks of the crop that will sprout from these seeds and thinks of himself. It is only a matter of time...

"See how the Koingsung and his Sower stand up to this," Nicaia says.

"It's good to be back out here," Jeko says, breathing deep. Yes, the feeling of the sowing satchel feels right slung over his shoulder, even if it is in the middle of the season today when no seeds are sown. "And to think that my grandchildren are already picking up the trade. Well done, my son, and my daughter." He smiles warmly at both Reydeyn and Acacia.

Several other servants are out with them inspecting the crop.

"Sower," Qodei says, "didn't you sow good seed in these fields? Why do we keep seeing weeds? And weeds that look so much like the crop planted?"

"An enemy has done this," Jeko says.

"Then we should gather up the weeds, shouldn't we?"

"No," Jeko says.

"Because the good crop might be uprooted with the weeds," Reydeyn explains.

Jeko nods. "Yes, let it all grow together. Then, at harvest, the reapers will gather the weeds into bundles for burning while the good crop will be stored away."

"Very well," Qodei says.

Jeko looks away to the western horizon and says to himself, "And so it will be at the end of this age, the herald-warriors of the King of that glorious city will divide the children of his enemy from those who are his citizens. A fiery furnace. Deep sorrow, great rage. But the righteous citizens of that glorious city will shine like the sun in the Kingdom of their Father, the greater King."

Prince Siohtion twists the ring around his finger. Comastasia? Has he really been back for months? Is it already harvest? And Nicaia is still at the vineyard, refusing to see his father or mother or anyone yet loyal to the king with the force of the wall set around the property. Loyek has been sent by the king to obtain the fruits of the reaping, the beginning of the harvest celebrations, a token of the relationship between the king and his son. But how will Nicaia respond? Can he still be angry about how their father received Siohtion?

Siohtion's thoughts are interrupted by the announcement of Loyek's return. His limping gait and empty hands tell the story. The king receives his servant, washing his wounds himself.

Les Pariablues

Siohtion feels sick. This is his fault. He looks over at Tebala as his sister places her hand on his shoulder.

"Father's reception of you hasn't changed Nicaia's heart for the worse. It has simply revealed who he's been all along."

"Send me, my lord," Yaren addresses the king.

And so the prince who has not returned for his ring continues to reveal his heart through his reception of the king's servants at his inherited vineyard.

Quietly, Prince Azaryada approaches his right hand. Nicaia's mistreatment and murder of the king's servants has worn them all down, but now, Nicaia has beaten Acacia and killed Jeko. Azar lays his hand on Reydeyn's shoulder.

"My father has asked me to go. Will you accompany me?"

Slowly, Reydeyn– once a nameless slave– raises his head to meet eyes with his lord. "Of course."

And so they depart in the king's final effort to be respected. Princess Tebala travels with them. Their journey is a silent one. At their destination, the noise of thundering hooves jolts Reydeyn from his numb daze.

He begins to cry out that they should flee when their horses are shot out from under them. They scramble to their feet. The prince's right hand fumbles for his daggers to defend the prince and princess.

"Let him go!" Reydeyn cries. "Don't you know who this is?"

"I have been waiting for this day," Nicaia gloats.

Reydeyn cries out as his hands are pinned behind him. Tebala finds herself in the same state and jerks violently against the unrelenting grip.

"Don't struggle, Reydeyn. You cannot win. The inheritance is mine," Nicaia says.

Reydeyn turns his face away. He cannot watch Nicaia put the crown prince to death with all of the brutal cruelty that years of bitterness have stored up. All the while, Tebala weeps.

"Go, little lady, carry the news to your father!"

She stumbles away, and Reydeyn is glad that at least she is allowed to keep her life for now.

"And as for you," he hears Nicaia say from somewhere far away, "you will return to being what you have always been. A slave."

But Reydeyn is too numb to feel the rod as it falls on his back. All he can think about is the murdered prince.

Pari surveys the scene. The murderers have now been put to a miserable death. His own son...

"Your Majesty!! Your servant yet lives!!!" It is Qodei and he carries a limp figure in his arms. "Reydeyn yet lives," he says breathlessly.

The king rushes to meet him and puts his arms around Reydeyn. "Good and faithful, Reydeyn." He stoops and kisses his servant's forehead. "Yada ues," he whispers.

And so, this vineyard he planted years ago will be passed on to others who will give him its fruits in the season of harvest. Others like Siohtion, who wasted his inheritance but now will

Les Pariablues

be crowned king after Pari. Others like Onxwade, who valued money above his own soul. Others like Lazarus, who disregarded the truth. Others like his daughters: Thuis and Teakim, who walked away for a time; Tres, Tengithae, Tekoa, Taei and Tebala, as well as servants like Reydeyn and Acacia, who, in trusting his love, have stayed faithful.

Epilogue

"*A*iwa!!"

It is an hour none of them are expecting. The trumpet blast is mighty, announcing his coming like a thief in the night, yet as unmistakable as lightning illuminating the blackness of midnight. A horrific crash resounds as the sky is rolled up like a scroll and the heavens and earth are folded up like a worn out garment. All earthly kingdoms once for all flee away in the face of the coming of the greater King.

"Aiwa!! Lelal granel canel."

"Make way!! Behold the bridegroom comes."

And do His people ever rejoice. He sits upon his throne with all of the nations gathered before him. He separates them: the sheep on his right, the goats on his left.

To those on his right, the blessed, he invites them into the kingdom prepared for them, recounting the fruits they have borne in his service by his power. As for those on his left, he sends them, the cursed, away into the fires prepared for his enemy where there is deep sorrow and great rage.

He himself bore our sins in his body on the tree, that we might die to sin and live to righteousness. By his wounds you have been healed. For you were straying like sheep, but have now returned to the Shepherd and Overseer of your souls. This Jesus is the stone that was rejected by you, the builders, which has become the cornerstone. And there is salvation in no one else, for there is no other name under heaven given among men by which we must be saved."

And he said to the disciples, "The days are coming when you will desire to see one of the days of the Son of Man, and you will not see it. And they will say to you, 'Look, there!' or 'Look, here!' Do not go out or follow them. For as the lightning flashes and lights up the sky from one side to the other, so will the Son of Man be in his day.

He who testifies to these things says, "Surely I am coming soon." Amen. Come, Lord Jesus! The grace of the Lord Jesus be with all. Amen.[1]

Additional resource:

Tell me the Stories of Jesus: The Explosive Power of Jesus' Parables by R. Albert Mohler

---

[1] 1 Peter 2:24 - 25 (ESV), Acts 4:11 - 12 (ESV), Luke 17:22 - 24 (ESV), Revelation 22:20 - 21 (ESV)

Les Pariablues

Novel playlist:

"Wineskins" by Cloverton
"Prodigal Like Me" by Jonny Diaz
"The Golden Boy and the Prodigal" by Jason Gray
"99" by 7eventh Time Down
"House Divided" by Josh Wilson
"Letter from the Grave" by Shai Linne
"The One" by Cade Thompson

Especially to my fellow members of Gen Z and to all of the generations who come behind us: That you may know the Truth and that he may make you free. And, to those of us who already know him, that we may stand firm and steadfast, ever looking to him.

To the glory of God. – January 2023

Jesus' Parables as recorded in Scripture

New Cloth on an Old Coat (Matthew 9:16; Mark 2:21; Luke 5:36)
New Wine in Old Wineskins (Mark 9:17; Mark 2:22; Luke 5:37–38)
The Lamp on a Stand (Matthew 5:14–15; Mark 4:21–22; Luke 8:16, 11:33)
The Wise and Foolish Builders (Matthew 7:24–27; Luke 6:47–49)
The Moneylender forgiving unequal debts (Luke 7:41–43)
The Rich Fool Building His Bigger Barns (Luke 12:16–21)
The Servants Must Remain Watchful (Mark 13:35–37; Luke 12:35–40)
The Wise and Foolish Servants (Matthew 24:45–51; Luke 12:42–48)
The Unfruitful Fig Tree (Luke 13:6–9)
The Parable of the Soils (Matthew 13:3–23; Mark 4:1–20; Luke 8:4–15)
The Weeds Among Good Plants (Matthew 13:24–43)
The Growing Seed (Mark 4:26–29)
The Mustard Seed (Matthew 13:31–32; Mark 4:30–32; Luke 13:18–19)
Yeast (Matthew 13:31–32)
Hidden Treasure (13:44)
Valuable Pearl (13:45–46)
Fishing Net (Matthew 13:47–50)
Owner of a House (Matthew 13:52)
Lost Sheep (Matthew 18:12–14)
The Master and His Servant (Luke 17:7–10)
The Unmerciful servant (Matthew 18:23–34)
The Good Samaritan (Luke 10:30–37)
Friend in Need (Luke 11:5–8)
Lowest Seat at the Feast (Luke 14:7–14)

Les Pariablues

Invitation to a Great Banquet (Luke 14:16–24)
The Cost of Discipleship (Luke 14:28–33)
Lost Sheep (Luke 15:4–7)
Lost Coin (Luke 15:8–10)
The Prodigal Son (Luke 15:11–32)
The Shrewd Manager (Luke 16:1–8)
The Rich Man and Lazarus (Luke 16:19–31)
The Early and Late Workers in the Vineyard (Matthew 20:1–16)
The Persistent Widow and Crooked Judge (Matthew 18:1–8)
The Pharisee and Tax Collector (Luke 18:10–14)
The King's Ten Servants Given Minas (Luke 19:12–27)
Two Sons (one obeys, one disobeys) (Matthew 21:28–32)
Wicked Tenants (Matthew 21:33–44; Mark 12:1–11; Luke 20:9–18)
Invitation to a Wedding Banquet (Matthew 22:2–14)
The Fig Tree and Signs of the Future (Matthew 24:32–35; Mark 13:28–29; Luke 21:29–31)
The Wise and Foolish Virgins (Matthew 25:1–13)
The Talents (Matthew 25:14–30)
The Sheep and the Goats (Matthew 25:31–46)[2]

---

[2] https://www.kevinhalloran.net/a-complete-list-of-jesus-parables-in-the-new-testament/

About the Author

*L*oving the gift of story for as long as she can remember, D. N. Dettwiler now weaves God's truth into fictional tales that through them her readers may know him.

Printed in the USA
CPSIA information can be obtained
at www.ICGtesting.com
JSHW010223040224
56451JS00002B/4